For all intents and purposes, this book was not written under any Mercury retrogrades, void-of-course Moons, or seriously adverse transits.

About the Author

Christine Rakela is an internationally known astrologer, lecturer, and writer. She is officially recognized as a certified astrologer through the National Council for Geocosmic Research and has had a full-time practice for over twenty years. Christine has produced and hosted the independent television program "Astrology Connection" for a wide audience for seventeen years. She has also been a featured guest on national television and radio, and lectures throughout the country. Christine currently resides in New York City.

To Write to the Author

If you wish to contact the author or would like more information about this book, please write to the author in care of Llewellyn Worldwide and we will forward your request. Both the author and publisher appreciate hearing from you and learning of your enjoyment of this book and how it has helped you. Llewellyn Worldwide cannot guarantee that every letter written to the author can be answered, but all will be forwarded. Please write to:

Christine Rakela
℅ Llewellyn Worldwide
P.O. Box 64383, Dept. 0-7387-0424-5
St. Paul, MN 55164-0383, U.S.A.
Please enclose a self-addressed stamped envelope for reply,
or $1.00 to cover costs. If outside U.S.A., enclose
international postal reply coupon.

Many of Llewellyn's authors have websites with additional information and resources. For more information, please visit our website at
http://www.llewellyn.com

the love Relationship formula

predicting

Romantic

success

with

Astrology

christine Rakela

2004
Llewellyn Publications
St. Paul, Minnesota 55164-0383, U.S.A.

First Edition
First Printing, 2004

Cover photograph © SuperStock
Cover design by Lisa Novak

Thanks to Dell Horoscope Magazine for permission to use material originally published in a May 1994 article entitled "The 15 Keys to Romantic Compatibility," written by Christine Rakela.

All horoscope charts used in this book were generated using Win*Star © Matrix Software.

Library of Congress Cataloging-in-Publication Data

Rakela, Christine, 1955-
     The love relationship formula : predicting romantic success with astrology / Christine Rakela.—1st ed.
         p. cm.
     Includes bibliographical references and index.
     ISBN 0-7387-0424-5
         1. Astrology. 2. Love—Miscellanea. 3. Mate selection—Miscellanea. I. Title.

     BF1729.L6R35 2004
     133.5'864677—dc22

                                                                                    2004044116

Llewellyn Publications
A Division of Llewellyn Worldwide, Ltd.
P.O. Box 64383, Dept. 0-7387-0424-5
St. Paul, MN 55164-0383, U.S.A.
www.llewellyn.com

Printed in the United States of America

This book is dedicated to my late brother, Frankie Rakela.
His words of wisdom will inspire me forever.

Acknowledgments

First and foremost, I would like to thank God for the opportunity to write and have my book successfully published. I will always consider this book to be one of my greatest achievements in life.

Secondly, I wish to thank all of my spiritual teachers for their exceptional guidance in expanding my consciousness to further grasp the true essence of the human being, while working on this creation.

Thirdly, I am so grateful to all of the people who have supported me and more importantly believed in me and this wonderful project. Throughout my years on this planet, it has been my intention to write a book where many, many people would benefit. The days, months, and several years that went into the making of this book will be remembered for the painstaking yet incredibly exhilarating journey it has been. To become immersed in the world of words is an unbelievable experience that those who are lucky enough to find themselves in should relish each and every moment, regardless of the tremendous amount of work involved.

The people who have supported my effort include: my parents, Frank and Mary Rakela, my siblings, Nancy, Kathy, Teresa, and Jim Rakela, Jan Shulman, Nelly Nazario, Sarah Shaines, Susana Puglise, Mary Lou Falconey, Nicky Zann, Tony Leroy, and the entire staff at Llewellyn, especially Dr. Stephanie Clement, who was instrumental in assisting me in the manifestation of this book.

And for those who have lent minor support, too many names to mention, in offering their encouragement may the publishing of this book be their reward as well.

Contents

charts

introduction

For one human being to love another;
that is perhaps the most difficult of all tasks,
the ultimate, the last test and proof,
the work for which all other work is but preparation. *
—*Rilke*

All of life is a relationship. We have a relationship with ourselves, others, planet earth, our solar system, and our God. Being in embodiment, as opposed to being a soul, is a rare opportunity for connecting with others and exploring and understanding the concept of relationship. Forming an alliance with the one we love calls upon the depth of our every experience. Hopeful, yet never sure of the outcome, we proceed. It is the unknown that beckons us. Yet take the risk we must if we are to discover our own humanity. Our inner desire to love and be loved cannot be suppressed. It is also here that we grow and further our understanding the most, for with love there is greatness and sorrow.

---

* From *Letters to a Young Poet* by Rainer Maria Rilke, translated by M. D. Herter Norton. Copyright 1934, 1954 by W. W. Norton & Company, Inc., renewed (c) 1962, 1982 by M. D. Herter Norton. Used by permission of W. W. Norton & Company, Inc.

Sometimes this unique opportunity to cultivate a relationship is seen as a curse instead of the blessing that it is. This is usually due to unresolved issues with difficult, abusive, terminated, or nonexistent relationships. However, even the pain or disappointment, as great as it may be, should be viewed as a means to help us become more aware of who we are as individuals. In this case it is not a matter of being "stuck" in the pain, but finding a way to see through it.

Relationships are based on feeling. Although we think we can hide from our emotional feelings, we are only fooling ourselves. It is the shadow within that constantly seeks to be recognized. How often we avoid what we need to address because of the fear and anguish involved—the memories that we embrace if we were once in love, and the hate we feel due to the heartfelt pain of loss. Or perhaps we have never experienced love. But in learning from our emotional experiences, we are never taught how to find and maintain lasting romantic happiness in a relationship, which is how and why "The Love Relationship Formula" came into being. We end up suppressing this emotion, and suppressed feelings lead to internal anger.

Anger is the rage that wants the feelings to be known. Sometimes we hang on to our anger, for it is a matter of survival; otherwise our feelings might die. This fear seems far worse than anger itself, for at least we are feeling something! We are conditioned to believe that anger helps us separate, but this does not empower us; surrendering to the idea of just letting go does. Bringing disappointments from the past into our next relationship will only keep us from experiencing what we truly desire—love.

The most powerful attraction is our personal happiness, which can only be experienced through inner feelings of self-love. Love and all its worthiness validates our existence. But the inspiration behind love is not in pursuing the ideal person, but rather in becoming one. Having a wonderful relationship with ourselves will attract exactly what we are looking for—that same thriving relationship. All limiting patterns can be broken. This starts by expressing our feelings, so we become more aware of ourselves. Feelings are truly the essence of our existence, allowing us to give meaning to life and meaning to our relationship with another.

The relationships we encounter in life, we attract through the subconscious mind. Ridding ourselves of the pessimistic experiences that have taken up residency here allows us to create in our mind the right intention. This objective, finding the "ideal" relationship, eventually becomes our mind's reality. Since awareness of a universal rhythm allows us to live life more effectively, when visualization of the ideal union is combined with the rhythmic science of astrology, we obtain successful results for our efforts.

Delving into the summation of my clients' experiences involving synastry, I discovered a common thread that beautifully describes a soulmate relationship. This is reflected in the Love Relationship Formula. In this realization, I conceived a global breakthrough that truly benefits couples. This astrological formula gives a precise understanding of what is going on between a couple, and identifies the aspects of their relationship that they need to enhance.

Every relationship is unique. At times, we may wonder what one person sees in another. The cosmic chemistry between a couple is a strong drawing card that may even relate back to prior lives. Behind this intense attraction is a greater purpose that can be explained with the Love Relationship Formula. Unraveling your relationship destiny by understanding the significance of your bond with another will bring tremendous depth and meaning into the union. The fifteen points of the Love Relationship Formula, which describe a couple's "perfect" synastry, have been specifically formulated to improve your relationships beyond expectations. It is based on over two decades of research into the true meaning of love. My sincere hope is to share this vital, unparalleled information with you so that you may live a more joyous life with another.

In this book lies the spirit of my mind, heart, and soul. Those who read it, and read it well, will be rewarded with hope, inspiration, and lasting love.

—Christine Rakela

part 1

the journey to love

I ♥ understanding
the Love Relationship Formula

We are all looking for the "right" relationship—the one that works! Timing, fate, and your astrological connections have everything to do with it. For a relationship to really prosper, however, both parties must have some sense of stability in their lives, have no other involvements, and have a desire for each another, as well as a desire to make it work. But what signifies a good, lasting relationship? Have you ever wondered if there is some kind of secret to having a great relationship? Well, there is.

What if we could come up with a formula that could lead to the "perfect" relationship—one that truly satisfies the needs and desires of the two people involved? Now you have the opportunity to benefit from the Love Relationship Formula, which has all of the right ingredients for the relationship you are looking for and more. So often we think we know what we want, but then we are disappointed in our romantic encounters. Why? Because the Love Relationship Formula is incomplete. Once you understand what the formula is, you will attract and maintain a winning relationship. The Love Relationship Formula is actually a reflection of your finest self.

One of the most important findings is that the Love Relationship Formula is consistent in relationship after relationship. Since the formula is based on the mathematical angles used in astrology, with a specific composition of planets, if a (cosmic) mathematical pattern is consistent, it cannot be denied. Why? Because math is a form of perfection. Therefore, it is possible for a relationship formula to exist that is based on math for precision, yet fluctuates to the needs, desires, ideas, and emotions of being human.

But what makes the Love Relationship Formula even more valid is that you will find the formula not only in a couple's synastry, but also in first meeting charts, marriage charts, and composite charts of long-term unions, and even in the solar and lunar return charts. The consistency of the Love Relationship Formula is what validates its credibility and love potential for all.

Before we explore the world of synastry and understand our Love Relationship Formula in its entirety, we must first discuss relationship challenges. What emotional blocks are keeping us from a lasting love? In this process we will learn what works, what doesn't, and why. The next few pages will allow you to release emotional blocks, get back in touch with your feelings, understand love, and confront your relationship beliefs that may be inhibiting you from finding true love. Once we rid ourselves of all this relationship baggage, we may enjoy the Love Relationship Formula to its fullest.

Without getting into any astrological specifics, here are four questions to ask yourself.

1. Do you communicate well with your partner, or is only one of you calling the shots?

2. Does your partner meet your needs, or are you constantly meeting his or her needs, and thus your needs are neglected? (We will talk about your desires later.)

3. Do you feel secure and comfortable with your partner, or do you need to control or monitor him or her?

4. Are you pulling all the weight in the relationship emotionally, physically, and financially, or are the responsibilities equally divided?

However you answered these questions, now we will find out why.

In relationships, good communication is of prime importance. Mental needs are just as important as physical needs, and must be fulfilled. You have to be able to express your feelings and opinions with your partner, and if a disagreement is in order, then fine. A client once stated to me how she was so afraid to express herself, because otherwise, she thought, her spouse might leave her. With his Saturn (restriction) in adverse aspect to her Mercury (communication) and her Venus (affection, self-esteem), I could understand why. However, if she did not face up to this challenge, her self-esteem would continue to diminish and he would eventually leave or neglect her because she didn't think she was worthy enough to express how she felt. Yes, he might leave her, but he might also stay and give her the respect that she deserves, because she thought enough of herself to speak her mind. This challenge, of course, was not an accident. It came into her life to transcend her low self-esteem, fear of rejection, and need for approval to validate her existence. Once she confronted this episode in her life, either her significant other would change, or she would attract a more supportive relationship. Expressing how you feel, talking issues out—these are musts. If you find yourself in a relationship where you are experiencing verbal repression, than you need to seriously reevaluate your relationship, for one thing is for sure—you are not happy. Why? *Because you can't be yourself.*

♥ what challenges our relationships

Needs Versus Desires

We all have desires. But desires are short-lived and *needs must be met.* Forget about what you want or what you think you should have—stop twisting God's arm! Concern yourself with your needs, because otherwise you will never be fulfilled. How often is it that we go running after our desires? Yes, the grass always looks greener on the other side— but is it? *When you get what you want, but not what you need, the longing within continues. What we desire is fulfillment, not greed.*

Thanks in part to the media, it almost seems to be easier to go after our selfish desires then deal with our needs, which furthers sexual promiscuity, unwanted pregnancies, co-dependent relationships, and fatal attractions. What we really want is long-term gratification. It is something that we all yearn for in life and it comes through a deep, meaningful union with another. This happens when we recognize our needs through the Love Relationship Formula.

It's not always easy to get in touch with our needs, and sometimes we are surprised by our discoveries. Why? Perhaps they are not in line with our "ideal" relationship, the one that our parents, grandparents, and, worse yet, society has programmed into our heads—that image of how it is "supposed to be." Remember, the whole idea behind relationships is that they are an illusion, like ornaments on a Christmas tree. It's romanticism—it's happy connotations of what life can be like with someone. This is not real. There is no such thing as an ideal relationship. The ideal is what we may strive for, but it should not rule over or confine us in any way. The ideal relationship does not exist in dense reality; it can only be found in God.

In *The Divine Romance* by Paramahansa Yogananda, he writes about how we seek that special union with another human being, but what our soul is really looking for is union with our divine selves. We should never lose sight of this fact, for in doing so we give our power away to another. In seeking the divine romance, looking outside of ourselves for love is a very unfulfilling experience. It's like setting ourselves up for a disappointment.

Sometimes we have to come to terms with the fact that we may be madly in love with someone, but they may not be the right person for us. Why? Usually it's because our needs are not being met. *If we neglect our needs, we are neglecting ourselves.* When we find ourselves attending to someone else's needs and loving too much, we are probably neglecting our own needs.

Giving your power away to another leaves you with nothing, and eventually they leave you too. For you end up giving away the very thing your lover was attracted to in the beginning of your relationship. You feel that if you shower them with love and attention, then they will not abandon you. But what is happening is that you end up abandoning yourself in the process. Givers always attract takers, and taking advantage of someone, controlling someone in a relationship, is not love. In any relationship, we give to a point, but we also need to learn when to cut off our efforts and let the other person help themselves, so we in turn can help ourselves if necessary. *The strength of a relationship depends on the two people involved. Both must be able to stand alone, yet stand together.* The Love Relationship Formula encourages you to get in touch with your higher self and your needs.

The "Fix"—Ignoring Relationship Issues

We are prone to ignoring relationship issues. Even though we don't intend to repeat this mistake, at times we do. Looking for ways to escape, we continually distract ourselves from the truth. The problem stems from the fact that we are constantly looking for the "fix" instead of looking for a way to reunite with our divine selves. *The "fix" never allows us to arrive at the point of relationship realization.* Awakening from this delusive state, we can then truly unite with another. Remember that romance is a delusive state of mind.

To bring romance into an awakened state, we can begin to create a positive romantic ideal. I often hear, "All I need is the right person, Mr. or Ms. Right, and then everything will fall into place." It's time to take off those rose-colored specs and start dealing with your issues, for the work really begins with you. So much of my own personal discovery and transformation was learning about myself through my own astrology chart and struggling to change the adversity. It's called "turning squares into trines," and you can achieve this much easier than an alchemist turning base metals into gold.

What Are Your Beliefs?

As you strive to become a better person, you will attract a better partner—one in line with who you really are. For in life we attract what we are. I had a hard time recognizing that like attracts like when I attracted someone into my life who I felt exemplified qualities or behaviors that where *unlike* me. After much soul-searching, I came to realize that a certain thought/belief system pulled these emotionally unsettled individuals my way. I finally concluded that yes, thoughts are things, and their importance is not to be underestimated. For our thoughts are more powerful than we realize. So be careful of what you are thinking, because it may come true for you!

Getting control over your thoughts is easier said than done. You can become very comfortable being angry with someone, or feeling life is out to get you, or that life is unfair. This will not help your situation. What will improve your circumstances is working on yourself to change the old pattern. You may need to find healthy ways to release the tensions, resentments, or anger, and how you deal with it will lead to your success or failure. The choice is yours.

Timing

Timing has everything to do with securing a relationship. When our timing is off, one or both parties are unavailable on some level: emotionally, physically, psychologically, spiritually, or financially. You will not find security in someone who is unavailable or prefers a love affair or third-party relationship. Both can be highly regrettable, especially the triangle. I have seen women wait for years, as he tells her he's going to leave his wife someday. In most cases, he never will, for the pattern is set.

Going from one relationship to the next can also burn you out. The only way to recuperate is to be with yourself. Celibacy is not a curse! It is a time to get your act together on the emotional front. The more you are with yourself, the more time you have to check in to your own issues—to change. The dating merry-go-round of attracting individuals who are not right for you is a reflection of something in yourself. But you will continue to attract what is in your life blueprint until you transcend it.

Part of the healing process is dealing with your issues and not being *distracted* by another relationship. Although romance sounds nice, it doesn't usually solve your dilemmas. However, there are some rare cases where someone you meet is a part of that healing process. But don't count on this. For after a recent breakup, one tends to be vulnerable and hurting, and therefore needs to take time to heal the wound. If you look for someone to do that for you, you might well become prey to someone else's vindictive tendencies, and the cycle continues.

Space between relationships can be a very important time and can be just as significant as the time spent in a relationship with someone. Hopefully, we take what we have learned into our next relationship. For as the saying goes, if you don't learn from your mistakes, you are destined to repeat them until you do. There is nothing worse than going through the same painful experience a second time around. The more you work out your issues alone, the less you will have to work them out in a relationship. *The idea is to enjoy your relationship.*

Besides the timing and the cosmic connections, to have a relationship succeed you must feel you are worthy of love and a wonderful relationship. If you take a good look at yourself, you may find that you are too critical of yourself and maybe of others too, thus making it difficult for anyone to get close to you. Or perhaps you are always trying to meet with someone else's approval or are living someone else's life.

You must feel good about yourself. Otherwise you will not feel happiness with another. Don't expect that you can depend upon another person for your happiness. No one is required to provide this joy for you. Being an adult is being responsible for your own happiness. The Love Relationship Formula allows your personal happiness to thrive as you incorporate timely choices.

Control and Denial

There are two kinds of emotion in life: love and fear. When fear dictates, we deprive ourselves of love and happiness. In this instance love is a one-way street, for people who do not fully love themselves attract partners who exemplify those same feelings. This can also be said for the emotionally detached and noncommittal individuals who attract people who are already spoken for, or unavailable. This only further promotes a fear of love and intimacy. Sabotaging ourselves keeps us from what we want. These are conditioned patterns that must be addressed, for what one tends to attract in this state is essentially an abusive relationship in either a verbal, physical, psychological, or emotional manner, sometimes all of the above. What we do for love!

At times, due to karmic retribution, we find ourselves in an abusive relationship. If we are not able to work things out, hopefully we learn not to tolerate this kind of treatment—that we deserve better. Ridding yourself of anyone who negates your self-esteem will signify that you do not accept this behavior. Therefore, you are less likely to attract this detrimental conduct into your life again. Once you take action, your life will change for the better. Don't think that you can wave a magic wand and change a person. Wouldn't life be so great if that were possible! But how a person sees you can rarely be changed, especially if they want to have a certain control over you, which is due to their own selfishness and insecurity.

Usually when one person is calling the shots in a relationship, they are also projecting their issues onto you, which will soon erode your self-esteem along with your potential. *When we fall in love with someone who controls us, we give our power away.* If and when you regain your power, your relationship will either move to a new level or dissolve if the other party continues to want to overpower you. *Relationships are growing together and sharing, not conquering and controlling.* I have seen many love slaves in my time and I always urge them to move on. At times, however, it's not until they are either fed up or totally devastated that they break the chains. Sometimes many years have gone by and an emotional price has been paid.

One of the hardest things to do is to move on when a relationship is or has become destructive, because you have made a tremendous investment of time and energy. But abusive relationship situations may need to end if the couple cannot resolve their differences. The longer you wait, the longer your recovery will be. I am certainly not an advocate of terminating relationships. You can possibly save your relationship by working on it. The people whom we meet in life and become intimate with, we have much to learn from because they mirror what is going on within ourselves. Many times it is not what we care to see. This is why some people can't seem to stay in a relationship, because they start to see the reality of who they really are and want to believe otherwise.

Many of us come from dysfunctional families. We learn to adjust, and therefore survive. So often to survive we enter the world of denial. We block out scenes of physical and/or verbal abuse, drug or alcohol-related incidents, love affairs, or a lack of emotional support (love). We *rationalize* that it's okay if dad drinks, because he's stressed on the job. It's okay that mom has an affair, because she needs love and attention.

People in denial blind themselves from the truth. *They don't want to feel.* They don't want to face themselves. *And if you cannot feel, how can you possibly love?* When we take this behavior into our relationships, it becomes an issue of control, abandonment, or a need to take care of someone. *What we really need to do is take care of ourselves!* If love and respect are not forthcoming in our earlier years, we need to take time out to understand our feelings—not deny them. The Love Relationship Formula allows you to avoid unhealthy obsessions and be aware of control and denial issues so that you fully appreciate yourself.

What Is Love?

True love is respecting and deeply caring for someone.

Venus, the goddess of love, depicts for us a picture of heavenly romance, which love certainly can be. But this illusive state does not touch upon the realities nor the responsibilities involved. The cherub, resourcefully armed with bow and arrow, symbolizes the innocence, truth, and love that we experienced in our childhood. But as we take this into adulthood, we begin to learn otherwise.

When we wish to establish a romantic bond with someone, we start by showing responsibility toward them. In time trust is earned, which leads to love. *When we love, we become the truth. We become real.* Love is tapping into the depths of our soul, connecting with our essence. Once we realize our oneness by reuniting with our divine selves, we can unite much more easily with a significant someone. *The word divine describes a heavenly yet spiritual understanding that inspires in us a desire to fulfill an essential need that will greatly improve our life.* Divinity is an exalted state that we must strive for to enhance our relationship potential.

Mother Teresa said that of all the places she had visited, there was a great hunger for love in the United States. To end that loneliness that is so prevalent in our society is not an easy feat. So many are starved for love and appreciation. But behind this human desire is one longing, and that is to fill that emptiness, that void, with divine love.

So often the problem is that *we are not seeking love, but what love can give us.* Self-gratification, me-me-me, does not lead to love. We can only fill that empty void with divine love. This is the love that does not involve just you and another, but our spiritual Creator as well. The Love Relationship Formula encourages a compassionate, spiritual love that embraces and supports a relationship.

Triads or Dyads

Relationships are dyads, male and female energies. But just experiencing the polar opposite of one another is not enough. For true fulfillment, a third entity of divinity is needed. It enhances as well as embraces the totality of this relationship experience.

In a relationship, two people are a duality. The divine must be a part of this duo for the relationship to prosper. Then it can become the triune reality of love.

Even the composite chart, which is created by finding the midpoint between a pair of planets and other significant points of interest of the two horoscope charts, describes the subtlest details of a relationship. A relationship (two) emanates a third entity (three) described in the composite chart. This third entity is the *spirit* of the relationship. How that spirit affects the two people involved depends on what they are individually able to contribute to the relationship. The more they improve themselves, the more the dynamics of the relationship as a third entity, as *spirit*, will prosper.

In astrology, we relate to the triplicities, based on energies conceived of a triangle that relate in harmony and therefore promote unity. The three horoscope signs in each element, such as the fire signs, Aries, Leo, and Sagittarius, relate to this experience. The three compatible horoscope signs in one element indicate the triad principle, as the trine in astrology is a harmonious angle connecting one element to another. Therefore, the more trines or sextiles (half of a trine) that you have in your compatibility analysis of all of the planets or significant points of interest, the better off your relationship will be. With the Love Relationship Formula intact, we can rate your interaction as a couple with the help of the triad principle.

Our Relationships Reflect Our Parents

If we look into the past, we usually find a situation or series of situations that have caused an inner difficulty to develop, grow, and fester until it is addressed. So often this goes back to our relationship with our parents. The interaction you had with your parents will directly reflect what is going on in your intimate relationship.

Mental conditioning has occurred when we attract people into our life who exemplify our parents. There is no escaping this pattern. Once you realize that you have attracted someone who mirrors one of your parents, then you can begin to change the pattern that started in childhood. Since most of us come from dysfunctional families, most patterns need to be changed.

Paul, a handsome and well-to-do client, came for a consultation and told me that within six months of meeting and developing a relationship that seemed to be going great, the woman would decide to leave him. This had happened several times, and he was devastated and could not bear for this to happen again. My first question to Paul was, what happened to your relationship with your mother? There were some adverse aspects in his chart indicating a definite problem. It turned out that at a young age, Paul's mother died and he felt terribly abandoned. He said that he was angry and hurt, and being just a child he didn't know how to deal with his loss, so he repressed this trauma.

Unfortunately, Paul has such a fear of being abandoned by a woman that his fear attracts the very thing he fears. *He has a belief system that women abandon him, and has created a pattern of female abandonment that is true to his beliefs.* This belief system can be changed. If we look at Paul's astrology chart, his aspects clearly depict the situation that he finds himself in, and also indicates how he can begin to transcend his astrological karma. He has a Moon-Neptune (mother/emotions–spiritual/illusion) conjunction in the tenth house in Scorpio, the sign that rules over transformation and death, in sextile aspect to Uranus in Virgo (progressive, detailed insights). Here Paul would have experienced his mother not being around, possibly due to her passing away. Now that he is older, he needs to understand his strong connection with his mother, which, although suppressed, is still there. With a Moon-Neptune conjunction, Paul was meant to experience his emotions, not suppress them. A spiritual way of looking at his situation along with some counseling or psychotherapy can lead to a new understanding. *The women in Paul's life were leaving him not to hurt him, but to get Paul to finally own up to his suppressed emotions that were wanting to be felt and heard.* Sometimes we need to be broken to finally find our way. Paul surrendered to his emotions and cried. I knew from that point on his life would change for the better.

So often we block or control our feelings, and thus may block and control the people who come into our lives. Surrendering to our feelings, to love, is not a failure—it's a success. It can be scary to extend ourselves and be open to love. But if we are not receptive to love, it doesn't have a chance to enter our lives.

The problem with many relationships is that an unwanted pattern starts to take hold, and instead of addressing the issue, the person who is being undermined goes into denial. Once you lose touch with your feelings, you are not able to confront the initial problem. *The relationship pattern is what is now controlling you.* You can begin to set the pattern right with the Love Relationship Formula. This formula sheds light on all of these personal issues. If you find that you are overlooking these issues, then you are overlooking your relationship.

part 2

the love relationship formula

3

The Love Relationship formula —introduction

Happiness and love are designated so eloquently by our karma. Thus, the actions that we consciously take, predetermine our future. *In the end, what we are all looking for is happiness. But happiness is actually a fleeting moment. Love, however, is a constant.*

I once read an article in Vogue magazine entitled "The Happy Pill Question" by Erica Goode. It was about whether you would take a pill that would make you happy all of the time. Well, to my surprise, in the article the panel concluded that they would *not* take the "happy pill." Why? Because if they could not feel sadness and pain, they would not know what happiness and love truly were. They would not be able to experience the gamut of emotions, the agony and the ecstasy. And not to feel is not to love. It seems that we need our sad and painful experiences so that we have a reference point—something to compare love and happiness to, to fully appreciate them. We all have our ideas about love, but we must be in touch with our feelings in order to experience it. For love is the ultimate expression of feeling.

How many of us come from dysfunctional families that have created denial issues of one kind or another? Denial on any level blocks our true feelings. Once we become aware of and purge ourselves of denial issues, then our inner feelings can guide us toward love. *Our tendency, however, is to create patterns that are the same dysfunctional situation that we grew up in. Since it feels comfortable and familiar, we feel we can handle it. Even from a dysfunctional perspective, we know what's coming. Yet dysfunctional is just that—you are not functioning in a balanced manner. This is not what you want to become more familiar with, for it denies you personal happiness.*

By being in touch with our feelings, needs, and desires, we are able to choose a more suitable and loving mate. Synastry, or astrological compatibility, can help piece together the emotional foundation of finding that special someone as well as improving a current relationship. Through astrology, because it is a science, we can come up with a formula that comprises the ideal relationship. Like anything, you have to believe in the formula for it to work. You can have the astrological mechanics, but if your belief system is creating unavailable relationships for you, then that is what you will continue to attract.

The formula for relationships, however, is basically two-fold, involving both science and artistic expression or emotion. It is the art or emotion that gives rise to the formula. Einstein wasn't great just because of the formula, but what he added to it—the finesse. Just as he had a tremendous belief in what he was doing, so must you. What's nice about the human being is that we are emotional—flexible. It has to be that way for this is the functioning of any relationship. At no other time is flexibility more vital than when you are interacting with another human being.

Formulas help us make sense out of life. The formula for relationships based on science and art or emotion can also be found in the Golden Ratio—the formula of transcendence. On some level, life is a mathematical equation, otherwise known as the Golden Ratio—"phi" 1:16:18 . . . "Phi represents a divine ideation—an etheric formula for transcendence and beauty superimposed by the Creator upon the physical plane, (us). The Phi ratio describes with numbers and geometry the universal formula for growth. Its resulting pentagonal symmetry is found only in living forms."*

---

* Reprinted with permission from *The Coming Revolution: A Magazine For Higher Consciousness*, L. R. Productions (Fall 1981): 44–45. For further information, contact Summit Lighthouse, P.O. Box 5000, Gardinar, MT.

It is through this mathematical equation that we have form, beauty, and harmony. We can also have this in our relationships, which can be derived from the Love Relationship Formula.

Pythagorus once declared, "All is number."* But why does life express itself in certain consistent mathematical patterns, especially the Golden Ratio? We find that it is because the vibration to these numeric ratios are pleasing and work in accordance to man's and woman's soul, thus bringing them in touch with their higher selves, especially involving a relationship. Implementing the Golden Ratio into our lives allows us to become more centered or aligned with the universe. The further we get away from this principle, the more scattered we become. This is why it is so important to seek out true perfected forms, for here harmony prevails.

There are many formulas that make sense of our existence, such as Einstein's interchange between mass and energy, $E=mc^2$. *Astrology is also mathematical and is also a formula.*

Astrology is a reflection of life, and better yet, it makes sense out of life. Through astrology a formula within a formula can be derived that makes sense out of love relationships. You may ask yourself, how could this be? There are so many variables. But not if you stick to the basics. The science of astrology gives us a foundation on which to base our Relationship Formula. But with this formula comes intellectual, emotional, physical, and spiritual depth. That is why it is so unique. It allows us to go beyond Sun sign compatibility, for I'm sure you have found that unlikely duos, such as Pisces and Sagittarius, or Scorpio and Gemini, do get together. So we don't want to limit ourselves with Sun sign astrology. The Love Relationship Formula allows for this flexibility as you rely on the guidance of true, perfected, numeric forms.

Striving for the ideal, the "perfect" relationship, helps us set a standard so that we may eventually attract the right relationship. *This attraction is based on your belief system from your conditioned past, your karma, and the compatibility of your astrological connections based on the Love Relationship Formula.* When you combine all three methods, you will be successful in attaining the right relationship. Now we will delve into the universal principles of astrology to find out what signifies a good, lasting relationship.

To start with, and as a general rule, Sun sign compatibility is a strong contributing factor. However, we are not just relying on Sun sign astrology, but on how the planets

---

* Reprinted with permission from *The Coming Revolution: A Magazine For Higher Consciousness*, L. R. Productions (Fall 1981): 45. For further information, contact Summit Lighthouse, P.O. Box 5000, Gardinar, MT.

and significant points in two charts interact with one another. It is this interaction that will create a certain dynamic that will make or break a relationship.

Throughout my twenty years of counseling singles and couples, I have come across a group of compatible planetary influences, used in the Love Relationship Formula, that reflect a truly fulfilling relationship. There are fifteen aspects that comprise the ideal relationship—the one that works. If you don't have them all, don't fret. Your relationship can still survive. But the more compatible planetary connections you have, the better off you and your partner will be. *Because this is backed up by the mathematical science of astrology, make no mistake, this is the perfect formula. As in any formula, when you have all of the right ingredients, it works!*

4

♥

THE LOVE
RELATIONSHIP
FORMULA

In the beginning of your relationship, it is important to establish a pattern that will bring the union to its highest potential. As you read through the following pages, recognize what is going on in your relationship and what needs to be addressed. If you are single, this will prepare you for what you want to attract into your life in a long-term partner. Every point described here is a reflection of the relationship you are having with yourself and what you have to offer. Therefore, whatever each person is willing to give to the relationship will become the inner spirit of the relationship, which is the third entity that you create as a couple. This "spirit" may be found and understood through the Love Relationship Formula, along with other challenging planetary influences.

1. "Venus-Mars"—Romantic Attraction and Desire
2. "Sun-Moon"—Strong, Enduring Bond
3. "Sun-Venus"—Showing Affection and Respect

4. "Sun-Mars"—Energized, Passionate Goals

5. "Sun-Ascendant"—Mutual Approach to Life/Similar Interests

6. "Sun-Jupiter"—Confident, Supportive, Expansive Goals

7. "Moon-Venus"—Sensitivity to Feeling

8. "Moon-Jupiter"—Emotional Happiness

9. "Mercury-Jupiter"—Positive Communication

10. "Venus-Jupiter"—Compliments, Favors, Positive Self-Esteem

11. "Venus-Saturn"—Long-Term Security

12. "Venus-Uranus"—Exciting, Lasting Attraction

13. "Venus-Pluto"—Deep, Intense Love

14. "Mars-Jupiter"—Motivated Desires

15. "Jupiter-Saturn"—Friendship Ties

(The ideal and lesser ideal aspects are listed in order of importance. For more information, refer to chapter 19, "Aspects and Orb.")

(1) "Venus-Mars"—Romantic Attraction and Desire

The ideal: conjunction, trine, and sextile

The lesser ideal: square, opposition, semisquare, sesquiquadrate, and inconjunct

I am sure you are probably familiar with the two classic symbols representing the male (♂ Mars) and the female (♀ Venus). They, like astrology, have been around for a long time. You could relate Venus and Mars to positive and negative ions just waiting to link up. When you meet up with a romantic encounter under this passionate, attractive influence, your whole life is enlightened by the experience. Being human, you can't help but embrace the idea of falling in love.

The first planetary influences that support the Love Relationship Formula are Venus and Mars, the planets of romantic attraction and desire. As Venus represents the feminine mystique and Mars the masculine drive, these two planets need to be in aspect to each other in order for the social/romantic connection to occur. Whether it be a conjunction, square, trine, opposition, etc., any kind of angle is significant as it links the two planetary influences. Of course a square, a hard aspect in astrology, involving Venus and Mars as opposed to a trine, a soft aspect, may bring out a more passionate and challenging exchange of energies. The tighter the aspect in orb, 0 to 6 degrees, the stronger the influence. The harmonious angles create a more compatible romantic rapport where both people are fully enjoying the romantic/sexual dynamics. Uranus involved with this planetary duo will also enhance the sexual excitement.

The planet Mars denotes men, aggressiveness, desire, and passion. I also call Mars the planet of identity, for how we assert ourselves and approach our goals establishes who we are as individuals. The planet Venus denotes woman, beauty, attraction, self-esteem, social/romantic life, and comfort. Venus represents how we value ourselves. This is a very important influence, for how we value ourselves is what we are going to attract into our lives. If your self-esteem is well defined, you in turn will like who you are and will therefore attract love, beauty, harmony, and comfort into your life.

When the planets of love and passion merge, the desires of the Mars person are satisfied by the Venus person. Mars is driven toward the attraction (Venus) both socially and romantically. Venus is receptive and loving to the Mars person's ego assertiveness.

Mars indicates how you approach life. Being the planet that wishes to identify with someone, Mars seeks out its opposite—Venus. Mars is attracted to Venus, and Venus is receptive to Mars' actions. Therefore, you can extend yourself through Mars, to find out more about your own true identity. Mars needs to be in strong aspect to your partner's astrology chart in order for Mars to feel at home. This zestful planet will motivate you to pursue and get involved. Once you (Mars) establish your connection with Venus, you can relate more romantically to your partner.

Most men feel that they cannot identify with their Venusian side. Men identify with Mars, masculinity, and women identify with Venus, femininity. So men naturally project their Venusian side onto women. This creates an attraction, man to woman. However, if he wants to compliment her further, he needs to expand upon this idea by bringing out more of her femininity, her beauty, and her attractiveness. Truly, a man who compliments a woman, compliments himself! This concept is one of the most important factors in the ideal relationship. He can do this by respecting and appreciating the woman he loves.

The physical magnetism of Venus and Mars represents male and female coming together in a partnership, usually in marriage. This marital union is not only designed for a romantic relationship, but also procreation. Venus is the planet of fertility, and Mars is our male sexual counterpart, the sperm. So if you are interested in having children, it is necessary to have these two planets in aspect. Jupiter, the planet of expansion, opportunity, and good fortune in aspect to Venus or the Moon, is also favored for having a family. On the other hand, a Saturn aspect to Venus may limit the amount of children. Usually one is enough. A Mars-Saturn aspect may also curb the affections and block fertility unless other romantic Venus-Mars aspects are pronounced.

Inharmonious angles between Venus and Mars may actually enhance the romantic dynamics between you as long as there is mutual cooperation in the act of lovemaking. Dancing and loud music can release any emotional tension and lead to an evening of intense love, provided your relationship is in good standing to begin with. Finding a balance may be required, as one of you seeks out sexual relations and the other prefers an affectionate exchange.

Venus and Mars in aspect are essential to a close, passionate relationship. The romantic sparks created with this male/female pairing are a driving force toward a loving partnership.

(2) "Sun-Moon"—Strong, Enduring Bond

The ideal: conjunction, trine, and sextile
The lesser ideal: square, opposition, semisquare, sesquiquadrate, and inconjunct

A Sun-Moon aspect is a powerful and enduring combination in a couple's compatibility. It is highly supportive of lasting ties. The conjunction is the most significant because it's like a new Moon, which tends to enhance our ambitions in life by creating a fresher outlook. Usually it's a man's Sun in aspect to a woman's Moon, as the Moon will find support and reliability with the Sun. A woman can therefore depend on her man. However, in this day and age when sometimes the woman is the breadwinner, or at least his equal, a man's Moon aspecting a woman's Sun is a possible find.

The Sun and Moon are known as the luminaries. They light up the astrological experience, especially when the Sun and Moon are in favorable aspect in a couple's compatibility. The Sun represents the masculine luminary, and the Moon represents the feminine luminary. In a relationship, each of us possesses both the male and female energies. You may identify with one or the other, but both are inherent within. Therefore, the woman could be in the role of the masculine luminary (the Sun) and the man could be in the role of the feminine luminary (the Moon). The fact that the Sun-Moon connection exists is what is most important. This does not take away from a man's masculinity or a woman's femininity; it only encourages a strong link in the relationship that will last through the years.

Here, one's long-range goals (the Sun) work easily with the other's habitual patterns (the Moon). The Moon's intuition understands the Sun's wishes. The emotions, the Moon, and the ego, the Sun, are at home with each other. An ideal aspect between the Sun and Moon, especially the conjunction in the same element, encourages you to compliment each other. It's a smooth ride as the emotions and ego set sail together.

The Moon person can depend on the Sun person. But that doesn't mean you should lose yourself in the Sun person and then become totally dependent. Co-dependent behavior leads to a limited relationship, so don't let your partner become your entire life. Your partner should be an enhancing force, encouraging you toward continued personal growth.

When the Sun and Moon are in adverse aspect, you are sometimes not willing to compromise. You experience frustrations and disappointments. The struggle here is trying to find a way to balance the emotional needs with the willful ego needs. Adverse aspects, especially the square aspect, create a dynamic attraction in the relationship, for one feels compelled to get involved. Yet getting along on a daily basis can meet with obstacles. Both people must learn to be patient in addressing the issues so that their needs, emotional and wordly, can be satisfied. The polar opposite aspect allows you to explore and struggle with who you are as individuals and in a relationship. In attracting our opposite, we learn to see ourselves more clearly and understand the give and take that promotes the continuum of our life experience

A Sun/Moon midpoint has a strong impact on a relationship as well. If a Sun-Moon aspect is not present, usually a Sun/Moon midpoint in aspect to the Sun or Moon is, to strengthen the union. This significant bond generates an attraction between the emotions and the ego that endorses long-term prospects. (For more information about the Sun/Moon midpoint, see chapter 17.)

(3) "Sun-Venus"—Showing Affection and Respect

The ideal: conjunction, trine, and sextile
The lesser ideal: square, opposition, semisquare, sesquiquadrate, and inconjunct

Attraction may inspire, but demonstrating love and respect in a relationship is an absolute priority. This occurs when Venus, the planet of love and values, aspects the Sun. In a Sun-Venus aspect, the Venus person displays love, affection, and respect toward the Sun person. Being demonstrative will let your partner know how you are feeling about them. If you hug someone, you want to feel the hug back. If you say "I love you," you want to hear it in return. Mutual Sun-Venus aspects indicate that both parties are inclined to address each other in a caring, loving manner, which in turn shows respect for one another.

Only fear can get in the way of expressing your true affections toward someone. Sun-Venus aspects help break through feelings of fear surrounding set patterns from the past. Without question, you will feel love and fondness for the person. When you fall in love with someone, a Sun-Venus influence is usually present. The loving qualities of Venus are receptive to the Sun's purpose of being. The Sun empowers Venus, and Venus loves the Sun. You feel more than inclined to show affection and nurturing. In admiring your partner, you compliment their self-esteem. Fond devotion (Venus) is inspired by the Sun. Amorous Venus increases the fortitude and stamina of the Sun person. The Sun is flattered by Venus' display of affection. Venus attracts the Sun's rays that spotlight all of the feeling and love Venus has to offer. *Harmonious angles and the opposition are highly effective in creating a scenario of true love.* Social values are also emphasized. This combination works best when in favorable aspect and when it's mutual.

Even in adverse aspect, the Sun-Venus combination can be respectful and loving, especially if there are many other positive planetary pairings in the Love Relationship Formula. The tendency, though, is for either person to get too involved with themselves, thus not being able to fully respect the other. The Sun, which represents the ego, may become self-absorbed when the Venus person attempts to demonstrate their affections. Venus then feels ignored, as the ruler of Libra prefers the idea of sharing the love given. The Venus person would garner hurt emotions, as if what they have to offer is being shunned. The Venus person may also become rather self-indulgent, attracting the Sun's vitality to bolster their Venusian image. The Sun's pride would be slighted in this instance. In either case, one needs to recognize when one is concerned only with oneself and not one's partner to gradually improve upon the mutual respect that is needed in a loving relationship. Nevertheless, the presence of a Sun-Venus influence inspires an affectionate, loving rapport that presides over the lifetime of a relationship. No other influence will allow you to experience such fond, heartfelt feelings for the one you love.

(4) "Sun-Mars"—Energized, Passionate Goals

The ideal: conjunction, trine, and sextile
The lesser ideal: square, opposition, semisquare, sesquiquadrate, and inconjunct

As feelings are awakened through Sun-Venus, passion is aroused through Sun-Mars as well as Venus-Mars aspects. Many couples have a Venus-Mars aspect. If you don't, the

Sun-Mars aspect is the next best thing. Mars is associated with a masculine image, aggression, and passionate sex. Mars is our desire nature and how we take action to satisfy our desires. The Sun represents our vitality, pride, ego, achievement, and purposeful goals that bring us joy and recognition. In the physical body, the Sun relates to the heart and represents the capacity to generate warmth to those around us. When these powerful forces link up, Mars, the planet of energy and passion, lights up the life, vitality, and purpose of the Sun person.

When you are in the company of someone whose Mars aspects your Sun, you feel energized. As Mars optimizes the Sun's ambitious goals, oftentimes we attract people whose Sun relates to our Mars. We can't help but feel that revved-up drive and passion. The Sun literally glows, especially when in harmonious aspect to Mars. The Sun represents pride and ego. Here, Mars can motivate the Sun person to succeed, and perhaps win. The Sun person likes taking the lead and being fully recognized by the Mars person.

The Sun prefers being in the spotlight as Mars pursues a more passionate exchange. A man's Mars is especially favored when in aspect to a woman's Sun, as the male drive can be expressed toward the woman and therefore compliment her—the Sun loves attention. As Mars is our identity planet, the Sun's influence allows the Mars person to be more in touch with independent goals. Therefore, the Mars identity feels secure to move forward, to be assertive. The Sun, already shining brightly, will throw a spotlight on Mars. Thus Mars feels driven even further toward the self, as the identity is strengthened.

In adverse aspect, Mars may try to conquer and challenge the Sun person, becoming competitive or, in extreme cases, combative. This drive for dominance needs to be curbed. How this works out depends on the individual. Self-awareness and personal growth can lessen the effect of this challenge. The attraction is there, yet we need to channel the energies so that both parties benefit. Couples with a Sun-Mars aspect need to be active, either sexually or with other activities such as sports. On a positive note, goals are achieved through mutual cooperation and drive. The passionate embers of Mars are ignited by the Sun to enhance a romantic relationship and to motivate the couple toward success.

(5) "Sun-Ascendant"—Mutual Approach to Life/Similar Interests

The ideal: conjunction, trine, and sextile
The lesser ideal: square, opposition, semisquare, sesquiquadrate, and inconjunct

Another complementary pair is the Sun in aspect to the Ascendant. The conjunction has the greatest impact, as the Ascendant is the reflection of the Sun person's personality.

Therefore, the Sun person will see himself or herself in the Ascendant person. Remember, the Ascendant, or rising sign, is what you are projecting out into the world. This is how others see you. If you have Capricorn on the Ascendant, others see you as conservative, practical, and proper. If you are a Capricorn, you would notice someone who has this influence and feel a like-mindedness that would make the relationship more compatible. Therefore, your Ascendant plays a very important role in attracting the right relationship. This is not always a lasting impression, but it does make for a strong initial attraction. What lasts is your ability as a couple to capitalize on a parallel approach to your goals. When a couple is involved with similar interests, the relationship has an opportunity to bond more. Shared activities, such as a recreational or leisurely pursuits, will not only fortify the union, but also allow the couple to continually interact through the years.

The Ascendant reveals your perspective of the world and how the world sees you. The Ascendant represents the self, the personality, and physicality, and describes by sign what course of action you take in approaching life goals. Everything we experience— our birth into a certain set of circumstances, our childhood, and our environment— conditions our outlook on life. It is the indicator of how we will approach everything in life, because through the sign's energy this is the way in which we have learned.

The Ascendant signifies the mask people wear. This facade will describe quite accurately the personality and how the individual will achieve their aims. When your Sun connects with your partner's Ascendant, you feel as though you can identify with this individual. The Sun's purpose relates to the Ascendant's analogous methodology about pursuing one's objectives in life. What is nice about the Sun-Ascendant influence is that it is also tempered by the Sun being in opposition to the Descendant, a Venus Point, which emphasizes a display of love and affection. Therefore, the mutual approach to a couple's aims instills a shared fondness as well. The Sun-Ascendant aspect, preferably a conjunction, promises an enduring connection through similar interests and ideas about your outlook on life, which will promote the continued growth of your relationship.

(6) "Sun-Jupiter"—Confident, Supportive, Expansive Goals

The ideal: conjunction, trine, and sextile
The lesser ideal: square, opposition, semisquare, sesquiquadrate, and inconjunct

For both sexes, a Sun-Jupiter aspect brings support and enthusiasm to one's aims and purpose in life, especially when it is in harmonious aspect. If you do not have a Venus-

Jupiter connection, then make sure Jupiter is at least aspecting the Sun. Jupiter will make the Sun person feel important, so he or she can advance in life. Being the planet of abundance, expansion, and opportunity, this uplifting influence wants you to succeed. Jupiter builds confidence and provides opportunity for the Sun's achievements and wants you to expand upon your goal-oriented role in life.

In a relationship, auspicious Sun-Jupiter aspects will help strengthen the union. The Jupiter person is acting in your best interests when in aspect to your Sun. In turn, the Sun person will approve of Jupiter's expansion and prefer Jupiter's optimistic outlook. You are encouraged to move ahead on certain projects or career pursuits. This shows your partner's appreciation for your skills and talents and promotes your self-esteem. You now have the support to achieve recognition and prosperity. These days, most women will have a career, and they, like men, have a strong sense of pride in their accomplishments. When Sun-Jupiter aspects are mutual, both parties truly benefit, as their intentions are to further each other's goals. Materialistic aims are improved. Any shortcomings are tolerated as your image is bolstered. A shared success is felt for every goal reached. This favorable relationship influence can help alleviate any difficult aspects that are found between your charts.

When adverse Sun-Jupiter aspects are present, you may receive encouragement from your partner with high expectations, but not always the follow-through support. You may find yourself somewhat on your own, feeling the desire to expand or proceed, but not sure if you can trust it. This may put some stress on your relationship. There may also be times when Sun-Jupiter in discordant aspect may promote overconfidence, causing you to be blinded from the truth. In such cases, expansion always needs to be determined by realistic guidelines. Calculated risks are the way to go. Those who possess inner strength and confidence may be able to balance an adverse Sun-Jupiter influence by enjoying the positives and avoiding overly speculative ventures that yield an illusive victory. Either way, your relationship has an opportunity to prosper from this encouraging influence. You are able to bring out the finest in one another by offering your fullest support.

(7) "Moon-Venus"—Sensitivity to Feeling

The ideal: conjunction, trine, and sextile
The lesser ideal: square, opposition, semisquare, sesquiquadrate, and inconjunct

Besides encouragement, showing sensitivity is essential in unlocking the true essence of one's feelings. In a relationship, we always want to enhance feeling, which is described by the Moon-Venus aspect. Both are planets of emotion. When in aspect with one another, they activate nurturing, warmth, and sensitivity toward your partner. It's where you take that extra step or go that extra mile to be supportive and sensitive to your partner's needs. Here, the Moon feels and understands Venus' values. Venus is comforting and receptive to the moods and feelings of the Moon. The Moon-Venus aspect in a compatibility reading brings out the finer qualities of the relationship. To contribute in a productive way to your relationship, you need to be in touch with your feelings. Showing sensitivity means wanting to understand your partner's needs and desires. A lack of sensitivity, or just ignoring your partner, does not indicate concern or appreciation. Hurtful feelings and resentment may arise from such negligent actions.

People who are in denial suppress their emotions, thus they cannot truly feel. They are unaware of others' needs and feelings because they are unaware of their own. Therefore, a person in denial may experience great difficulty in relating to their partner. Such people may need to find someone with whom they can begin to discuss those buried feelings. Only then can they have a successful relationship. The Moon-Venus aspect creates an environment where just that can happen. When the Moon and Venus are in positive aspect, they reflect a nonthreatening nature. When you experience this in your relationship, you feel comfortable letting your guard down and expressing what you are feeling. The Venus person is able to comfort the emotion emanating from the Moon person. In turn, the Moon person is open to receiving this kindness and affection from the Venus person. Displaying sensitivity toward another indicates that you care for them. What are you feeling? What is your partner feeling? If you don't know, ask. Start showing consideration for your partner and the union you both share.

In this day and age, men need to become more in touch with their hidden feelings. They are repressed because they have been conditioned to hide them. But this is changing, for it is no longer the norm for a woman to lean on her man for support, and he doesn't always have to be the strong, responsible one in the relationship. It is more of an idea of sharing the responsibilities. In this way, as men become more in touch with their feelings, they can fully appreciate their relationship. It has been documented that a man gets in touch with his feelings through having sex and a woman through nurturing. A balance is really what is required here for a mutually fulfilling relationship. The warm sensitivity of Moon-Venus aspects indicate care and consideration that will always enhance the bond between you.

Discordant Moon-Venus aspects sometimes instigate jealousy or a fear of losing your significant other to someone else. This may induce possessive behavior that will not be appreciated by your partner. Both of you may have this tendency. Continuing to show sensitivity to your partner's feelings will win them over much more easily than exercising possessiveness. Try capitalizing upon a warm, caring attitude that is always accessible. The sensitive qualities of the Moon-Venus angle will enable you to reach out to your partner in a manner that is caring, endearing, and well received, especially as you grow closer through the years.

Since Venus is exalted in the sign of Pisces, feeling has an opportunity to be expressed in a higher spiritual essence. A similar effect occurs when the compassionate influence of Neptune, ruler of Pisces, is exalted in Cancer, the sign governing the Moon. This links Venus and the Moon with Neptune, which induces a romantic soulmate connection. As we all yearn to find heavenly, compassionate love, we must be aware that Moon/Venus/Neptune aspects are also prone to deception. We learn through Moon/VenusNeptune aspects that the truth counts. The spiritual essence experienced between a couple grows out of honesty. Suspicion and dishonesty will only erode your relationship. A positive Moon/Venus/Neptune aspect shows that you can express a sensitized compassion for your lover that knows no bounds. Being in touch with your feelings enhances the spiritual bond between you, as a caring and loving disposition finds its way to both hearts. If you do not have a Moon-Venus influence in your synastry, a favorable Venus-Neptune aspect will bring added sensitivity into the relationship.

(Venus-Neptune aspects are covered in chapter 14, "Karmic Relationship Connections," and can enhance the Love Relationship Formula.)

(8) "Moon-Jupiter"—Emotional Happiness

The ideal: conjunction, trine, and sextile
The lesser ideal: square, opposition, semisquare, sesquiquadrate, and inconjunct

The Moon-Jupiter aspect enhances emotions. In a committed partnership, this aspect promotes happiness and brings out your sense of humor. There's a lot to be said for a man or woman who makes you laugh. Laughter alleviates stress. In the medical field, Dr. Bernie Siegel, who wrote the book *Love, Medicine & Miracles,* clearly explains how laughter relieves stress and can actually heal. This is certainly a great commodity to have in your relationship. We speak of how we want to enjoy our relationship. If your interaction brightens one another's outlook, you will both feel optimistic about your relationship and your future together. By sharing your internal joy, you enhance the long-term outlook of the union.

Jupiter emanates such happiness that even an adverse angle will encourage the Moon to attain a brighter outlook. Mood swings caused by other planetary crossings can be corrected by Moon-Jupiter pairings. The Moon (emotion) is receptive to optimism (Jupiter). Tensions and past issues find peace. When your Moon is around Jupiter, you relax, for you know everything will be alright. Such wonderful reassurance will draw you to your partner as he or she lightens your load, making all the difference in the world. Interacting with your partner becomes a pleasure. The generous spirit of Jupiter will pamper the sensitive Moon. The inner personality of the Moon opens to receive the wonder and goodwill that Jupiter has to offer. The Moon person will encourage the Jupiter person's high standards, philosophical ideas, and adventuresome spirit. Jupiter wishes to make the Moon person feel good, and will go out of their way to do so. You will operate on a positive instinctual level in understanding one another.

If an adverse Moon-Jupiter aspect is prominent, the Moon may be demanding of Jupiter's good fortune. Jupiter may impose its over-optimism onto an unreceptive Moon. The sensitive Moon is overwhelmed by Jupiter's higher quests. The Moon's needs clash with Jupiter's desire for freedom. Regardless of some discordant feelings, the Jupiter person will still brighten the Moon person's day. Although Jupiter's giving may be overdone, the Moon in some manner will be amenable to receiving its cheerful attitude. There is nothing more treasured than restoring someone's happiness. Bringing joy into your relationship will alleviate tension and anxiety, building a cherished bond of contentment between you. Thus, you are able to provide happiness that lasts through the years.

(9) "Mercury-Jupiter"—Positive Communication

The ideal: conjunction, trine, and sextile
The lesser ideal: square, opposition, semisquare, sesquiquadrate, and inconjunct

Whether you are relating through laughter or sadness, social interaction is a human need. You can have a great sex life with someone, but if you cannot communicate, your relationship will eventually fall apart. Besides our physical needs, mental needs must also be fulfilled. You have to be able to express your feelings and opinions with your partner, even if it means a disagreement or argument every now and then. When Mercury, the planet of communication, is in aspect to Jupiter in a compatibility analysis, this creates an atmosphere for positive verbal exchanges. Here, Mercury (communication) is met with enthusiasm (Jupiter). Your ideas are expanded upon. Social opportunity will also be enhanced when Mercury is in aspect to the Sun, Moon, Venus, or Uranus. These planetary connections will allow you to express your thoughts and feelings, especially when in positive aspect. Mercury-Jupiter aspects are essential in a business partnership as well.

Mercury's influence can be described as nonsexual—platonic. When a relationship is platonic, you can be friends. The bond of friendship allows you to communicate your thoughts and feelings to your partner. We all want and need someone to relate to in life, and Mercury-Jupiter aspects create an intellectual openness that enhances the interaction with your partner. The communicative rapport between you flows easily as the conversation expands upon the ideas being expressed. When mutual, both will enjoy conversing with each other. Mental blocks are nonexistent here. You will find that the right intellectual rapport is also a drawing card in developing a relationship. For as a couple, you seek out one another to relate to, and the relationship continues to benefit.

Where we may get into trouble is when Mercury is in adverse aspect to Mars, especially if Saturn, Neptune, or Pluto is involved. Look out! If you are experiencing difficulty with stressed, blocked, or evasive communications in relating to your partner, an adverse Mercury-Mars, Mercury-Saturn, or Mercury-Neptune aspect could very well be the reason why. Also be cautious with a discordant Mercury-Pluto aspect as this can promote manipulation, an undesirable attribute we can all do without. Mercury-Jupiter aspects encourage a couple to bond on a communicative level, which enhances the rapport between them. Intellectual interaction is the thread of a relationship.

(10) "Venus-Jupiter"—Compliments, Favors, Positive Self-Esteem

The ideal: conjunction, trine, and sextile
The lesser ideal: square, opposition, semisquare, sesquiquadrate, and inconjunct

Communication is a necessity and compliments are a must. We all like to be around someone who makes us feel good about ourselves, and this is just what a Venus-Jupiter aspect can do. A Jupiter aspect to Venus compliments our image and our social/romantic life. Since Venus is the planet of femininity, it's highly favorable to have a man's Jupiter in aspect to a woman's Venus, as Jupiter will bring out her Venusian qualities.

This is what to look for, ladies, for this means beautiful flowers on birthdays and holidays, and nights out on the town. He makes her feel good about herself by emphasizing her attractive appearance. When a woman's Jupiter is in aspect to a man's Venus, she builds his self-esteem and also expands upon his Venusian image of her. Jupiter and Venus are givers. Their benevolent natures are well-received. Jupiter expands upon what Venus would like to share. Jupiter compliments Venus' beauty and charm, and Venus attracts and is receptive to Jupiter's generosity. Affection is greeted with happiness. Venus values what Jupiter wishes to expand upon, especially higher-minded pursuits.

Because Jupiter is the planet of abundance, this influence will bring out more and more of what Venus has to offer. Here, the Jupiter person appreciates and highlights the Venus person's artistic talents and potentials. When in mutual and harmonious aspect, the image of the relationship is enhanced tremendously. Social festivities and leisure life will also be thoroughly enjoyed. Venus-Jupiter aspects allow you to compliment your partner in a meaningful way so that he or she feels appreciated by you. As you are inspired by the Jupiter person to feel your best, you in turn reciprocate the compliment. Where in the past compliments may not have been forthcoming, this relationship will benefit greatly from the mutual appreciation.

When men project their Venusian side onto a woman, man is attracted to woman. A man who compliments a woman, compliments himself, for she is a reflection of his Venusian side. If she looks good, he looks good. Only a man can truly compliment a woman by aspiring toward her beauty, grace, and talents. Making love to a woman compliments her. A man who cannot compliment and appreciate the woman in his life may sour the whole relationship. Chances are he is looking elsewhere to project his Venusian side.

Even on adverse angles, Venus and Jupiter still work well together to flatter the relationship. However, excessive tendencies involving self-indulgence or an extravagant lifestyle indicate that Venus may not be able to appreciate what Jupiter has to offer. Venus may also show signs of jealousy if Jupiter is too successful, thus stealing the spotlight away from Venus. Regardless of the circumstances, in any relationship you need to be aware of interacting on a complimentary level with your partner. For in offering them goodwilll, you are paying attention to them. As your mate is open to receiving this attention that you are giving, it improves the loving rapport between the two of you. A

Venus-Jupiter aspect allows you to sincerely compliment your partner. Praising your partner will brighten your entire relationship.

(11) "Venus-Saturn"—Long-Term Security

The ideal: conjunction, trine, and sextile
The lesser ideal: square, opposition, semisquare, sesquiquadrate, and inconjunct

Besides feeling appreciated, we also need to feel secure in our relationship. There are two aspects that can provide us with that security. The first is a Venus-Saturn aspect, which can engender a long-term alliance. Saturn, our planet of fears, insecurities, and burdens, is comforted by Venus, the planet of love and affection. It usually works best when a woman's Saturn is in aspect to a man's planet of Venus. Women need to feel secure in a relationship. She wants and needs to know that her mate is going to be there. A man is able to offer comfort and love to his mate, knowing that he can provide, and she can rely on him. Under this influence he will demonstrate dependability. When this influence is mutual, both partners have an opportunity to be there for one another.

A Venus-Saturn aspect will allow you to feel at ease with your partner. When meeting for the first time, you feel as though you have known the person before. This level of familiarity brings such contentment that you are free to be yourself. Feeling this comfortable lends itself to a lifelong companionship. In most instances you will find Venus-Saturn aspects in a couple's comparison, especially those who have been together for many years. More often than not, couples, especially men, will marry under Venus-Saturn transits and progressions as they are destined to become serious in love.

Reciprocal Venus-Saturn angles tend to reveal very karmic relationships indicating you have met before and are meant to spend time together to balance the pros and the cons of your relationship. When mutual Venus-Saturn aspects exist, it can be acceptable as long as the man's Jupiter is in aspect to the woman's Venus, so he can compliment her and bring out the beauty and attractiveness that she possesses. If this is not the case, the man's Saturn will tend to suppress the woman's Venus—her femininity, self-esteem, and creative expression. This can in some instances lead to a controlling situation. Saturn needs to learn to respect the love and comfort of Venus.

Because Venus is also the planet of self-esteem and self-love, your partner's planetary influences need to activate Venus in a positive manner, such as Uranus trine Venus or Jupiter conjunct Venus, to let you know they are attracted to you and appreciate you.

Even though you may feel secure in the union, too much Saturn and its restrictive influence will gradually smother the self-esteem of the Venus person. Eventually the Saturn person will react negatively, as Venus' charm and attractiveness become dull and undesirable. The Venus person must react to and change this conditioning, or the relationship will suffer. Otherwise, the Saturn person may find themselves controlling, taking for granted, and even rejecting the Venus person. Unless a man or woman sees this pattern in themselves, they cannot learn to appreciate their partner.

Being too comfortable in a relationship does not mean that you appreciate what is there. Unless you do with your actions and say with your words that you love your significant other, your relationship will experience unfortunate setbacks. Never take your partner for granted. Although Venus-Saturn aspects denote long-term security, you still need to demonstrate appreciation for your partner. To ease this influence, a Venus-Jupiter aspect needs to be present. Where a Venus-Saturn aspect has a tendency to become too comfortable, a Venus-Jupiter aspect encourages your partner to acknowledge your presence with compliments.

Adverse Venus-Saturn aspects may not only show a lack of appreciation, but the Saturn person may be especially demanding and critical of the Venus person. Control tactics evolving from the Saturn person keep the Venus person in his or her place. Although Venus may try to revolt, Venus has little control and may be overwhelmed by Saturn's restrictive and disapproving ways. If you decide to remain in a relationship where a person's Saturn is in hard aspect to your Venus, you are destined to earn your love, hopefully without compromising your dignity. Only a Jupiter influence to Venus can help alleviate some of Saturn's pressure, which is part of the Love Relationship Formula and why they work so well together.

Finding a balance between Venus-Jupiter and Venus-Saturn indicates why it is so important to love and respect yourself and to establish a positive image. In doing so we have the opportunity to attract a more productive as well as committed relationship. Through Venus-Saturn aspects, you can secure a comfortable, lasting relationship, where loyalty is highly valued. (For more information on Venus-Saturn connections, refer to chapter 14, "Karmic Relationship Connections.")

(12) "Venus-Uranus"—Exciting, Lasting Attraction

The ideal: conjunction, trine, and sextile
The lesser ideal: square, opposition, semisquare, sesquiquadrate, and inconjunct

Security, relating, sensitivity, and love are all important, but how does a couple find one another and stay interested in one another? There needs to be a compelling, lasting attraction. One that makes you feel as though you cannot take your eyes off the person you find so intriguing. This type of romantic meeting will lift one's spirits as well as touch one's depth, the reason being that we become so intrigued that we need to tap into our deepest resources to understand the attraction. Here, we are suddenly interested in another human being who allows us to feel excited and more aware of our feelings. In that one moment, we forget ourselves and experience a part of the essence of life—connecting with another to enhance our romantic understanding on this planet.

Very often a couple meets under a Venus-Uranus transit, which is a love-at-first-sight contact that is usually lasting when on a positive angle, such as a trine or sextile. Unlike Venus-Mars or Mars-Jupiter transits, which also arouse a couple toward meeting, Uranus will suddenly excite a social/romantic attraction with Venus. One feels completely drawn to the other person. If a couple does not meet under a Venus-Uranus transit, they may very well have a Venus-Uranus aspect within the compatibility of their two charts that is activated in the meeting.

Here, the Uranus person is attracted to the Venus person. Uranus finds Venus exciting, charming, and appealing. Venus finds Uranus fascinating. In this case, it is more desirable if a man's Uranus is in aspect to the woman's Venus as your man will always be attracted to you, almost never allowing his eye to wander. Mutual attraction is a definite plus. It's like only the two of you exist. Here, one's attractiveness (Venus) flashes out to another (Uranus). An example would be Uranus in Leo trine Venus in Sagittarius. Since the Uranus person desires the Venus person, Venus may enjoy being noticed and in control, as Uranus continues to impart romantic intrigue.

Attraction on some level in a relationship is a must for it keeps the other person interested in you. This usually stems from Venus and Uranus in aspect. Along with this attraction, there needs to be good relating, comfort and security, romance and sex, friendship, respect, sensitivity, understanding, and depth, all of which are a part of the Love Relationship Formula. All of the ingredients need to be there. An attraction alone will not uphold a relationship, but is needed in order for the couple to notice and become intrigued with each other. The love story of Romeo and Juliet exemplifies this sudden, fervent attraction. Uranus in aspect to Venus were surely mutually present as the two young lovers were captivated with each other's presence.

Very exciting attractions may occur under adverse Venus-Uranus transits, but they may not be long-lasting. Rarely do I see these attractions hold up over the years. Sometimes the romance is experienced as a flash in the night. Romantic fascination is ignited in the thrill of the moment, only to suddenly and indifferently cease. Unless other factors of the Love Relationship Formula are strong, abrupt endings are indicated. Adverse

Venus-Uranus transits are categorized under "love affairs." However, in synastry an appealing attraction will be indicated throughout the life of the relationship, whether it is a positive aspect or not.

Inharmonious Venus-Uranus aspects challenge the relationship. You need to be careful to avoid becoming too detached or burning out from all of the romantic excitement. Space is required so you can experience excursions of self-discovery with the understanding of bringing new and interesting ideas into the relationship. A striking attraction will still be evident between you.

When a Venus-Uranus aspect is present, you will pay attention to the person you find so desirable. Feeling drawn to the object of your affection furthers romantic possibilities that enhance the bond between you. A lasting attraction will promote a long-term relationship, especially with favorable angles.

(13) "Venus-Pluto"—Deep, Intense Love

The ideal: conjunction, trine, and sextile
The lesser ideal: square, opposition, semisquare, sesquiquadrate, and inconjunct

Once we experience attraction, there is a gradual desire for greater depth and meaning. Very deep and intense feelings arise with Venus-Pluto aspects. Through lovemaking, we experience a merging of souls that cannot be explained or understood, only felt. We may sense that a past-life connection has once again been reestablished. Reliving this bond of love can be quite dramatic.

Under favorable aspects, the power of love and what it has to offer is such a moving experience that it reaches beyond our reality as we know it. The Venus person is receptive to and feels the depth and transformation persuaded by the Pluto person. This is where love and sex come together for the ultimate in lovemaking. The objective is to evolve through sexual intimacy to a higher plane. Sex without love is a limited experience. Pluto without Venus is very alone. Pluto represents not only sex but isolation. We evolve through isolation just as much as we evolve through sexual intimacy. Pluto encourages us to become in touch with the deepest core of our being. Here, transcendence can occur. Venus becoming involved with Pluto sensitizes this transcendence through the sexual act. Thus lovemaking is everything it should be. It's always best when it is mutual. If not, it is preferable to have the man's Pluto influencing the women's Venus, as he will be able to express his deep, passionate interest toward her.

This convergence heightens a sexual awareness that will only enhance a long-term relationship. Fated meetings happen under Venus-Pluto transits and progressions. Love (Venus) is intensified (Pluto). The Pluto person is driven toward sensuous and desirable Venus for sexual relations, and Venus (emotional feeling) is transformed by Pluto as two souls embrace in the act of love.

Inharmonious influences between Venus and Pluto can be challenging. Pluto may be too driven to merge with Venus. Venus, being receptive to Pluto's advances, is eager to please, yet may not approve of such aggressiveness. Venus' personal overtures may be inhibited by Pluto's alienation, due to a fear of a deeper emotional involvement. Venus may want all of Pluto's attention, as Pluto desires his or her own company. Tensions may arise if the couple is not sensitive to each other's needs. A primitive interaction will not achieve the desired result, which is to bring each other to a point of transcendence through the act of lovemaking. Oppositions and conjunctions in particular can indicate very karmic relations. In these cases the couple is meant to come to a deeper under-standing of one another through sexual intimacy. Difficult changes may lead to personal growth or break-ups. If the couple cannot reach a mutual understanding, they will go their separate ways. With the support of the Love Relationship Formula, even adverse Venus-Pluto aspects can be directed toward a meaningful exchange, where lovemaking is a deep, genuine experience.

(14) "Mars-Jupiter"—Motivated Desires

The ideal: conjunction, trine, and sextile
The lesser ideal: square, opposition, semisquare, sesquiquadrate, and inconjunct

The depth of love experienced in a relationship places an importance on sex. A Mars-Jupiter aspect in compatibility emphasizes ardent lovemaking. This influence can boost the passion of both sexes. Since women need more of a sense of security in a relationship, whereas men need to be physically attracted to their partner, it works best when a women's Jupiter is in aspect to a man's Mars. As Mars rules the masculine identity and sex-ual desire, Jupiter wants the woman to be able to expand upon this concept. She will not only be able to motivate him to get things done, but will also arouse his passionate side. Desires and physical cravings (Mars) are encouraged and fulfilled through Jupiter. Oppor-tune situations are also acted upon, thus promising financial gain. A Mars-Jupiter aspect between two peoples' charts does not replace the Venus-Mars connection. It enhances what is already there with a more dynamic exchange of love. Mutual Mars-Jupiter aspects encourage a motivated and active relationship. You just might enjoy doing everything together! If a Mars-Jupiter connection is lacking, a Moon-Mars or Mars-Uranus aspect will create emotional and sexual excitement as well.

In any formula, you have to have all of the ingredients. If you only have Mars square Jupiter, or Mars square Sun, the person with whom you are interacting could become overly aggressive with you if the affection (Sun-Venus) and sensitivity (Moon-Venus) are missing from the relationship. Mars, in ancient astrology, is known as the planet of war. Jupiter's influences may intend to expand upon this combative idea when in adverse aspect. If a negative Mars-Saturn crossing is also involved, the situation could become abusive. Mars always needs an aggressive outlet. In a loving, substantial relationship, Mars will most likely be used constructively to attend to certain activities that are a part of daily living. Mars combined with Jupiter will support a passionate exchange as well.

At times, daring Mars may become reckless, or overly optimistic Jupiter may take uncalculated risks. Much play and no work could be the result. Hasty business deals may also not come to fruition. Differences will have to be reconciled. One's temper may erupt, as the other's successes increase. Jupiter may want to go out, whereas Mars may be in the mood for sex. Although Mars may want to conquer, Jupiter's spirit will continue to encourage intimate exchanges.

The power of sex can sometimes push one to become involved in an affair with little chance of longevity. Make sure the Love Relationship Formula is secure before sex occurs. I have seen so many men and women devastated from having had sexual relations that I encourage a longer union before having sex. You think that you can handle an unemotional yet sexual attachment, but I have seen the brightest minds become emotionally wiped out when the sexual union takes a turn for the worst. I encourage men to be more responsible and women to not be so sexually vulnerable. Become more acquainted with your partner first, while applying the Love Relationship Formula. This takes time. Since sex produces children, a committed relationship is a responsible couple. Mars-Jupiter influences will promote the physical and sexual dynamics of a relationship that inspire a thriving, motivated couple.

(15) "Jupiter-Saturn"—Friendship Ties

The ideal: conjunction, trine, and sextile
The lesser ideal: square, opposition, semisquare, sesquiquadrate, and inconjunct

A relationship will last longer when you are friends as well as lovers. A good friend will listen to your issues and want to help you when in need. Mutual and favorable Jupiter-Saturn aspects are a real plus to any relationship, establishing a good, supportive friendship throughout the duration of your relationship. If a Venus-Saturn aspect is not present, security and comfort can be found with a Jupiter-Saturn aspect. Jupiter is the planet of optimism, support, opportunity, and expansion. The Jupiter person will take on the burdens and issues of the Saturn person, and also encourage the expansion of their social foundations. Jupiter's desire is to make Saturn feel secure with venturing out and interacting with others. Jupiter inspires one to go beyond any Saturnian fears, so that life goals can be attained. Saturn offers wisdom and guidance to Jupiter's hopes and dreams.

Jupiter's generous nature offers support and protection, while Saturn adheres to what is proper to achieve substantial results. With reciprocal harmonious Jupiter-Saturn aspects, the accomplishments of the couple not only inspire mutual respect, but also lead to long-term rewards. A solid foundation for their future plans is established. Sound investments generate security and a level of comfort within the partnership. When you are friends, you can rely on each other, discuss what is needed, and reach for your dreams.

When Saturn is in adverse aspect, it will restrict Jupiter from pursuing his or her wishes. Too many rules and regulations could discourage Jupiter from reaching for new horizons. Saturn needs to keep in check a controlling attitude that limits optimistic Jupiter from achieving new ambitions. In any situation, fear is limiting, but especially if it does not allow you to progress toward your desired objectives. On the other hand, Jupiter may want to pursue risky ventures that Saturn considers to be pipe dreams. Balancing out each other's objectives will lead the couple down a more constructive path where goals can be accomplished for the benefit of both parties. Jupiter helps alleviate personal issues that cloud the Saturn person's perspective. Saturn, if used constructively, can devise realistic plans that enable one to reach the desired objective. What you are destined to work out together will open up the dialogue to enhance your lifelong connection.

Using the Love Relationship Formula

The fifteen combinations of the Love Relationship Formula are designed to work to-gether to exalt your relationship. Even if adverse aspects, such as a square or opposi-tion, are present, the remaining influences that comprise a lasting relationship will help support the couple in addressing and working out the challenges that may exist. The link between the two planets enables a certain reaction to occur that is further directed by the aspect involved, be it a trine (positive) or a square (adverse). In some cases, ad-verse angles are needed to create sparks or challenges that allow the couple the chance to understand each other on a deeper level and grow closer together as they work through issues. There is much to be learned and gained. As the couple strives to bring harmony into their relationship, the surrounding influences of the Love Relationship Formula promptly assist them. Although all fifteen components of the formula are needed to have a loving and lasting union, having the following nine combinations in mutual aspect would put your relationship in good standing: Sun-Moon, Sun-Venus, Sun-Jupiter, Moon-Venus, Moon-Jupiter, Mercury-Jupiter, Venus-Mars, Venus-Jupiter, and Venus-Saturn.

The ideal relationship would be comprised of a mutual conjunction, trine, or sextile of each of the fifteen combinations of the Love Relationship Formula, preferably within 1 degree of orb. In our imperfect world, we allow some flexibility with varying degrees of orb and the inclusion of adverse angles with planets in the Love Relationship For-mula only. All of these planetary ingredients in the Love Relationship Formula in favor-able aspect will bring you the desired relationship you are looking for. More informa-tion to further your understanding of the complexities of a relationship can be found in the following chapters.

The Love Relationship Formula is a planetary guideline that will lead you to a won-derful, loving relationship. To share our lives with another is something we all yearn for—it's our birthright. Therefore, demand that it happen, for your journey to love has every opportunity of being a success.

part 3

aspects
of synastry

5 ♥ an up-close-and-personal look at the moon in synastry

The Moon nurtures, protects, and absorbs. Its receptive capacity promotes an instinctual awareness of one's environment. The Moon represents not only our emotions, but any type of a mother image. We can be the mother image ourselves, and/or we can project this image out into the world, thus looking for the one that will nurture our needs and satisfy our hunger for the emotional connection that brings fulfillment. If our Moon is activated, it brings up our feelings and therefore our needs. Here, sensitivity, nurturing, or a sense of obligation become a part of a relationship.

Moon-Mars—
Emotional Arousal and Initiation, Agitation, and Angry Feelings

Motivation comes in many forms, but when we are emotionally motivated, we experience a strong desire to accomplish a personal objective. Moon-Mars pairings in harmonious aspect usually inspire us to take action and be productive. In a relationship, our emotions become an integral part of acting out in a physical manner, where a passionate exchange between a couple is emotionally rewarding. Feeling (the Moon) is receptive to ardent desire (Mars). One's emotions (the Moon) are stimulated (Mars) toward intimacy. Mars is able to channel his or her desires through the sentimental openness of the Moon person, so both experience a level of satisfaction. The Moon's emotional outlook can find expression through Mars' amorous zeal. Emotion and passion ignite to enhance the romance in the relationship. This cosmic interplay allows the couple to accentuate the male and female personas, where both are exalting the sex of the other.

Both planetary influences symbolize an identity exchange as well. The Moon represents the inner emotional desire to connect and nurture, and Mars represents the assertive, worldly self that looks for comfort in identifying with a significant other.

Mars is better known as the initiator. Just as it can initiate passion, it can also initiate rage. Irritability and anger are the result of adverse Moon-Mars aspects. Volatility exists when the Mars person provokes the Moon person toward emotional fury, or when the Moon person is not receptive to the advances of the Mars person. Mood swings that provoke quarrels can arise unexpectedly. Usually this is caused by suppressed anger of one kind or another that is touched off by Mars. The natural instinct of Mars is to compete and dominate, but in a relationship this conquering attitude is not seen as agreeable. The Moon will become increasingly annoyed with the lack of consideration from Mars.

If you where born with a Moon-Mars aspect, you are more susceptible to this kind of temperamental behavior. I would suggest following a vigorous workout program or keeping very busy. Take the reins and direct this unsettled energy to help improve your life. Otherwise oversensitized emotions may get the best of you.

The energetic mannerism of Mars needs to be properly channeled so that tensions do not build and become explosive in a relationship. If other encouraging planetary factors are present, Mars can tame its restless manner, where constructive interaction leads to an exciting involvement. A passionate exchange will bring the satisfying result you desire.

Moon-Saturn—
Serious, Controlled, and Repressed Emotions/Co-dependency

The Moon is a reflection of our personality that was established during childhood. The early conditioning that we experienced as children is directly related to our emotional needs as well as our fears. Being raised with a certain emotional conditioning, we end up attracting this pattern in our relationships, for better or worse, until it is addressed.

The Saturn aspect to the Moon causes us to fear, control, and block our natural emotional response. This fear is more pronounced if a nurturing environment in childhood was not forthcoming. Unfortunately, Saturn influencing the Moon may encourage an unhappy relationship situation unless other supportive astrological factors exist. But this may not be so evident at the beginning of a relationship.

At first, the Saturn person will feel a sense of obligation toward the Moon person. Being responsible will anchor Saturn into the relationship. But if there are emotional imbalances with the Saturn person, he or she may like the idea of controlling the emotional response of the Moon person. This allows the Saturn person to feel secure and more in control, a condition that was most likely lacking in childhood, which is now a strong part of the relationship.

In turn, the Moon person acknowledges Saturn's personal obligation and feels comfortable setting up a home life. Even though the Moon person is aware of the controlling mannerisms of the Saturn person, the Moon person may seem comfortable as this does represent some type of stability. As time goes by, the Moon person will induce more and more of a family attitude, gradually bringing up Saturn's insecurities. Whereas Saturn may begin to fear the responsibilities involved with family life, projecting a worrisome attitude onto the Moon. The Moon person begins to feel emotionally blocked and therefore unable to discuss the lack of fulfillment with his or her emotional needs and domestic issues that continue to mount. The Moon person feels that he or she cannot express himself or herself emotionally, but then Saturn feels that his or her emotional needs are also not being met.

Saturn clearly feels a sense of obligation as the role of the provider, yet may not fully want the responsibility of taking care of someone. But because Saturn wants to control, in order to feel secure, he or she will end up staying in the relationship out of fear and emotional insecurity. This becomes a co-dependent relationship.

Mutual Moon-Saturn aspects cause both people to feel obligated in the relationship. But when emotional needs are not being met and you are staying in a relationship out of a sense of duty and/or fear, you are not happy. Moon-Saturn aspects represent sad, repressed, or controlled emotions. In most circumstances, this mirrors a dysfunctional family environment that systematically ends up affecting your adult life and intimate relationships. This can be appeased under a Moon-Jupiter influence. Nevertheless, Saturn may continue to be impersonal toward the feelings of the Moon, as the Moon is indifferent to Saturn's needs.

Eventually Saturn, under too much pressure, may be forced to leave the relationship, even though in most instances Saturn, still feeling co-dependent, does not want to part. The karmic connection involved with this Saturnian influence could cause the relationship to last for many years. Living under such pressure is not the ideal in a relationship. If this influence exists in your compatibility, you are being given a chance to recognize what emotional issues have been restraining you throughout the years, and now is your chance to release this fearful, co-dependent behavior.

We attract situations like this where we need to face up to our deepest fears for a reason, to finally confront them. Moon-Saturn connections indicate where co-dependency, abandonment, and rejection issues can be further understood. The co-dependent factor that is involved with this planetary combination will keep people together too. If there is a need to be co-dependent, this can be fulfilled when your Saturn is in aspect with another's Moon. You may not even know this issue exists until it happens. But clinging to each other is not the ideal in any relationship situation. If this is the case, addressing co-dependent issues will only improve your life in the future. Harmonious Moon-Saturn aspects will derive better results in working out emotional issues. Adverse aspects with this cosmic pair are intense, where a serious approach to one's hidden emotional self is a must.

Moon-Uranus—Emotional Excitement, Unpredictable Feelings

Early on in a relationship, the thrill of having a Moon-Uranus aspect in a couple's synastry will inspire emotional excitement. Whether a couple can channel this influence to keep those charged feelings alive may depend on both parties. Nevertheless, an exhilaration will arouse the couple toward wanting to enjoy and be moved by this electrifying appeal. This magnetic attraction will arouse great interest. The enthusiasm generated creates an atmosphere of surprise that is titillating. The Moon (one's emotions) is fascinated by Uranus. The Moon person is receptive to the surprises of the Uranus person. But what may excite one may also split one apart as feelings become unpredictable and indecisive. If Uranus acts in an erratic manner, the Moon will feel frazzled by the experience.

When this pairing is in adverse aspect, tensions build as the Moon may become upset over the lack of sensitivity from Uranus. An impersonal approach will not fare well with the open intentions of the Moon. The erratic behavior of Uranus may unknowingly cause undue stress. This dynamic influence does not guarantee a long-term connection. More substantial astrological connections are needed. If it is the man's Moon, he may have a new, eccentric vision of his woman.

Moon-Neptune—Mutual Identity, Obligation, and Emotional Illusion

I have always felt that positive Moon/Neptune aspects in synastry represent a sense of mutual identity where you can relate emotionally and telepathically to your partner. Since Neptune's etheric influence knows no bounds, emotionally you can sense what your partner is feeling. But that does not mean that you can understand what you feel, for Neptune also emanates a very nebulous energy.

When we are obligated in our relationship, we usually exercise compassion toward our partner, especially if we are aware of a sensitive underlying connection with them. This sympathetic bond that exists between the couple helps support a long-term alliance, but the couple might form a platonic association as opposed to a more romantic involvement. Nevertheless, the empathy shared by the couple is a special addition to the relationship. The Moon trusts Neptune's compassion and flows with his or her vision. Neptune finds that he or she has an emotional channel on which to impart his or her otherworldly, magical charm. More sensitive human beings will have an awareness of their spiritual oneness with another.

The creative side of Moon-Neptune aspects ensures that the Neptune person will project an intriguing, illusive quality over the receptive Moon. In turn, the Moon person will be fascinated by Neptune's idealism, inspiring the Moon's imagination to explore a world of fantasy.

Adverse aspects involving the Moon and Neptune in synastry create a distorted emotional rapport between the couple. When we have empathy for someone, we don't expect to be sucked into all of their problems and become completely overwhelmed. But having an insane compassion for a loved one can become an emotionally draining experience. The opposite can exist as well, where there is an obvious lack of compassion but still a strange feeling of obligation that leaves both feeling quite disturbed and frustrated. The Moon is not impressed with Neptune's unreliable nature. Neptune is not sure it can handle the extreme moody tendencies of the Moon. Falling into an emotional abyss is certainly not desirable in any relationship. However, adverse Moon-Neptune aspects may be another indicator of the relationship mirror that exposes our susceptible, hidden emotions. Once dealt with, a spiritual bond can be maintained.

Moon-Pluto—
Intense Understanding, Emotional Depth, and Manipulation

The intentions of Pluto cannot be denied as this cosmic force will invoke emotional depth in another when in aspect to the Moon. Our emotions are already heartfelt, but may lack the deep understanding that is required to find answers to life's many questions. When the Moon is in harmonious aspect to Pluto, we are better able to explore our inner self, developing and capitalizing upon helpful insights that mold our future. The Pluto person instinctively understands the feelings of the sensitive Moon. The Moon person will feel attracted to the mystery and depth that Pluto provides. The emotional impact of this karmic bond is truly felt and experienced.

Adverse aspects involving the Moon and Pluto will intensify the emotions, but the manipulative tendencies of Pluto are triggered. Pluto's profound insights could turn on the Moon person, where one is plotting away with secret tactics. The vulnerable Moon person could fall prey to a hidden agenda. These underhanded strategies will not benefit either party in the long run.

Perhaps if buried emotions need to surface, a Plutonian influence is helpful, but not at the expense of toying with another's feelings. If you love the person, your objective would clearly be to assist in unraveling that which is an emotional hindrance. This means working in the best interests of your partner, not using manipulation as a means to an end. A man's Moon will feel the powerful strength of a women, personified by her Plutonian influence.

6

♥

more on
mercurial
exchanges
in synastry

We have already established that Mercury-Jupiter aspects expand upon the communications to the greatest degree. Mercury may also be enhanced through influences from the Sun, Moon, Venus, and Uranus.

Sun-Mercury—Highlighted Communications

The Sun person will emphasize a communicative exchange with Mercury. Willing to listen, the Sun encourages Mercury to express his or her thoughts by providing a platform on which to converse. Mercury appreciates the Sun's understanding and proceeds with sharing his or her ideas and opinions.

When under an adverse influence, the Sun may not take Mercury seriously. Scattered thoughts are in need of direction and may make relating difficult. Mercury may feel that the Sun does not comprehend the witty yet unstructured mannerism that Mercury demonstrates. Under favorable aspects, the creative ideas of the Sun can be clarified through Mercury, as the Sun can be supportive of Mercury's intellectual skills. Highlighting communications causes a significant interaction between a couple.

Moon-Mercury—Sensitized Communications

There is an excellent balance in a relationship when the mind and the emotions come together in a harmonious angle. Feelings (the Moon) are expressed in an intellectual way (Mercury). Ideas (Mercury) are received in a sensitive manner (the Moon).

If Mercury and the Moon are afflicted or in difficult aspect, there may be some confusion, as Mercury may not understand the feelings of the Moon and the Moon may not be receptive to Mercury's ideas and opinions. Mercury may need to be more sensitive to the Moon, capitalizing upon his or her intellectual approach to ease the communicative rapport. The receptive Moon needs to be open to discussing Mercury's concepts and using his or her intuitive capabilities to guide Mercury if necessary. When a couple agrees mentally and emotionally, decisions are easily made, which in turn supports a lasting tie.

Mercury-Venus—Agreeable, Profitable Communications

Congenial conversation occurs under Mercury-Venus aspects. Ideas (Mercury) are accepted and appreciated (Venus). The intellectual approach of Mercury supports Venus materialistically and with shared incentives, so they both profit. Venus agrees with what Mercury has to say, and Mercury understands the feelings of Venus. Smooth communications allow the couple to relate quite well.

Under adverse aspects, Venus may continue to cooperate when Mercury is in error. Indecision about how to relate to Venus may baffle Mercury and promote a critical assessment of Venus' pursuit of pleasure. To counteract the adversity, Mercury needs to capitalize upon his or her wit to understand the desires of Venus, as lovely Venus has an opportunity to comfort and assist Mercury with ideas that benefit both of them. Sensitive, cooperative communications will lead to personal and monetary gain.

Mercury-Uranus—Excited, Intuitive Communications

The interaction between Mercury and Uranus inspires the mind to want to learn more by communicating one's thoughts and ideas. The mentality (Mercury) is intrigued with what Uranus has to offer. Mercury's ideas are stimulated by Uranus. Intuitive thought (Uranus) has an avenue to express itself intellectually through Mercury. This mental and intuitive acceleration can greatly assist a couple in understanding one another.

Inharmonious aspects create mental discord where Uranus will cause too much stress for Mercury. Uranus may want to break through Mercury's old way of thinking, and Mercury will judge Uranus for being indecisive or overly progressive. Nevertheless, Uranus will fuel Mercury with new concepts, as Mercury is fascinated with Uranus. Both may complement each other, providing a stimulating rapport between the couple.

7

challenging/ malefic combinations in synastry

Combinations to Look Out for or Totally Avoid

Malefics are the opposite of benefics. The benefic planets are Jupiter and Venus. The more benefic planetary combinations you have, the better off you are with developing and enjoying that wonderful relationship. In most cases, however, there will be some malefic aspects in a compatibility analysis. These are the areas that will need more attention in order to keep the harmonious balance in a relationship. Usually there are some karmic lessons connected with the experience of these malefic planetary influences. Therefore, here is the relationship that can help you rid yourself of this past-life burden.

You can learn a lot from a partner who is giving you a difficult time. The Dalai Lama has stated that your enemy, or the person you are at odds with, is your best teacher. Of course, we don't want to be enemies with our spouse. However, if we look at the seventh-house sector of close relationships in an astrology chart, this is the area of intimate conflicts *and* open enemies! This clearly indicates that issues will surface that must be addressed. This one-on-one encounter can actually strengthen the relationship, driving you together as opposed to driving you apart. Here, each of you will give to the relationship, creating stronger bonds.

Since we wish to evolve through our interaction with others, we need to understand differing ideas and opinions. I am not speaking of abusive situations, although we can learn much from such circumstances. Ralph Waldo Emerson pointed out in his essays how we learn from our shocking experiences. If all of life were the ideal of happiness, we would never learn anything. We can still have peace in our relationship, yet learn from the differences, the criticisms, and the conflict. I am not talking about a battlefield, but a stage where you can open up the dialogue.

Sun-Saturn—Constructive, Criticized, and Difficult Goals

When transiting Saturn aspects your Sun, everything seems "heavy" or more difficult than usual. In compatibility, Saturn's stern mannerisms are projected onto the Sun person. Here, the Saturn person has an opportunity to be constructive about pointing out the shortcomings of the Sun person. Let's keep in mind that we all have our weaknesses. As they are revealed, we should be given a chance to correct this shortcoming or turn our weaknesses into strengths. In this case, much depends on our partner. Are they going to be helpful or are they going to further criticize a weakness, thus debasing their loved one? Saturn can be quite hard on others, thus undermining their efforts. Not everyone is going to meet your expectations. Concentrating only on your partner's inadequacies will diminish the romantic rapport between you. In extreme cases, casting a fear of failure onto your partner will paralyze his or her efforts. If you are constantly criticizing your partner, he or she will feel insecure and unappreciated for everything he or she does. Unmistakably, the tendency for Saturn is to criticize when it is in aspect to the partner's Sun. To criticize constructively, however, may require some patience and understanding. Then both people will benefit. Once you offer constructive criticism, you may need to give your partner some space to apply that advice or wisdom.

Many times, the Saturn person has been too hard on themselves and will project their own shortcomings onto their partner. If you are hard on yourself, you will surely be hard on others, thus isolating yourself from the very acceptance and interaction you are looking for in life. If this sounds like you, you may need to explore your past and find out who's rating system you had to measure up to for acceptance. Then give yourself a break, so you can be more accepting and patient with your partner, which will only deepen the bond between you.

Saturn is known as the teacher planet, and a good teacher will emphasize discipline and responsibility to help organize and improve another's ambition toward any goal. In applying Saturn's influence, we can always aim toward constructive improvements in our life, but how others assist us is a reflection of how they really feel about us.

Although adverse Sun-Saturn pairings in compatibility are known to be karmic, unless the Saturn person's Venus is in aspect to your Sun, and perhaps your Moon as well, thus promoting affection and sensitivity, I do not recommend this combination for a relationship. It's just all too critical. A couple may also experience brief periods of financial loss, illness, lack of intimacy, or difficulty parting from a prior love. Nevertheless, the bond between you will be strong. A separation does not necessarily mean that it is over, yet much time could pass before a reconciliation. If you find that a Sun-Saturn combination is part of your synastry, ideally both of you will be evolved enough to channel these influences and benefit from a rewarding relationship that stands the test of time with patience and understanding.

Sun-Uranus—Exciting, Unpredictable, and Disruptive Goals

When the Sun and Uranus link up in favorable aspect in synastry, exciting ideas can be pursued. Your spirit will be revived while in the company of your Uranian partner. Reciprocal Sun-Uranus aspects perpetuate a progressive lifestyle that eliminates boredom and restraint, allowing both of you to experience the ideal scenario. You will seek out adventure and enjoy the thrill of self-discovery. If you feel stifled in your day-to-day life, meeting someone whose Uranus aspects your Sun will inspire you to see life in a whole new way. The Sun person is encouraged to move in new directions and feel his or her independence (Uranus). Breaking away from tradition will invite a better future as the Sun is stimulated to explore other avenues. Uranus' fresh outlook will promote a lasting companionship.

All of this excitement can have unfortunate setbacks under adverse aspects. The erratic nature of Uranus may create such tension that the relationship could become explosive. The eccentric behavior of Uranus may not be tolerated by the Sun. A couple adamantly wanting to pursue their own aims will move in separate directions. A clash of wills could suddenly bring the union to an end unless both parties are willing to give each other needed space. When you are able to allow your partner the freedom to attain his or her own objectives, the relationship has an opportunity to prosper. Having the independence to pursue your ambitions and be who you are is a must in any commitment. If you encourage your partner's individual growth, it will only improve your relationship. *Remember, setting someone free gives them the opportunity to come back to you.*

Sun-Neptune—Idealistic and Deceptive Goals

The creative, spiritual influence of a harmonious Sun-Neptune aspect will attract opportunities that improve your circumstances. These idyllic conditions encourage your vision where your ideals can become a reality. Neptune's unearthly and captivating manner will continually intrigue the Sun. The Sun person will be inspired by Neptune to take the lead in creative pursuits. Neptune may look upon the Sun as the ideal person to follow. When in positive mutual aspect, the couple is fascinated by what each other has to offer. Finding fulfillment in each other will only encourage the longevity of the union. Shared sympathy will warm the Sun's heart and reveal Neptune's innate compassion.

The presence of unfavorable aspects may create a tremendous uncertainty about each other's objectives. The Sun may question Neptune's reliability. Neptune may find the Sun too egotistical and demanding. Being overly interested in oneself causes ignorance of the complicated relationship issues at hand. If you feel you are being misled, the trust factor may dissolve, leaving both of you stressed-out. Neptune will have to earn the Sun's trust by directing his or her imagination toward the well-being of the union. A spiritual approach to understanding each other's objectives may help channel this illusive influence. As you find yourselves through each other, you may even be able to rekindle the tie. A platonic friendship may arise that will help base the union on honesty. Your relationship gains from maintaining its integrity.

Sun-Pluto—Involved, Powerful, Transformed, and Manipulative Goals

A powerful bond may occur when the Sun and Pluto are in positive aspect. The couple may feel that destiny has brought them together. These forces will induce a strong physical attraction as well. Pluto encourages the Sun's confidence. The Sun brings to light the deeper motives of Pluto. Partnerships are supported along with the restructuring of one's personal agenda. Psychologically, the differences of both influences challenge each other. The Sun wishes to express his or her outgoing, creative side, while Pluto wants to maintain his or her privacy. A clash of interests may be the result.

Deep-rooted issues may prevent the couple from cultivating a lasting relationship under adverse aspects. The struggle for a superior position will undermine the relationship's compatibility. The Plutonian influence will force the Sun person to transform his or her ways without his or her consent. Feeling undermined, the Sun will expose Pluto's secrets and take advantage of jealous tendencies. Not backing down, Pluto will want to conquer and gain supremacy over the Sun's ego by taking advantage of any weaknesses. As the two become rivals, there is little hope of renewing this tie. To avoid such power plays, a couple needs to use their commanding qualities to transform old issues and build a strong foundation of self-assurance that supports the couple's growth. As Pluto becomes more understanding in prompting the Sun to change, and the Sun carefully guides Pluto to transcend subconscious drives, this may encourage the evolvement toward a more rewarding union. The personal growth that one experiences can never be measured by time, but only by the repercussions that hold lasting value.

Mercury-Mars—Assertive, Agitated, and Angry Communications

We tend to be mentally invigorated when Mars influences Mercury. There is a desire to say what is on one's mind without holding back. This may cause you or your partner to be rather abrasive in speech, or interrupt you as Mars does not possess a great deal of patience. Nevertheless, this mental alertness will encourage lively conversation. It's important to direct the communicative energy so that a constructive rapport develops between both parties. One may need to exercise some control over the commanding influence of Mars, who may want to dominate the conversation.

Harmonious Mercury-Mars aspects will allow the couple to express their ideas and opinions, and act decisively. Intellectual exchanges are stimulating and productive. If everything begins in the mind, Mars can activate Mercury to be driven toward excelling to your highest potential. Otherwise, you can be as offensive as you wish to be.

When a couple is not able to channel the Mercury-Mars influence, different points of view lead to angry exchanges. Discussions turn nasty and in some cases provoke verbal abuse, especially if adverse Mars/Saturn aspects to Mercury are present. Disagreements in a relationship are fine, but they should not turn into shouting matches where Mars declares victory, though he or she has actually lost. Yelling at your partner will destroy your relationship. Since Mars likes to conquer, lying may become a part of this communicative scenario. In some cases, this may be unintentional and allow for more motivating conversation. *Lying, however, will eventually erode the trust factor in the relationship. When it comes to a relationship, trust is pretty much everything!*

Accentuating only your ideas and pursuing plans your way is not the concept behind a relationship. It's sharing and compromising. You want to be assertive in conversation so that both of you benefit, not because you want to win. The dialogue needs to unfold as a win/win situation. You can express your thoughts and accomplish your aims so that your relationship has an opportunity to meet even greater expectations.

Mercury-Saturn—Serious, Blocked, and Fearful Communications

I have found that many couples have Mercury-Saturn aspects, especially when raising children is a part of their lifestyle. Saturn can encourage the couple to bypass frivolous conversation and get to the point. An agenda is discussed, and rules or chores around the house are decided. Plans are laid out for the present and future, and a serious attitude toward one's objectives is applied. Saturn acting in such a positive manner is usually the result of favorable synastry to the Mercurys of both individuals, such as Jupiter conjunct Mercury or Uranus trine Mercury. In this case, their minds are stimulated toward conversation, and the conversation can move in a more serious direction if necessary.

In any relationship, being practical and working together as a team attracts stability. This leads to an orderly life where an everyday agenda allows us to accomplish and gradually attain our sought-after aims as a couple.

Saturn does not have a reputation for being well liked. Its depressing, restrictive, burdensome, and frustrating influence we can do without. We may at times feel that Saturn has failed us. Usually the reverse is the case. In a relationship, when Saturn is interacting with Mercury we might feel that if we lose control, our fears will overwhelm us. Therefore, some of us might attempt to control what our partner says when discussing matters. But if you are dominating the conversation and blocking what your partner would like to contribute, the relating is going to become one-sided. Your partner is going to start to feel that they cannot say anything for fear it will upset you, or just not go along with your plan. If you continue to project your Saturn onto your partner, the fears will grow and fester. Eventually your partner will feel isolated from you as you persist in calling the shots. Controlling the strategy of the relationship is not working as a team. This must be overcome if too much Saturnian force is restricting the rapport of the relationship.

Time and patience may be required to slowly and thoroughly discuss the issues at hand. Although Saturn will push you to work harder than what you thought would be required of you, this meticulous planetary teacher will always find a way to reward you for a job well done. This is not a material reward, but one of value that will give your relationship the meaningfulness that it deserves.

Mercury-Neptune— Nebulous, Confused, and Deceptive Communication

I have seen many relationships end that had adverse Mercury-Neptune aspects. The couple could not communicate and work out the misunderstandings that continued to plague the relationship from the start. Even if you have great synastry, Mercury-Neptune aspects may erode the rapport between the two of you. This further confirms that good communication between a couple is of vital concern for a long-term alliance.

Although Neptune emanates a creative and spiritual influence, when in aspect to one's planet of communication (Mercury), one's thoughts become vague and forgetful. The Mercury person will have a difficult time expressing himself or herself as thoughts drift and misunderstandings begin to occur. The Neptune person will get frustrated with the Mercury person, feeling that Mercury does not understand him or her, for Mercury is probably not listening in the first place. The intellectual rapport encounters confused ideas that misrepresent what is truly going on with the relationship. In time, the connection will dissolve, leaving one or both feeling that they deserve someone to whom they can relate.

If this is a part of your relationship experience, I would suggest that you write down what needs to be discussed, and listen carefully to what your partner is saying and respond to it.

Jupiter aspects to Mercury will certainly help the situation, encouraging favorable verbal exchanges that support the relationship. Occasionally, Saturn aspects to Mercury can also help you look at the situation from a practical perspective. In most instances, only an evolved couple can channel these Neptunian energies.

In comparing Neptune and Jupiter to Mercury, Jupiter always encourages financial gain, whereas Neptune is not economically supportive and tends to dissolve any monetary resources. People are rarely hired under Mercury-Neptune transits.

In synastry, you will find that the Neptune person seems to drain the Mercury person's funds. This may not be intentional, but it happens. Financial stability is a must if a relationship is going to prosper. Continually having money dissipate from your account will either slowly put you into debt or make you feel like you cannot get ahead. If the Neptune person is not contributing to the couple's pocketbook, the Mercury person will start to become resentful. If both people can contribute to the monetary growth, then they should. It's respecting the future investment that you will be spending together. Money isn't everything, but it sure helps. When you accompany your partner down the path of life, financial stability must be present.

Mercury-Pluto—Deep, Pensive, and Manipulative Communication

When we are immersed in deep thought, we become very involved with our thinking processes. We are inclined to probe the subconscious mind to gather information that can assist us in our life choices. Favorable Mercury-Pluto aspects allow a couple to understand more of the intellectual depth of their relationship. The Mercury person will be intrigued by the mysterious insights of Pluto, and wish to intensely explore them. The Pluto person, after having reexamined Mercury's concepts, will encourage profound thinking in the Mercury person. However, Pluto's influence is so deeply rooted in the underworld that even with the trine or sextile one might encounter adversity. Being that it is difficult to channel this powerful influence on any angle, Mercury needs to be aware of the hidden attributes that could seek to undermine him or her.

Adverse Mercury-Pluto aspects in synastry will initiate mental power plays that are exhausting and quite destructive. Through the manipulative tendencies of Pluto, the Mercury person will be overwhelmed and end up giving into coercive, power-driven tactics. Pluto may embellish the truth or lie to acquire what he or she wants. Continuous scheming will gradually erode the lines of communication. Once these lines are severed, very little can be done to save the mental rapport of this union. The Pluto person is convinced that it is okay to manipulate the conversation to his or her point of view. Thus, one person ends up making most of the decisions. Mercury feels deprogrammed. These forceful, secretive ploys indicate an intellectual quest for power. The use of such tactics with your partner signifies a tremendous imbalance in your relationship. The word *relationship* holds the functional importance of the word *relating,* which is interacting on a positive level with your partner, not manipulating them.

Those who wish to harness the power of Pluto through selfish means risk the chance of this influence backfiring on them. This in turn will damage the communicative foundation that you want in your relationship. The mind is where everything starts. Therefore you want to use this transformative influence to engage its highest potential so that both partners may benefit. Such is the power of Pluto, to destroy and rebuild. Ridding yourself of an old consciousness and establishing a new, productive one is the most cohesive way to enhance your relationship.

Mars-Saturn—Restricted Motivations and Desires/Abuse

Mars-Saturn influences are very difficult to handle in any union, especially when in adverse aspect. Mars is our identity planet, and how we assert ourselves or take action establishes who we are as individuals. To keep Mars functioning at a proper level, we must feel an inner sense of freedom so that we can move forward in the pursuit of our goals and exercise an ability to stand on our own. When Saturn aspects Mars, the Mars person feels restricted in some way by the Saturn person. At first, they may find themselves encountering delays with their personal, daily agenda. Then frustrations set in that cause the Mars person to begin arguing. The Mars person needs space and feels restricted by the Saturn person. The Saturn person expects the Mars person to go along with their plan. If the Saturn person recognizes that the Mars person needs some space, as opposed to being in control, this can help the relationship tremendously. If not, as time goes by more frustrations set in and eventually the Mars person needs to regain their personal freedom. If this is mutual, there can be major differences that are difficult to resolve, especially if resentment is building.

If one's identity is suppressed over long periods of time, resentment turns to anger, and anger can lead to an abusive relationship. Arguing, yelling, and physical violence may become the pattern of the relationship. You may wonder at times, how did this happen? If conflicting issues are not being addressed, eventually there is an explosion. Suppressed energy cannot be contained. When I see any Mars-Saturn aspects in a compatibility analysis, I always let the person know what they are in for, and then it's their call.

At times you will encounter a couple who continually argue, yet stay together for years! What usually is going on here is that they feel comfortable in the relationship because they know the person so well. This is usually a reflection of a Venus-Saturn contact, which implies a past-life connection. They may not like what is going on, but they feel inclined to stay in the relationship. *Even though they may feel emotionally miserable, at least they know what they are dealing with here—there are no surprises. It's the same old situation, but better this than having to go look for someone new!*

Our fears are certainly warranted, but staying in a relationship that is depleting the core of your being will gradually destroy you. Better to part, knowing that you deserve a loving, supportive relationship.

Since Mars is more widely known for its passionate side, our passion for a person or personal quest needs an outlet. As Pluto is our planet of involvement, sex, and intimacy, Mars arouses us toward this purpose. But Mars may need to be supported and guided to reach this goal properly. Usually a favorable aspect such as Jupiter trine Mars will motivate Mars in a productive manner so that passion is an enjoyable experience.

When an adverse Mars-Saturn aspect exists between a couple, their timing is off. Mars wants to exert himself or herself, whereas Saturn wants to slow down, be conservative, or in control. Either force could become extremely upset with the other. Mars may not feel motivated to reach out to Saturn and express his or her passionate side, while Saturn may reject or want to put restraints on Mars.

In a romantic or passionate exchange, timing is important. You want to experience arousal, intimacy, and sex so that both people are satisfied. In synastry, the Saturn person or the Mars person may block this timing. Mars may need to be more patient with Saturn, and Saturn may need to be more spontaneous and flow with Mars. Or Saturn may want to control Mars, and Mars may want to express unprompted passion. If Jupiter is involved with this Mars-Saturn pairing, you have an opportunity to work out the differences.

A woman's Saturn in aspect to a man's Mars will allow the woman to feel in control of her man's drive. Yet, she may find that she has to initiate romance. Saturn here is restricting the man from his natural inclination to take the lead, be assertive, and express his passion. If her Jupiter is in aspect to his Mars as well, then a balance can be created between the two influences, as Jupiter will help expand upon his drive and motivation.

Difficulty in having children is often associated with adverse aspects from Saturn, Uranus, Neptune, or Pluto to a woman's Venus, the planet of fertility, which may create an unstable or disagreeable environment for conception. *However, in synastry this lack of conception is often caused by a women's Saturn influencing a man's Mars. This is especially evident when Mars and Venus are not found to be in aspect. The Saturnian aspect to Mars can limit a man's sexual advances and/or performance. It also restricts the sperm from reaching a fertile environment. The reverse could also be the case where the fertile environment is experiencing difficulty in accepting the sperm. To override this restrictive influence, the Venus-Mars aspect must be strong.*

The attraction of Venus and Mars encourages people to stay together, whereas the interaction of Saturn and Mars does not. Venus and Mars promote intimacy and conception, but Saturn and Mars block one's desires and can lead to restrictive, controlling, and abusive relationship situations if not properly channeled. How interesting it is that conception takes place frequently with couples who have Venus-Mars connections, and almost never with couples who have adverse Mars-Saturn connections and no Venus-Mars connections present. I can see children benefiting from their parents staying together with a Venus-Mars connection. Could there be a higher plan here? The problem is that oftentimes couples may have both Venus-Mars and Mars-Saturn combinations, and their relationship has difficulty surviving.

When you fall in love with someone who has Saturn in adverse aspect to your Mars, you're in trouble. A similar effect may occur with Saturn conjunct or in adverse aspect to your Ascendant, a Mars point. You will find the Saturn person wanting to control or monitor you, and knowing that they can. If Saturn is influencing your Ascendant, it is also in aspect to your Descendant, a Venus point. Saturn-Ascendant and Saturn-Mars connections represent a karmic obligation that may need to be confronted and resolved.

Mars/Uranus—Excited Passion/Sudden Anger

Adding to the attraction of Venus and Mars is the stimulating force of Uranus. When this Uranian influence interacts with Mars, our passions are suddenly aroused. Throwing caution to the wind, we are highly motivated to pursue our desires. An immediate, dynamic attraction will draw a couple together like magnets. In favorable aspect, the spontaneous Uranus person overwhelms the passionate Mars person with excitement. The intrigued Mars person acts assertively to capitalize upon the impulsive spirit of the Uranus person. Mars accentuates the unique Uranian qualities. The strong fascination that characterizes the relationship augments the magic. The couple will thrive on this sexual stimuli, looking forward to every intimate experience.

Adverse Mars-Uranus aspects may provoke a turbulent challenge, along with the sexual excitement. Full of surprises, Uranus will end up clashing with the straightforward approach of Mars. Freedom-loving Uranus will rebel against the dominating Mars, who wants to run the show. A sudden display of anger will be the result as neither will want to give in to the other's demands. Minor irritations can turn explosive as tempers flare. Although this could cause an interesting change in one's normal routine, the compounded tension could breed resentment and anger. Violent arguments may also interrupt sexual relations. This rage needs to be harnessed before hostile actions destroy the good of the relationship. It will take two determined souls to channel this erraticism down a constructive path. Each person needs to be able to express their individualized self. Therefore, when they are in close company, both will direct this spontaneous influence to enhance personal intimacy.

Mars-Neptune—
Romantic Mystique or Nebulous, Deceptive Representation

Most relationships are built around some form of romantic intrigue. Our imagination becomes intertwined with an idealistic interlude of passion and romance. This illusion is something into which we all enjoy escaping to experience relationships in a different realm.

When we meet someone whom we are attracted to, we may come to find that we have a certain fantasy about them. In other words, they seem to fit our ideal in a man or a woman with whom we would like to be intimate. In harmonious aspect, Mars, the identity planet, will assert himself or herself toward the mysterious desire he or she sees in another. The Mars person is enraptured by the Neptune person's qualities. Thus intrigue sets in. The Neptune person is able to channel the Mars drive in a more understanding and compassionate manner not only for themselves, but also for those around them. Mars is able to guide Neptune to reach his or her ideals.

A couple who possesses this dynamic in a stable relationship can enjoy the fantasy, but also deal with the reality of daily living and still appreciate one another. Without stability, the fantasy can take on deceptive forms. Mars can become so caught up in an amorous illusion that confusion is the result. Mars may become disillusioned with the vague, confusing behavior of Neptune. The compassionate ways of Neptune may clash with Mars' aggressive, direct, and self-centered behavior. Neptune can tease Mars, as a provocative, romantic illusion that is just that—unattainable. In extreme cases, the aura of seduction can lead to rape. For those who are emotionally unbalanced, Mars-Neptune aspects can lure one, whether it be victim or perpetrator, into such a destructive, savage act. Since the aggressive abuse of power is more evident in the male species, women need to develop a stronger awareness of their male counterparts. Men need to be more responsible in controlling their desires even when they are shrouded in sexual deception.

We always want to be careful of projecting our romantic fantasies onto another, otherwise we may be disappointed if they don't measure up to our expectations. Whether you are under the influence of Neptune in aspect to your Mars, or if a Mars-Neptune pairing exists in your natal chart, you must keep your desires in check. For your ideal may not be a true reflection of what you originally thought.

A problem relationship exists when the Neptune person feels they always have to acquiesce to the drive of the Mars person for fear of strife and mistreatment. Neptune, on the other hand, may flirt with Mars with no intention of involvement. Balancing their different ways of approaching goals is what is required. The Mars person needs to develop an understanding, compassionate attitude. The Neptune person needs to appreciate a commanding, straightforward performance. We all have personal needs, and each person's needs want equal time. Pursuing the spiritual and emotional needs of the relationship in a direct manner will bring positive results.

Saturn-Uranus—Traditional Goals Define or Restrict One's Freedom

Our personal freedom is described by Uranus. As individuals, we are able to capitalize on our unique selves, freely expressing our ideas. There is no greater freedom than to be who we are. Uranus persuades us to be progressive. Its futuristic concepts will permeate our consciousness until we decide to individualize, to strike out in our own personalized direction.

When Uranus is feeling erratic and out of control, Saturn's maturity may be called upon to offer stability and guidance. In harmonious aspect, the Saturn person will help the Uranus person understand that being responsible will bring them the freedom they desire. Saturn's conservative ways will give Uranus a foundation on which to build their future. Clearly stated in the lessons of history, independence is earned. Uranus will instill in Saturn a progressive attitude.

Adverse Saturn-Uranus aspects indicate a clash between the old and the new. The youthful spirit of the Uranus person may be severely quelled by the Saturn person. Uranus may totally upset Saturn's traditional outlook by unexpectedly lashing out at Saturn's conventional behavior. Saturn wishes to tone down Uranus' erraticism so Uranus will be accepted into mainstream society. Uranus will feel inclined to break free of tradition, and Saturn may be lost in the historical dust. Saturn may look upon Uranus' eccentric behavior with disapproval and not understand why Uranus wants to be so unconventional. Uranus, feeling out of step with Saturn's restraint and customary ways, will distance himself or herself from outdated priorities. A lack of sensitivity may push the couple further and further away from each other, unless other compatible aspects support an affectionate exchange. Such differences can also prevent a couple from getting together in the first place.

Although Saturn and Uranus clash, they still need each other to accomplish their goals. In establishing a means to an end, Saturn needs Uranian insight to keep tradition moving with the times. Uranus needs Saturnian pragmatism to realize its futuristic inspirations. This bridge between Saturn and Uranus can be described by the asteroid Chiron, wanting to take the past into the future. From a psychological point of view, the old structures of Saturn can be released through the self-discovery of Uranus, allowing us to come more fully into our own. If the views of both Uranus and Saturn can be respected as well as integrated, a couple will not feel so torn between traditional and progressive values. In any relationship, a couple needs to agree on the values of the past and the present.

Saturn-Neptune—Structured or Blocked Ideals, Realism versus Idealism

Neptune's influence has always enhanced our life by allowing us to dream of what could be attained. Dreams are important because they impress upon us a hopeful attitude about our future. We have all witnessed people who have lived an impoverished life pursuing their dream and, in a moment of grandeur, have accomplished this hard-earned goal. Dreams instill hope. Hope gives credence to the spirit of life.

When Neptune is in harmonious aspect to Saturn, our dreams become realistic, and therefore have more of an opportunity to be attained. In most cases, the Saturn person can offer a successful strategy for Neptune's vision. The Neptune person, attempting to grasp an illusive pursuit, will appreciate Saturn's disciplined and focused approach. Neptune will loosen up Saturn's strict behavior so that Saturn will be more open to compassionate and creative ways of living.

Since Saturn's influence is not one of wishful thinking, Saturn could project a harsh attitude toward anyone pursuing a dream. Especially when in adverse aspect, Saturn will dull and in some instances completely restrict a person from their vision. Disillusionment sets in, and the Neptune person feels blocked from achieving their ambitious goals. Creative and spiritual aims are subdued as well. Saturn may feel frustrated by Neptune's lack of responsibility. Neptune may feel disappointed by Saturn's cold, materialistic stand. Saturn may question Neptune's sense of integrity as promises are not always delivered.

Neptune is known for its idealism. The planet of love, Venus, is exalted in Pisces, Neptune's ruling sign. Thus Neptune encourages us toward romanticism. To be a romantic, one has to dream. In parting from reality, one can experience the mystique of romance. Life and love become more colorful. As a couple, romantic ideals add to the relationship. An amorous rendezvous, a picnic in the park, or a candlelight dinner is time out for the two of you to enjoy your relationship. When Saturn is present, it will cast a dark shadow over this loving, Neptunian ideal.

Adverse Saturn aspects will take the joy and the romance right out of the relationship. Too much reality creates a disillusioned state of mind that does not support the couple. This lack of inspiration will gradually dissolve the romantic rapport unless supportive influences exist. Without dreams, the human spirit would wither away.

Saturn-Pluto—Restricted Personal Growth/Intense Responsibilities

Pluto is our planet of transformation that represents the continuum of life—endings, yet new beginnings. This planetary influence also rules our personal growth. In life, we thrive when our growth is enhanced. Experiencing new stages of evolvement in this incarnation, we seek out events that change our life and bring more meaning to it.

In synastry, Saturn imparts its realization of, or limitation to, one or more of our needs. Favorable aspects depicted by Saturn will promote the use of solid, conservative planning. In this case, the Saturn person will constructively guide the determined Pluto person, insisting on a practical approach to personal goals. Saturn demands discipline and order from Pluto's involvements. Pluto appreciates Saturn's ambition and focus. Any Jupiter aspects would support Saturn's responsible behavior and expand upon Pluto's growth incentive.

In adverse aspect, Saturn's restrictive energies will tend to delay and even block Pluto from the personal growth it innately desires. In this day and age, we do not want to be in the company of someone who is preventing us from experiencing our personal transformation. The Saturn person will repress what needs to surface and be transformed through Pluto. The Pluto person will bring up fears and insecurities, thus curtailing Saturn's accomplishments. Total restraint, lack of evolvement, suspicion, and envy are worst-case scenarios. Saturn might feel responsible in directing and controlling Pluto. Yet Pluto, with its volcano personification, cannot be controlled and restricted for long.

The couple needs to adopt a responsible attitude that contributes to each other's individual growth. Otherwise, karmic patterns where there was an abuse of power in a past life may need to be resolved. One needs to embrace the process of life, transformation, so the relationship can evolve to a new level.

8 ♥

Noteworthy Benefic combinations

When in positive aspect, Jupiter-Uranus, Jupiter-Neptune, and Jupiter-Pluto influences can offer underlying support to any relationship.

Jupiter-Uranus—Enthusiastic Ventures, Joyful Independence

Favorable Jupiter-Uranus aspects bring enthusiasm where you are inspired by your partner to pursue aims that promote your uniqueness. As you discover yourself, your aura will shine. Not only do you receive encouragement from your partner, but Uranus will continue to be the recipient of Jupiter's goodwill, which includes supplying the capital to finance Uranus' inventive ideas. Jupiter will understand Uranus' unconventional approach, such as practicing metaphysical studies. Uranus' intuitive skills will offer guidance for Jupiter, furthering expansive plans. Even under adverse angles, excitement through inspired yet reckless spending, risky investments, or rebellious behavior is not uncommon.

Jupiter-Neptune—Expansive Ideals, Spiritual or Overrated Quests

When harmonious Jupiter-Neptune aspects are in effect, an intuitive understanding enhances religious beliefs, spiritual aspirations, and philosophical views. Neptune's compassionate nature will persuade Jupiter's philanthropic manner toward more charitable causes. A sympathetic, mutual appreciation creates a spiritual bond that holds great value.

Under inharmonious aspects, Jupiter's misplaced trust in Neptune's counsel leads to disappointments. Defraudation may take a toll on Jupiter's bank account. Exaggerated ideals promote visions of grandeur that never materialize. Jupiter can maintain stability by curbing overly ambitious expectations. Neptune, instead of taking advantage of Jupiter's generosity, needs to show appreciation.

Jupiter-Pluto—Expansive Growth and Empowerment

Jupiter, in favorable aspect, wishes to expand upon Pluto's growth, which over time will build great inner strength. Here, one is encouraged to explore one's more meaningful side to gradually become empowered by the affirmative insights. Pluto intensifies Jupiter's philosophical views and aims for a fruitful experience, which can only happen when one is involved. A keen focus on financial issues augments funds. This auspicious Jupiter-Pluto contact only contributes to an already enriching rapport between a couple. When challenging influences exist, Pluto's narrow-mindedness will limit Jupiter's expansive actions and refuse to accept Jupiter's philosophy and beliefs, and Jupiter will be annoyed by Pluto's cynical outlook. Compromise from both persons is needed to create unity.

♥

planets are the experience

The planet is the experience, the horoscope sign describes the experience, and the house is where the experience happens. In the Love Relationship Formula, we are dealing specifically with the planets—the experience. The signs, however, do give us some added information that may further describe the experience. But this description does not replace the influences that emanate from synastry. The houses indicate where this experience is taking place. We are concerned with understanding the experience of the couple, as one planet aspects another from chart to chart.

The Planets

Since the planets are the experience, their dynamics are of the utmost importance when interacting with other planets, especially in the compatibility of a relationship.

Sun

The Sun symbolizes your will, vitality, strength, purpose, and your goals. It indicates where you become aware of your purpose in the world and are encouraged toward great achievement. Honoring integrity, you recognize your importance and are able to express your fullest potential. In developing your skills and talents, true dignity is attained. In a man's chart the Sun represents his disposition toward manhood, and in a woman's chart the Sun represents her idea of the male role model. Having purpose and being proud of who you are allows you to find your place in the world and must be mutually respected in a relationship. Your will is your greatest asset.

Moon

The Moon symbolizes emotions, feelings, instincts, habits, the mother, and all female associations. Various emotional responses emanating from the Moon explain your mood swings. Your inner being will display behavioral patterns that describe conditions from early childhood and your relationship with your mother. Feeling out circumstances, you learn to adapt to new conditions and find emotional stability. In a man's chart the Moon represents his idea of the female role model. In a woman's chart the Moon represents her emotional femininity and her womanly ideal, which reflects upon the mother. Emotions play an important role in relationships where you learn to be sensitive to another's feelings because you have come to an understanding of your own.

Mercury

Mercury symbolizes communication, the intellect, learning, and analysis. Through the process of gathering information, you learn to analyze your ideas and develop a communicative rapport with others. Reasoning skills allow you to accumulate data that will augment your versatility. Mercury allows you to connect with your partner so that you can develop better relations. Strong one-on-one links are established that promote a lasting union.

Venus

Venus symbolizes love, attraction, self-esteem, values, and femininity. It is through the power of love that you learn to establish meaningful values, especially in learning to love and appreciate yourself as well as those around you. The magnetic appeal that Venus displays allows you to attract opportunity. Developing love and appreciation increases your prospects for success. Love is not only receiving but also giving. You are apt to seek harmony and beautify your surroundings. Venus by sign describes your self-esteem and, for a woman, her femininity. The house placement of Venus describes where you will show appreciation and what you will attract to yourself. In a woman's chart Venus indicates her womanhood, how she feels and relates to herself. In a man's chart Venus represents the woman whom he finds himself attracted to on a physical level and the feminine ideal he wishes to bring into his life. This planet represents our affectionate and sensual nature. In a relationship, wherever Venus is, there is comfort and love.

Mars

Mars symbolizes desire, energy, passion, independence, aggression, and masculinity. Here, energy can be used constructively or destructively. When it is properly channeled, you are driven to establish your identity by seeking out your independence and personal goals. How you approach your objectives will indicate how well they are satisfied. Your desire nature will invoke intense passions that can be directed toward a love interest or an important ambition. In a man's chart Mars represents how a man feels about himself and expresses his masculinity. In a woman's chart Mars represents the man she finds appealing, her masculine ideal. Mars brings out the passionate, sexual desire in a relationship.

Jupiter

Jupiter symbolizes expansion, opportunity, abundance, optimism, and wealth. It indicates where you look for opportunity to attract the good fortune that life has to offer. Always broadening your consciousness, you will look to expand mentally, socially, spiritually, physically, and emotionally. Jupiter instills an optimistic and confident persona that invites benefits. It prefers that you express your generosity to others, even as you are acquiring abundance. As long as you don't overextend yourself, augmenting your experiences will lead to fulfillment. This influence is highly supportive of a relationship, as it tends to bring out the best in a couple.

Saturn

Saturn symbolizes limitation, reality, discipline, maturity, and authority. Here you must confront reality and recognize your limitations. You will learn how to consolidate your goals by structuring your life appropriately. Applying discipline and hard work in some capacity will be required, but you will develop integrity and gain respect from others. Saturn's calculating manner may seem cold, but its intentions are to acquire solid results. Since it rules over the aging process, one becomes more settled and accomplished as one matures. As you cultivate a grown-up attitude, you will reap your rewards. What you will come to realize is that it is only through earning your own way that you will truly appreciate your life. Saturn may help generate stability in a relationship.

Uranus

Uranus symbolizes sudden change, the unpredictable, uniqueness, the unconventional, and one's individuality. There is much encouragement to be your true self, capitalizing upon your individuality. Due to Uranus' erratic tendencies, circumstances will be unpredictable and prone to sudden changes. There will be a breaking away of any limiting conditions that are hampering your progress so that you may proceed into the future and manifest your fullest potential. There is a desire to be free and escape the status quo. Imaginative and inspirational insights will enhance your existence as you continue on the path of self-discovery. Developing your individuality may lead you to engage in unconventional activities, yet awaken you to the truth that lies within. Uranus can be exciting and disruptive in a relationship.

Neptune

Neptune symbolizes illusion, idealism, creativity, compassion, spirituality, nebulousness, deception, and dissolution. You may pursue your greatest hopes and dreams, which inspire the imagination. Yet, because of the vague projection of Neptune, your belief is tested to see if you have sufficient faith in order for the goal to be realized. Creative aims and spiritual quests are highlighted. However, deception is lurking, and if you succumb to unscrupulous behavior, you will meet with disappointment. You will learn to cultivate perceptiveness to take advantage of the idealistic means of Neptune and to avoid the undermining world of illusion. The unreliability of this influence could erode the foundation of your relationship. You could also reach new spiritual heights that secure a compassionate bond forever. Embracing a sympathetic understanding of humanity will help you develop a caring nature.

Pluto

Pluto symbolizes intense involvement, transformation, regeneration, partnership, joint finances, sex, obsession, manipulation, and elimination. The process of transformation involves dramatic change that allows for a new phase to begin. It is the experience of death and rebirth that allows you to be reborn into new circumstances. Through Pluto you encounter the heights and depths that bring greater meaning to your existence. You are challenged to delve into the subconscious mind and regenerate undesirable conditions. Attitudes and expectations will change as society reflects itself upon you. Partnerships and sex are explored where one may become seriously committed. Because of

Pluto's intensity, when you become involved, there is a chance of developing obsessive attachments. In a relationship you will attract experiences that compel you to alter your behavior. Reexamining each other's psychology, you become aware of a deeper force working within that promotes your personal growth. When cooperation is present, you experience meaningful, intimate encounters that enhance your relationship. A lack of cooperation leads to dominating or manipulative behavior. Pluto seeks either alienation or unity.

10 ♥ Benefics in Aspect

Compatibility is always supported by the benefics, Venus and Jupiter, which attract opportunity and benefits our way. When two similar benefics, such as Venus-Venus or Jupiter-Jupiter, are in aspect, it helps create a sense of buoyancy in the relationship that may alleviate certain difficulties. Unlike Saturn-Saturn aspects, which generate pressure, Venus and Jupiter in similar aspect encourage the relationship to continue.

Venus and Jupiter in aspect to each other are a wonderful pair that will complement each other to the fullest. This combination was mentioned earlier as a significant part of the Love Relationship Formula. When Venus-Jupiter aspects are mutual, great happiness literally emanates from the couple. Others are pleased to be in their company. In health astrology, Venus and Jupiter in combination are known as the sweet-tooth planets. There is a definite sweetness here that adds to the rapport.

A Venus-Venus aspect under positive influences creates more warmth, feeling, and comfort between the couple, where they experience a relaxed atmosphere. Sociability is enhanced as both tend to be congenial. The couple will demonstrate a loving consideration toward each other as a fond companionship is encouraged.

When discordant Venus-Venus aspects exist, they may detract from the shared affection, yet they still support the relationship connection as two benefics are in aspect. A lack of appreciation, an uncooperative attitude, or possessiveness could put the couple at odds with each other. Mutual consideration needs to be restored by showing more sensitivity to one's partner.

A couple with a harmonious Jupiter-Jupiter aspect experiences optimism, abundance, and support within the relationship. Jupiter is always an uplifting influence that encourages the couple to enjoy each other's company. Since they are able to agree on philosophical, religious, and moral issues, the intellectual exchange reinforces the union. Both benefit by bringing out the best in each other.

When discordant Jupiter-Jupiter aspects exist, differences over religious pursuits, philosophical outlooks, or moral standards may cause disagreements, yet there is always an opportunity to work it out with the benefics in aspect. Reckless extravagance may be encouraged for the wrong reasons. Expansive behavior needs to be contained to balance this outgoing dynamic.

II

♥ same planets
in aspect

When the same planets are in aspect in a compatibility analysis, the impact of the influence is emphasized. If the planets are afflicted at birth, the two similar planets will be affected by the adversity. If the planets in question are in favorable aspect at birth, this will enhance the two similar planets involved.

A Sun-Sun aspect emphasizes the influences described by the Sun signs. Two Librans are more likely to find compatibility than two Aries. There can be a like-mindedness displayed if the Suns are in the same sign. If this energy can be channeled for the good of the relationship, the union can be successful. The ambitions and purpose of both will be similar, thus enabling the couple to understand one another better due to common interests.

Adverse angles to both person's Suns indicate a clash of wills that makes it difficult to compromise. Each Sun sign has its own agenda, yet both have skills and talents to contribute to the success of the relationship. If the couple can allow for and appreciate their differences, that could offer new options for growth in the relationship. Then conflicting views have an opportunity to be expressed and directed toward the continuance of the union.

A Moon-Moon aspect causes the feelings to be more pronounced between the two individuals. The instinctive habits are in sync, which allows for an innate understanding of each other. You will feel comfortable in each other's company. The emotional sensitivity is supportive of a lasting relationship. Mutual feelings ease and complement the domestic scene. You will respond in a similar manner to everyday situations, which increases the compatibility between you.

When adverse aspects are present, one person's moods may not agree with the other's, which will instigate a stressful environment. A lack of appreciation toward each other's responses will create distance between the couple. Differing habitual patterns may cause discord. Both need to be sensitive to one another in expressing emotional needs or opinions.

A Mercury-Mercury aspect enhances communication, especially when in favorable aspect. Intellectually, there will be a harmonious rapport, where common interests are shared. Both will inspire communication and appreciate what each other has to say.

Under adverse aspects there is an intellectual challenge, as their interests may be dissimilar. It may be a struggle to work out issues, especially if one's Mercury is in a fixed sign—Taurus, Leo, Scorpio, or Aquarius. Being too critical will not achieve the desired result. Learn to be flexible with your partner.

A Venus-Venus aspect under positive influences creates more warmth, feeling, and comfort between the couple, where they experience a relaxed atmosphere. Sociability is enhanced because both of you tend to be congenial. You will demonstrate a loving consideration toward each other as a fond companionship is encouraged.

When discordant Venus-Venus aspects exist, they may detract from the shared affection, yet they still support the relationship connection. A lack of appreciation, an uncooperative attitude, or possessiveness could put the couple at odds with each other. Mutual consideration needs to be restored by showing more sensitivity to one's partner.

A Mars-Mars aspect is very stimulating and can rev up the passions between a couple, even with challenging angles, as long as the Love Relationship Formula, especially Sun-Venus and Moon-Venus, is present. Together, the couple can utilize the energies to accomplish any job. How well they collaborate is dependent on other planetary connections to either Mars. The directness of Mars is highly effective. Under this energetic influence, you can become quite irritated when restrained. Physical outlets, whether they are aimed toward completing chores, working out, or engaging in passionate sex, help channel this active force. A joint effort to become involved in sports or physical fitness will engender a mutual bond.

Under adverse Mars-Mars aspects, the couple may not be in agreement on which way to assert themselves. Both will resist the demands of the other, defending their viewpoint until they win. However, in order for them to achieve success with any objective, one of them will need to compromise.

A couple with a harmonious Jupiter-Jupiter aspect experiences optimism, abundance, and support within the relationship. Jupiter is always an uplifting influence that encourages the couple to enjoy each other's company. Since they are able to agree on philosophical, religious, and moral issues, the intellectual exchange reinforces the union. Both benefit by bringing out the best in each other.

When in adverse aspect, differences over religious pursuits, philosophical outlooks, or moral standards may cause disagreements. Overzealous or reckless extravagance may be encouraged for the wrong reasons, thus causing unnecessary excessiveness. Expansive behavior needs to be contained to balance this outgoing dynamic.

A Saturn-Saturn aspect is known to create some adversity, especially when in challenging aspect, as this influence will put extra pressure on you. You both need to conform to the idea of discipline and hard work. There are many lessons to be learned. You find that sharing the responsibilities is difficult, particularly when one feels inferior to the other's success. Both may seek control and may limit the other's ambitions as well. A division of the responsibilities will allow you to implement your own strategy toward achieving any goal.

Saturn will test you, individually and together, thus highlighting weaknesses that undermine the strengths of the relationship. Passing this test will build a stronger bond between you. It may be your karmic duty to see it through to a conclusion. Shared responsibilities flow more naturally with the easier aspects, where each of you can rely on the other for support. Although Saturn-Saturn aspects provide a stabilizing link in a long-term commitment, as each can appreciate a responsible attitude in the other, both may need to pursue separate ambitions, especially under adverse aspect. As you learn from the experiences of each other, you can outline successful plans for monetary security and retirement. The couple's endurance will create a lasting foundation.

A Uranus-Uranus conjunction aspect is the most likely aspect, as other aspects require an age difference of approximately fourteen or twenty-one years. The conjunction, especially with positive aspects, will encourage the implementation of new ideas. You inspire each other to live a progressive lifestyle and feel the need to express your individuality, along with your freedom. If the desire for space is not respected, conflicts will arise. The fourteen-year gap qualified by the sextile and the twenty-eight-year gap that reflects the trine aspect will cause the younger person to be motivated by the older, experienced one. Creative, original aims will be encouraged. If both can appreciate the stimulating behavior of the other, much can be gained. As a new perspective is embraced and new ambitions are launched, an enthusiastic attitude will uphold this union.

Under adverse Uranus-Uranus aspects, erratic behavior will cause much dissension. You will disapprove of each other's actions. This clash will cause one person, usually the younger person, to rebel and pursue their freedom without a second thought. Trying to discipline this type of behavior may be unsuccessful. Yet you, the partner, must try, remembering that in order to experience life, some freedom is needed.

A Neptune-Neptune aspect is generational. Depending on other factors in the Love Relationship Formula, a couple is either prone to forming a spiritual connection that offers mutual compassion, or to a confused interaction that leads to disillusionment. Favorable influences to a Neptune-Neptune conjunction or sextile will instigate a sympathetic understanding along with support for each other's dream goal.

Adverse Neptune-Neptune influences lead you down an illusive path where you are easily deceived. The partnership lacks sensitivity, and stimulates illusive desires for what you cannot have. You need greater emotional awareness in order to develop a more compassionate nature.

A Pluto-Pluto aspect can only occur as a conjunction in a particular generation being that it takes anywhere from eleven to twenty-five years to move through one zodiac sign due to its irregular orbit. This being the case, you may experience the conjunction and sextile, and possibly the square, in one lifetime. The conjunction, which is more likely in a relationship situation, will enhance deeper feelings of attractiveness or the exact opposite, repulsion. The natal aspects affecting the Pluto-Pluto conjunction will indicate a favorable or unfavorable result. Nevertheless, the couple may feel a close affinity, with the opportunity to delve into subliminal issues.

12

♥

sun sign compatibility —signs describe the experience

Since it is the zodiac sign that describes the experience of the planet, we have more information on which to base our explanation of a certain person, place, or thing. In visualizing a more detailed picture, the signs further clarify the experience. Signs may support or detract from the Love Relationship Formula.

Suns sign compatibility indicates what type of a relationship one Sun sign will have with another. Although the Love Relationship Formula goes beyond Sun sign astrology, we must take it into consideration as an introductory link to attaining further astrological knowledge in understanding compatibility.

The Sun signs are categorized into two different groups called *triplicities* and *quadruplicities*. Both groups reveal the finer points of each astrological Sun sign.

Triplicities

Triplicities are derived from the elements fire, earth, air, and water. There are three signs in each element. When we speak of Sun sign compatibility, we are describing an interaction that takes place as the Sun sign of one person connects with another's Sun sign within the same element, such as a Sun sign in Leo experiencing a favorable connection to a Sun sign in Sagittarius. This same compatibility among all of the other planets is what supports the Love Relationship Formula, although it is not dependent on it.

The Fire Sign Triplicity—Aries, Leo, and Sagittarius

Aries

Aries likes a challenge when it comes to establishing a relationship. Their dynamic energy allows them to be aggressive in pursuing their heart's desire. Aries is driven to win you over with their enthusiastic and flamboyant style. Their fiery character and romantic appeal know no bounds. Possessing an outgoing nature and zest for living, they like to take the lead. A competitive streak propels them to strive to be the best. Their pioneering spirit encourages them to be risk-takers and seek independence. Aries will expect you to be self-reliant as well. As a partner you must be their equal, yet display excitement and assertiveness to have them maintain complete loyalty to you. Although Aries is emotionally and physically passionate, they need to learn patience. Their demanding and headstrong manner can put them at odds with their partner. A fluctuating temperament may also cause them to be pushy, unyielding, and easily angered. Nevertheless, Aries see themselves as strong and need to be physically and mentally challenged. Confrontation, to them, has its seductive appeal. They may have difficulty, however, in sympathizing with their partner's needs. To balance a relationship Aries must forego concentrating only on the self to establish a mutually satisfying rapport with their mate. Fortunately, their passionate wiles will never exclude them from having the love they desire.

Leo

Leos refuse to be inferior to anyone and want the best for themselves and their loved ones. Their prideful manner dramatizes their skills and talents so that they may acquire an even stronger position of importance. Leos are appropriately named the lovers of the zodiac. They wish to enjoy all of the sensuous pleasures that romance has to offer. Their idea is to have fun exploring the many facets of leisure life. The charisma and flair that a Leo projects attracts many romantic prospects. In a relationship they need respect and fond attention, and can be demanding when it comes to love. Leo has a way of intensifying the capacity to feel love. A high vitality gives them a strong sexual drive. Others find their commanding, fiery, and genuine love nature very attractive. Leos exude a regal persona that radiates self-assurance, and they love being the center of attention, but they will be especially grateful for your admiration. Leos are responsible, know how to manage their lives, and are an inspiration to all. They like giving orders and are convinced that, regardless of the circumstances, they will win. They will thoroughly appreciate flattery and may desire a glamorous romance that does not exist. Although they can be egotistical, showy, and stubborn, Leos will wine and dine you with their seductive charm until they win your heart. Leos at first may see love as a game, but their true challenge is to love with an open heart.

Sagittarius

Sagittarians are optimistic, purposeful, versatile, and adventuresome. Their fiery and freedom-loving energy compels them to explore new horizons intellectually, socially, physically, emotionally, spiritually, and psychologically. They are on a quest to gather as much knowledge as possible to broaden their experience. They are willing to travel the world with you, enjoying every romantic place. Sagittarians have an intuitive flair for attracting favorable situations their way. You will be drawn to them by their flirtatious manner and jovial spirit. In a relationship they expect you to be independent, but will appreciate an affectionate and caring nature. Besides being a great lover, Sagittarius will insist on being your friend. As much as they desire to be with you, the centaur needs its space. Their restless spirit wishes to be expansive as it searches for the ideal. Sagittarians enjoy any activity, especially when it is outdoors. They love a party, which affords them the social avenue they seek to have fun and interact on a communicative level. There is a tendency to become reckless and overindulge themselves in food, drink, or whatever inspires them at the time. They need to avoid biting off more than they can chew. Pompous behavior and blunt comments may be quite embarrassing when all is said and done. Sensuous and sexy, Sagittarians are not afraid to flaunt their natural style. They exude confidence and class in managing an office or running a marathon. An honest nature bypasses the games people play in relationships, for they are only interested in seeking the truth. They will want to understand your problems as well as cultural differences that relate to humanity on a larger scale. You can depend on Sagittarians, as they are loyal and trustworthy. Sexually, they want a powerful bond that will sweep them off their feet in love. They may be gullible, but they have a generous manner that is the envy of many. Their buoyant personality makes them resilient even in the worst of circumstances. You will thoroughly enjoy their company whether they are needing intellectual or philosophical stimuli, or frolicking in the streets at night. If they are not mentally challenged, they can become physically or psychologically ill. At times Sagittarians may be exhibitionists with glamour and glitter, but it will never take away from their down-to-earth persona. Maintaining an independent identity in a partnership may be difficult for them, yet it is necessary in order for them to feel right with themselves. Gambling on Sagittarians in love may seem risky, but their charming, provocative, witty panache is highly appealing. Best of all, they are sure to prove their love for you, knowing that your intimate adventure together is a timeless embrace few souls experience.

The Earth Sign Triplicity—Taurus, Virgo, and Capricorn

Taurus

Taureans prefer stability and loyalty when it comes to relationships. They are keen on commitment and desire a permanent relationship, expecting the same allegiance from their partner. Taureans seek a partnership that is financially and sexually fulfilling, but they need to avoid making their partner feel entrapped with their possessiveness and rigid ways. A self-righteous and stubborn attitude will limit their progress as well. Although Taureans wish to capitalize upon material resources to maintain their security, they want to enjoy leisure life to the fullest. Their selfish desires may draw them into experiencing a love of comfort and luxury. Expecting the very best when it comes to love, Taurus promises sensual delights. Their sensuality is not to be questioned as they seduce with their physical prowess and sexy voice. Taureans are never hurried, but learn slowly and deliberately with the intention of reaping rewards. A solid, practical, and conservative manner allows them to be extremely efficient on the job, producing hard-earned results for their efforts. Underneath their calm exterior, they must practice patience, as once driven to anger it will undermine their self-respect. Venus, which rules Taurus, represents the extremes of love and money. Taureans may be caught in the dichotomy of wanting a more peaceful and spiritual existence yet still desiring material gain. They need to transcend materialism and possessiveness to appreciate the true meaning of love and peace. Nurturing and affectionate, they have the capacity to care deeply for others.

Virgo

Virgos may be analytical and cautious, and possess a workaholic nature, but they are also intrigued with the sensuous delights that intimacy holds. A curious appetite will cause Virgo to want to explore all of the avenues of sexuality. The accumulation of such wisdom will only enhance their lovemaking prowess. Shy in public, you will not find such modesty in privacy with your Virgo mate. Although they are practical and trustworthy, they may find fault with your romantic approach and feel they have to retrain you to meet their expectations. They only desire the ultimate experience in love for the both of you. Their subtle seductions will lure you right into a relationship. You need to reassure your Virgo mate with your compliments and sensitive yet responsible lovemaking. Your performance together will be rated until it tips the scales of satisfaction. You may have to tolerate a judgmental attitude along with compulsive behavior. Their disciplined and reserved disposition may sometimes cause them to be emotionally repressed. Virgos are hardworking and adaptable, yet are disappointed when perfection is not attained. The dutiful manner of Virgo makes them more a giver than a receiver. Virgos want to serve and will make sacrifices to support their lifetime mate. Wanting to win your love, they have a tendency to be hard on themselves. You will find their well-groomed appearance very attractive. They can be messy at times just to balance out their need for orderliness. Reliable and responsible, Virgos prefer to understand all of the details. They will use their resources and mental abilities to advance in life. Virgos need an exclusive relationship where they can totally depend on their partner for love and emotional support. Once they warm up to you, you are destined for a lifelong relationship.

Capricorn

Capricorns are known for climbing the highest mountain to achieve the loftiest of goals. Their success rate outshines all of the other signs, and they will aim toward winning in their relationships too. Their approach to love may seem somewhat traditional, with courting and flowers, but old-fashioned manners are quite romantic and lead to lasting love. Since Capricorns need to feel that they belong, they will seek out a solid, reliable commitment. They are really looking for your love and approval. In a relationship, they prefer a loving, stable partner who works as hard as they do and is a powerful, ambitious social climber. Their shy, sexy persona can be very attractive. You will find them to be a loyal lover, aimed to please. Their persistent, regal, status-seeking manner will land them in a comfortable, and possibly luxurious, position. Hard-working beyond compare, they are keen on accomplishing something every day, which provides much stability in a union. A responsible friend and lover, they are dedicated to taking good care of you. Capricorns like to play as hard as they work, so you will find them out having fun and will truly enjoy their company. Highly sexed but timid, you may have to warm up your Capricorn partner with steady affection. They may be critical of your style, but they hope that you will be conscientious enough to improve your approach. Yearning for prestige, Capricorns are known to be materialistic. They will always be concerned about their own security first, since providing for themselves will support a relationship in the future. Capricorns are proper, realistic, organized, and accomplished. They are so engrossed in what they are doing that they seem unapproachable. A matter-of-fact public image may seem cold and uninviting on a personal level, yet greatly appreciated when it comes to business. In all respects they tend to be cautious and only take calculated risks. Although Capricorns are pragmatic, they still have a good sense of humor. Respect for traditional values and ancient understandings will be applied to the everyday world. Wise, efficient, and loyal, once they know your love is sincere they will let go of their fears. Their persistence along with lasting sex appeal will attract a romantic commitment that is worth their time and investment. If they can overlook their partner's shortcomings, they are destined to enjoy a warm, intimate union.

The Air Sign Triplicity—Gemini, Libra, and Aquarius.

Gemini

Geminis want to experience the versatility of life. They can rely on their cleverness to attract exciting exchanges with others. Their refreshing, charming personality is quite appealing. In a long-term relationship, they need mental stimuli to keep their interest. A boring partner will never do. Geminis have the ability to intellectually intrigue those around them. They are restless by nature. A moody, changeable disposition makes it difficult for them to stay in one place for too long. There may be the tendency to be unpredictable, avoid responsibilities, and wander in a scattered state of mind. Constant mental activity and involvements with everyone under the sun can wear them down. Such a rapidly moving mind causes a high-strung nature that needs to be directed. Acquiring more depth will help guide them. They will use their cerebral assets to land a partner. To a Gemini, sex definitely starts in the mind. Their mind as well as their love life can be complex. They need to channel their racing, powerful thoughts. Geminis must find a balance within themselves before they can find harmony in a relationship. The Gemini twins can display an angelic spirit and also play the role of devil's advocate. They have the ability to become their own worst enemy or raise themselves to new intellectual heights. They receive intuitive messages loud and clear, prompting them to take the leap, for regrets only happen when they don't listen to their inner impulses. Never at a loss for words, Geminis enjoy entertaining and selective teasing. They are always informed with the facts and are known to be great debaters. They have a knack for interrupting, but are wonderful conversationalists. Their dual nature makes them capable of handling many jobs or relationships at once. Labor-saving devices allow them to move even more quickly throughout the day. Geminis look for a relationship that will honor their freedom and enhance their multifaceted mentality. When they are seized with intrigue, they know it's a match.

Libra

Librans are sociable, charming, and attractive, and prefer a one-on-one relationship. They pride themselves on being diplomatic, always restoring peace and harmony where it is needed. They desire a relationship that is complementary to their own image and aspires toward being cooperative. Librans gain through interacting with others to find that important balance that makes a relationship work. They show appreciation for beauty, art, and culture. Librans are born with class and like to look good. Their attractive and seductive persona are very inviting. They wish to surround themselves with beauty and spoil themselves with luxury. In tune with the art of love, you are in for a pleasurable romantic experience, complete with soft music, candlelight, good wine, gourmet food, and sensual sex. In most instances a polite facade makes them well liked, but an overly sophisticated persona may deter interaction with those around them. The quiet side of Libra can be passive and sometimes depressed. Their ambivalent manner causes them to shy away from emotional risks. Indecision may be their worst attribute, as it paralyzes their efforts. Aware of the pros and the cons, they must evaluate everything very carefully. Librans are especially thankful for one-on-one feedback, which helps their objectivity so that they can make a decision. They will depend on you for this type of sharing. Seeking cooperation, they attempt to be nice all of the time, yet when confrontation arises they may expose their impersonal side and spew anger. As smooth talkers, they can be quite manipulative in wanting to control their environment. They look for the ideal relationship, yet are afraid to become too involved. There is a tremendous fear of being hurt that blocks Librans from making emotional commitments, but this fond connection is just what they really want. Once they realize that love is the act of sharing, they can release their fears. They desire a partner who is their equal, but they still need to give from their heart to bring balance into the union. When they learn to trust themselves, they will find their loving soulmate and feel comfortable in establishing a long-term union.

Aquarius

Aquarians are unique, fascinating, and independent. They are born humanitarians and want to be everyone's best friend. Blessed with original insights, they are progressive in thought and spirit, opening new doors for us all. They need to explore relationships and are sexually open-minded. Although Aquarians demand their freedom as well as their privacy, they desire a lover who will be their life companion. Their intriguing personality may challenge your intellectual insights yet remain appealing. They possess a passive, manipulative manner that you need to be aware of when interacting with them. In a relationship, you need to respect their offbeat, freedom-seeking ways. They prefer someone who is interesting, attractive, and intelligent. Aquarians fear intimacy, as they do not want to be so responsible for one person. However, an unpredictable and detached manner will not suppress their affectionate nature. They are easily sexually aroused and will use their mental prowess to guide them in lovemaking. Aquarians are not your everyday people and will project their avant-garde, individualistic style. They may be seen as activists wanting to reform old ideas and make way for the future. They are charitable, incisive, and conscientious. Behind a shy persona is a strong mind and self-confident nature. Their restless spirit has them on the go, trying to be there for everyone. Others may try to take advantage of their humane ways. Aquarians are politically minded and up on the newest information. They cheer for the group and not just the individual. Understanding unconventional concepts and the need for change, they seek inspired ideals that reflect who they are. Nonthreatening and nonjudgmental, others open up to their liberated views, and so will you. Their intuitive guidance could turn them into a therapist or sex counselor. They may have a few romantic tips for you. To make love Aquarius' primary goal, they must comprehend the true meaning of intimacy. By integrating love and friendship, they can release their fears and experience the feeling of a reciprocated love.

The Water Sign Triplicity—Cancer, Scorpio, and Pisces

Cancer

Cancers exude a shy sexiness that is very appealing. Their sensitive, changing persona may be difficult for others to understand, but is useful to their own character. Although their emotional life dominates, the intuitive powers of Cancer direct them intellectually. In a relationship, their protective and nurturing demeanor is reassuring, and as long as their needs are met they want to provide for your every need. Cancer's safe haven is their home, where they will shelter you with their love and affection. Candlelit dinners and snuggling up on the couch will warm your soul. They enjoy exercising their culinary skills and collecting memorabilia. Tending to domestic affairs, you will find them raising children, cooking, decorating, or landscaping, and loving every minute of it. Their receptive abilities allow them to understand you quite thoroughly. If Cancers feel insecure, they are inclined to become possessive, clinging, and controlling. They must establish their own inner feeling of security in order to balance this tendency.

Once Cancers are able to master their moods, they retain a powerful position in dealing with others. Cancers guide themselves by feeling out people and situations to acquire an in-depth comprehension. When they are upset, they will probe their inner being until the problem is resolved. As Cancers are extremely sensitive, they may experience emotional anxiety. Their protective nature does not preclude them from exploring their highly sexual demeanor. Dreamy, romantic escapades stimulate their lusty, sensuous side. In order for Cancers to express their feelings, intimacy is a must. A shining example of patience, they put most people to shame with their ability to wait. They do not care to be in the limelight and will withdraw into their shell if necessary. Cancers are skillful at manipulating others and need to avoid this sometimes unconscious tendency. They are prone to being clan-oriented, overly emotional, and defensive. When fear gets the best of them, they can be insecure and overprotective. They may at times be vulnerable to others' accusations. Self-doubt may bring fear of rejection and worry of becoming a victim. Wanting love's good fortune, they may become jealous if they do not have all of your affection. Cancers love unconditionally and are persistent, caring, and giving. They need to learn how to give love freely without possessing their loved one. Cancers will want to hold on to you and never let go as long as a loving rapport and home environment are present to fulfill their needs.

Scorpio

Scorpions are intense and magnetic, and exude a powerful persona. They have extreme likes and dislikes that either compel them to be in a committed relationship or cause them to be alone. Their commanding presence will entice you their way. When involved, they are the most passionate lover, willing to thoroughly enjoy sex. They are intrigued by the art of seduction, and so will you. The Scorpion's sexual prowess is not to be questioned. Because their emotional depth is tremendous, they feel sex throughout their entire being.

The extremist attitude that Scorpions possess causes intense sexual involvement or sexual denial. In a relationship, Scorpions are very selective, since once they are committed it might as well be forever. They desire a mate who is assertive, amorous, and admirable, and who is willing to understand their need for privacy, which includes their inner thoughts. Secretive and perceptive, they rely on their intuition to guide them. They are confident with their insightful powers that accurately describe people. Self-assured, capable, and able to dominate, they seek an influential position on the job. They are obsessed with power and adamant about attaining a higher status. Their stubbornness can lead you right into an argument that is all-consuming. Scorpions can be revengeful if someone crosses them, but karmic retribution will follow. Even if they are able to detach emotionally, they still become jealous and oftentimes obsessed. Destructive, self-indulgent habits will steer Scorpio into a negative, downward spiral. In order to achieve self-mastery, they must transcend themselves on every level. They are drawn to the unknown, seeking adventures that will add to their already challenging life. Since they desire power, it becomes a strong fixation in their life until they are ready to experience a transformation that enables them to rise above all earthly pursuits. Finding a deeper meaning, they one day hope to bring such depth into a relationship, to melt into infinity with another.

Pisces

Pisceans are compassionate and illusive individuals who need to pursue their ideals. Their participation in group situations may support this initiative. A mysterious aura follows them that is highly attractive yet triggers a degree of uncertainty. Nevertheless, you will find them intriguing. They are highly romantic and dream of the perfect love life. In a relationship, they appreciate a soulmate connection, which persuades them to be more open. Pisceans will expect you to express your desires and, through your sympathetic touch, free any personal inhibitions they may possess. As long as they feel loved, they are first-rate lovers with much to offer. Pisceans will tend to your needs with compassionate love. Full of surprises, their changeable persona makes them difficult to figure out, as you cannot quite tell whether they are coming or going. Yet, they are always aware that they need to be of service in some capacity. They are willing to make sacrifices and extend themselves to the needy and less fortunate. Gullible tendencies may have them chasing after rainbows, which are sometimes actually realized due to their strong, convincing faith. Their multifaceted manner allows them to love in many ways. They may be prone to romantic escapades, but their love is also expressed spiritually and platonically. Since they are highly devoted in love, they are easily hurt. Pisceans want to have it all when it comes to matters of the heart. But when they are idealistic in love, emotional and sexual fulfillment may elude them. They are able to juggle people and daily life situations quite well. If you care to join them in their adventure, they will inspire you along the way. They are creative, inventive, and sensitive. Still, you will be puzzled and not appreciate their indirect, introverted, and fickle ways, for their own confusion is projected onto you. Pisceans may become very depressed over unfulfilled dreams and desires. Suppressed, negative emotions may take a toll on their health and relationships. Pisceans believe in the unknown, intangible world, which may include mysticism, religion, or life-after-death experiences. Although they are vulnerable to escapism, they are wise and perceptive and will guide you with their intuitive skills. Their one desire is to have a relationship in which they are able to merge love and sex. This form of unity creates the ultimate experience for this idealistic sign.

Quadruplicities

In addition to categorizing the signs by the elements and triplicities, you can classify them by quadruplicities. There are three groups called *cardinal, fixed,* and *mutable* signs. The group the planet falls in, according to the sign it is in, will determine its function. Although signs falling in the same quadruplicity will conjoin, square, or oppose each other, I have often found this dynamic to be a part of the attraction and not necessarily a hindrance to the couple, as was originally thought. Remember, compatibility is not just based on your Sun sign, but it comprises all of the astrological elements of the chart, which is how and why the Love Relationship Formula came into being.

Cardinal Signs—Aries, Cancer, Libra, and Capricorn

Cardinal signs are known to be enterprising. They are initiators, as they represent the beginning of each of the seasons. Cardinal signs are very ambitious and tend to hold a position of importance in life. Possessing a self-assertive nature, they are able to make great strides. If the majority of your planets are in cardinal signs, you will be concerned with initiating action. Aries prefers to act independently, as a pioneer conquering new territory. Libra wants to initiate good relations to bring balance into any partnership. Cancer feels out a situation, knowing when to act and be assertive. Capricorn wants to accomplish set goals to gradually attain success.

Fixed Signs—Taurus, Leo, Scorpio, and Aquarius

Fixed signs are steadfast by nature and are known to be focused yet stubborn. They are persistent, committed, and dependable and do not like the idea of change. A proud persona emanates strong endurance capabilities, where they are determined to see a goal through to success. They are not easily distracted and work well under stress. When seeking powerful positions of authority, they can be relentless. If the majority of your planets are in fixed signs, you will be concerned with perseverance. Taurus is solid and trustworthy, desiring security at all costs. Leo desires a position that instills confidence and self-importance. Scorpio seeks to regenerate the self and experience a sense of unity with others. Aquarius promotes progress, with the goal of improving themselves and humanity.

Mutable Signs—Gemini, Virgo, Sagittarius, and Pisces

Mutable signs are changeable, so adaptability is required. They are flexible and versatile, and able to switch gears when necessary. Capable of adapting to many different situations, they are easier to interact with on an everyday basis. If the majority of your planets are in mutable signs, you will be concerned with learning to acclimate yourself to new circumstances by being resourceful and exercising your versatility. Gemini is inclined to explore new ideas that offer versatile communications. Virgo is adaptable in assimilating knowledge and analyzing data. Sagittarius seeks to broaden their outlook and experience variety. Pisces is open to accepting obligations and understanding the unknown.

13 ♥ Needs Attract —Venus Through The Zodiac

What constitutes attraction? Although opposites attract, many times attraction is determined by our needs. The signs in astrology describe our needs quite accurately. A person with Venus in Capricorn has a need for emotional and financial security. They may also want to control their relationship. Whereas a person with Venus in Cancer feels a need to give and nurture, and perhaps be considered as a provider. They may also become co-dependent. As stated earlier, we cannot ignore our needs—they must be met.

When our needs become dysfunctional, excessive, and destructive, we find ourselves in an unhealthy, undermining relationship, for our dysfunctional needs have attracted a relationship that exemplifies the disturbance that is going on inside of us. When we attract an unqualified partner, we need to ask ourselves what our needs are. Here again, the more we get in touch with our feelings, the more we understand our needs.

Venus in Aries

Your need to be daring and independent requires that you stand on your own two feet. You are determined to call the shots when it comes to relationships. Although Aries likes to conquer, there is great leadership ability in guiding a relationship, even through the tough times. An impulsive drive will push you toward the one you desire. You are convinced that if you are persistent, you will win. You prefer being the aggressor in the relationship, but dominating the one you love for selfish reasons is an unfulfilling experience. If you can learn to be more cooperative, a successful union lies ahead.

Venus in Taurus

Your needs will be based around financial security, for you are inclined to enjoy the good life and want to feel very comfortable in taking delight in earthly pleasures. With such a sensuous appetite in love, romantic dinners that lead to more intimate moments are high on your list. If you are going to extend yourself, you hope to get results. Whether it's a lively rendezvous or a lasting commitment, you intend to get what you want. Once a love relationship is established, you will need to guard against being overly possessive. Think in terms of sharing and being productive in your relationship, as opposed to having or owning your partner.

Venus in Gemini

You have a need for variety in the area of love that can become complicated if not channeled properly. Your curiosity will persuade you to look for new experiences. Since you want to experience the spice of life, one lover may not be enough unless somehow your partner can intrigue you enough to stay interested. Stimulating conversation will be a turn-on and will assist you in arousing a romantic response in the object of your affection. Sentimental exchanges are not your style. You will receive attention from your lover when voicing your thoughts poetically or expressing your heart's desire through writing. Remember, a revolving door of experiences without any meaning will not bring you the true satisfaction you seek.

Venus in Cancer

You have a need to love, nurture, and protect the one you love. You are concerned about your partner's moods, wanting to make sure that they are happy and healthy.

Your instincts are alert to protect your partner if a threatening situation arises. In return, you want to feel secure in a warm, loving environment. The need to provide and nurture can be given freely when you are in a comfortable monetary position. If emotional and/or financial security is lacking, you may worry and tend to cling to the one you love, thus smothering them. This co-dependent tendency can be avoided once you build a sense of security within yourself. Use your past experiences in relationships to nurture your future. Your sensitive approach will attract love and appreciation.

Venus in Leo

You need to express love in a creative, dramatic, and regal manner. You desire the spotlight as you indulge in life's luxuries. You need to feel important so your charisma shines. Your partner may have to cater to you, but you know you are well worth it. You prefer that your partner also dresses with style. If you are the one trying to do the impressing, remember that you don't have to spend a lot to win someone's heart. It's your devotion that counts! You exude a tremendous warmth that captures its own audience. Your loved one will be sure to applaud. You may require more attention to reaffirm your position of importance. Unless you are too demanding or self-indulgent, you will easily attract your desired love.

Venus in Virgo

You have a need to be of service to others, but when it comes to love you need to be careful not to overanalyze it. Love is a feeling and is not to be intellectualized. You prefer a well-groomed mate, for you are very particular about matters of hygiene. You may have a critical perspective so you can devote yourself to any problem. You are very reliable, but are perhaps overly concerned about getting your job done instead of spending quality time with your partner. Your shy persona is very appealing, drawing romantic opportunity your way, but your reserved nature curbs you from extending yourself. You discriminate between what has value and what doesn't. What needs your attention may not be the details, but the one you love.

Venus in Libra

You have a need to bring harmony and beauty into your relationship. Sharing ideas, conversation, and love is the ideal. You will show respect and politeness toward your partner. You are inclined to maintain a gracious, diplomatic attitude that is appealing to all. Always exercising poise and good taste, you attract romantic opportunity with style. Socializing with your partner will allow you to feel more in sync with them. But if you choose to relate on a superficial level, you may find yourself alone. Since we do not live in a perfect world, it may be difficult to take an opposing side if required. Remember, it's how you do it. Chances are you will charm others to your point of view. You need to think in terms of sharing, balancing, and cooperating, without losing yourself in another. A loving relationship complements your inner being.

Venus in Scorpio

You may have a strong need to get involved in an intimate alliance. Your feelings run deep and it may take someone extra special to understand your emotional depth. Once involved, you are committed. You may need to let go of past relationship experiences that can hold you back if not purged from your life. But do keep that which has value. You are encouraged to overcome possessive and jealous tendencies. Your evolution through relationships will allow you to know the true meaning of the power of love. You prefer private moments with your mate. Although you hold untold secrets, your sex appeal is noticed by all. You may need to share some of those hidden feelings with your partner to add to that already intense connection. Never alienate yourself from a meaningful experience.

Venus in Sagittarius

You want to broaden your horizons socially for there is a need to show the friendly side of love to everyone. You have a flair for flirting with those around you. Having fun is your style. Your partner will truly enjoy you being playful and sexy. Honest to a fault, you need to watch your tendency to be blunt. Make an effort to be more sensitive for the best results. Even though you need space, you wish to share your sense of adventure with your mate. You may still like to roam, but you need to understand the meaning of each relationship experience. Cultivating this wisdom will eventually guide you toward a wonderful union, as happiness in love flourishes.

Venus in Capricorn

Emotional and financial security define your needs. There is a strong yearning to feel secure in love, yet you may need to provide financially for yourself before you place your trust in another. Any diligent effort you make will be well rewarded. Nevertheless, you still desire a loyal, committed relationship and you will be keen on accomplishing this goal. Your formal manner toward love might make you seem unapproachable. Do extend your sophisticated self if you wish to be recognized. Once in a relationship, show your affection; otherwise your partner may feel you have lost interest. Saying "I love you" may be the most demonstrative gesture you make, and the response will secure your heart and soul.

Venus in Aquarius

Being unique when it comes to matters of the heart, you need to feel like a free spirit. You may fear the responsibility of being too close and committed to another. Therefore, you may detach from intimate situations to maintain your independence. It may be difficult for you to conform to a traditional relationship, but you are capable of making a commitment as long as you can express yourself in a unique, unconventional, and progressive way. You want to be different, yet share your intuitive wisdom so that you both gain. Although you wish to follow your own unique path, one day you will learn to love unconditionally in return.

Venus in Pisces

Your compassionate, loving nature needs to be expressed toward your mate. You are right at home with pleasing your partner, no matter what the occasion. Feeling obligated, you will make sacrifices for your partner. Giving unconditional love and helping those in need are innate qualities, yet at times you may also need to learn when to curb your efforts and let others help themselves. You must be wary of illusions in love. You may be so idealistic that no one can measure up to your expectations, so you end up imagining that they do and you are deceived by your own romantic fantasy. Developing wisdom in the process, you learn to appreciate reality. You must have faith in your aims and be willing to make a total commitment toward them so they can be realized. A greater perceptiveness evolves through your enlightenment. Give your partner the opportunity to love you as you love them.

14

♥

κarmic
relationship
connections

Karma is what tends to bring people together. When we meet up with a soulmate, the power of love transcends time and space. The flame is once again rekindled to allow us to join forces through the romantic merging of souls. The dynamics involved are beyond our human comprehension. *But what we do recognize is what we feel. It is this feeling of remembrance that compels in us a desire to be together, to experience the ultimate embrace of timeless love.* This universal law, which follows our every action, promotes our reuniting with a past love. We wish to connect once again with a soulmate whom we have either experienced a powerful bond of love with, or have not been able to forgive. Or perhaps we have wronged that person and wish to make it right. A soulmate connection does not always indicate a wonderful relationship. You may have known each other before or in a past life, but under what circumstances? There is a certain comfort felt when you are in a karmic relationship. You just feel, right from the start, that you know this person. They seem familiar because you have been with them before. Memories of our karma reside in the subconscious mind. This imprint, along with early childhood conditioning, will determine who we will end up attracting into our lives. These meetings are not accidents or coincidences, but strategically planned by the Divine Intelligence that guides us all. With such magnificent, omnipresent planning, you would think we would consider each meeting with great care, wanting to be grateful for the opportunity to relinquish our negative karma and not accumulate more of it.

Learning is referring back to the past. Many times it is years later that we understand what has really happened in a relationship. Once you see the pattern, your relationships can improve. *For in seeing the pattern, the lesson is learned,* and therefore the continuing karmic experience can be released. It's hard to understand why the human soul must go through such trying experiences in order for the soul to heal and recapture its essence. Our painful experiences are actually meant to heal us—not destroy us. Karmic repercussions can be indicated by specific planetary combinations in a compatibility analysis. The following karmic connections will provide keen insight into your relationships.

Sun-Saturn—Past Obligations, Difficult Situations

You may have a lot to learn with Saturn being the teacher planet. The first lesson for your relationship is to stand strong and channel Saturn's heavy impact. As the Sun person, you should not lie back and take the critical abuse, but try to redefine your Saturnian partner's objective. Saturn has the tendency to undermine the Sun person's confidence, thus humiliating them. As both planets are at odds with one another, especially in the opposition, the idea is to strike a balance with varying viewpoints, for each planet needs equal time. The Sun's pride will denounce instruction from Saturn, whereas Saturn feels the Sun has much to learn. Ideally, your Saturnian partner will aim to make constructive comments to assist you on your karmic journey. Your experience may involve brief periods of monetary loss, illness, lack of intimacy possibly due to sexual dysfunction, or difficulty parting from a previous love. Eventually, this will pass, strengthening the union due to the hardship.

A solid bond will be difficult to break and will secure your union for years to come. Even in parting you may find the return of a past love who feels the karma has not been relinquished. At times a difference in age will show the older person projecting their

Saturn, especially in the square or opposition, onto the younger person's Sun. Regardless of age, the effect is the same, indicating that karma accumulated in prior lives is seeking resolution. In a marital situation, an adverse aspect involving Saturn will compel you to stay together in spite of the past-life pressure that is built into the relationship. If a break-up were to occur, which certainly could be the result of such heavy demands, Saturn's restrictive force could cause a long separation, delaying a reunion that seems inevitable due to the karmic tie. Unless there is serious reason to terminate the relationship, you should continue to work out the differences.

Saturn in adverse aspect to the Sun promises that you will confront your past life burdens that you may learn to strengthen your character and improve yourself for other uncompromising encounters that you are bound to face. Until your karma is fulfilled you are destined to withstand the demands made upon you with only resolve in mind. In a relationship, genuine lasting love is usually acquired when a couple has been willing to bear life's pains and tribulations, thus earning them the honor of being two loving souls in a lifetime embrace.

Moon-Saturn (Saturn-IC)—Obligated/Co-Dependent Emotions

Karmic repercussions are clearly evident when you feel a compelling sense of obligation in a relationship. Such are the influences of Saturn aspecting your Moon. Saturn experiences the need to provide for and control the Moon, as it projects its authoritarian manner upon its lunar subject. Although Saturn may not care for such responsibilities, Saturn will continue to stay in a relationship out of fear and insecurity. The emotional dependency creates a co-dependent relationship. This karmic connection can cause a relationship to last for several years. During this time you will need to confront repressed emotions and needs not only in this lifetime but from past lives as well.

Favorable Moon-Saturn contacts in a relationship may allow a couple to work through co-dependent issues, even though emotional needs will still require attention. Adverse Moon-Saturn contacts, including the conjunction, force the Saturn person to deal with concerns of being overly responsible that come from dysfunctional family conditions that can be traced back through lifetimes. Hoping that their emotional needs will be met if they are a good provider and observe a sense of duty, Saturn feels overwhelmed with responsibility. Wanting to be in control, they are subjected to a co-dependent relationship that does not meet their needs. For Saturn is blocking the emotional sensitivity that the Moon has to offer, but can't. In some cases, when the lesson is finally learned, the relationship may end due to the indescribable stress that ends up destroying the love between you. When mutual Moon-Saturn aspects exist, both individuals are being given an opportunity to address co-dependent behavior. The karmic lesson here is to learn to provide for your partner without getting buried in an overly obligated situation that does not support your needs.

Venus-Saturn (Saturn-Descendant)—Past, Familiar, and Loyal Love

There is a feeling of comfort when you meet someone you have met before, especially from a past life. You feel as though you just know the person. You can relax. It feels so comfortable. You are in the presence of a karmic connection. Venus is the planet of love, affection, and comfort, emotionally and materialistically. Saturn, the planet of reality, fears, and insecurities, will find great comfort when in aspect to Venus. Saturn is at ease in Venus' warm embrace. Venus-Saturn aspects usually generate long-term compatibility. You feel so at home with the person that it feels natural to be together. There is a feeling of safety; our fears and insecurities are alleviated. Saturn is assured that Venus will be there.

Saturn must also learn to respect the love and comfort that Venus has to offer, especially if this love was not fully appreciated in a past life. Too many adverse Saturnian influences will bring up control issues and create an overly content environment. You feel so comfortable that you may end up taking your partner for granted. If your partner is being ignored, they will eventually feel unworthy. This is the beginning of the decline of your relationship. As a couple, you need to feel appreciated and loved.

Saturn may also be inclined to control Venus, by not appreciating or complimenting Venus. Saturn has a difficult time saying "I love you." Saturn may actually feel out of control if Venus is appreciated. Saturn worries that fears and insecurities will take hold if Venus likes himself or herself too much, for then Venus may not have any need for supporting and being there for Saturn. Saturn is definitely insecure, but as an adult, one needs to define one's inner self so that deep insecurities do not take root and affect one's relationships in a negative manner. If Saturn feels secure with himself or herself, Saturn will learn to respect as well as be responsible toward Venus. In turn, Venus must also show worthiness. A responsible love is a lasting one. Karma is a reflection of a lasting relationship that endures over time because one is reassured of the other's loyalty.

Many karmic situations are also the result of being unappreciated, unloved, and re-strained. These are conditions in relationships that must be addressed, for they are an indication that a past-life situation of neglecting and controlling someone has occurred. You must change the pattern of someone wanting to control or neglect you by telling them you don't care for their selfish, dominating behavior. Once said, you must con-tinue to fully appreciate yourself. The karmic feeling of being internally familiar with your partner supports a long-term union. If you are able to hold each other in high re-gard, your relationship will last a lifetime.

Venus-Neptune (Neptune-Descendant)— Heavenly, Nebulous, or Deceptive Love

If I were to add a 16th point to the Love Relationship Formula, it would be the Venus-Neptune aspect. However, since the element of deception is present, a couple will need to exercise great perceptiveness in channeling this influence.

Heavenly love can best be described as two soulmates coming together in a timeless embrace of love. This romantic dream is part of being human—to desire your perfect soulmate. We have established that human beings need to relate. But human beings also need to be intimate—thus the desire for love.

Mutual, harmonious Venus-Neptune aspects in synastry can set the stage for a lov-ing, spiritual connection between a couple. The compassionate aims of Neptune are fondly welcomed by the affections of Venus. Love is spiritualized. You feel in your heart what you know to be true in your soul, and your soul's desire. You are fulfilled by the presence of your romantic truth. Neptune's enchantment inspires perfected ideals of Venusian love and artistic expression. It is rare when we experience such a karmic op-portunity, but when we do we must appreciate the romantic dream as it is happening.

Love can be experienced in three ways. There is romantic love, unconditional or spiritual love, and deceptive love. Painful love is a form of deception. To love romanti-cally and spiritually is the ideal. When we are inclined to pursue a relationship, we hope to attain this sought-after goal. Since Neptune represents idealism and Venus love, when we are under this influence we think that what we are seeing is what we are getting.

Therefore, we are not always prepared for the illusions of love that permeate our world. We may end up wanting to believe that someone is right for us when they are not. We are caught up in the world of illusions, which is sure to disappoint. Acquiring a clear picture of what you want in a romantic relationship is paramount in avoiding deception in love, especially when we are yearning for that deep, meaningful relationship. A lack of love can easily lead us astray in our search for love.

Adverse Venus-Neptune aspects in compatibility will test your faith and your ability to see love clearly. Venus will find Neptune's tenderness deficient. Neptune misunderstands Venus' affectionate manner, which creates emotional tension between the couple. Your relationship must encompass true consideration, otherwise dishonesty could drive the union apart. Although the Neptune person may desire more of a platonic love, both may have high expectations of the ideal love due to the karmic tie. The couple needs to be more sensitive to and understanding of each other. Exercising spiritual love and devotion will attract romantic love for the right reasons.

When we are dealing with illusions, the best form of love is platonic. There will be times in a long-term relationship where friendship is stronger than the romance, yet ever strengthening the bond between you.

Venus-Pluto (Pluto-Descendant)—Deep Love, Possessive Attachment

In the act of lovemaking, when the experience cannot be understood or explained, it is said to be karmic. This intensified love allows us to go beyond what we think love and sex are to find that involving ourselves in the merging of souls is the act of love we are looking for in a relationship. For this is the profound sexual experience that will only strengthen the bonds between lovers. Pluto desires sex, and Venus desires a more loving exchange. The embrace of sex and love can only enhance a passionate union. The past-life connection is relived once again, reminding the couple of the depth of love two souls can experience. Because Pluto adds depth to everything it influences, when it affects Venus the love experience becomes so meaningful that the couple wants to be there for each other in every intimate moment. In synastry, when this aspect is mutual, both lovers will enjoy making love to one another.

Many couples have met under Venus-Pluto transits, especially the conjunction and trine. Love is transformed and allows the couple to join forces of love that could last a lifetime. However, if you have not transcended old, buried feelings from the past, love may be withheld until you do.

Pluto may have great expectations when in adverse aspect to Venus, thus wanting to experience the depth of intimacy that Venus might feel threatened by right from the start. If such a demonstrative display of sexual feeling is tempered, Venus may not be so defensive, as more of a compromise between sex and love is established. As always, respect for your partner is of prime importance. Pluto needs to think about the Venusian idea of sharing, otherwise Pluto may be swiftly alienated by Venus. The Plutonian desire for sex needs to be understood by Venus. Pluto becoming sexually obsessed with Venus is an unhealthy attachment that could destroy the whole relationship. When we become so involved that we lose touch with ourselves, there are deep psychological issues that need to be addressed. These challenges are often seen in relationships and need to be transcended so that sexual intimacy and affection continue to enhance the romantic union. Under Venus-Pluto aspects, a past-life bond only grows deeper.

Mars-Saturn (Saturn-Ascendant)—Restricted Desires, Abusive Actions

Abusive relationships destroy lives. In the world today, we yearn for love and find too mush abuse. It always amazes me when someone, male or female, thinks they have a right to obliterate another's life by their abusive words and actions. Obviously something from the past has triggered this type of behavior and the perpetrator feels justified. We can certainly verify situations where abused children become abusers as adults. But then there are those abusers who come from decent families and just have it out for you. This can be described as a karmic situation where someone, whether from an abused background or not, feels they have the right to verbally or physically harm you. Their objective is to control you, lower your self-esteem so you can't stand up for yourself, and then verbally and/or physically abuse you. They make you feel guilty for causing the situation, which makes you feel like you are supposed to tolerate the mistreatment. We see or hear of examples daily of those who are abused. It is a disgrace to human evolution.

Karmic circumstances, however, will bring up abusive situations that our soul needs to confront. Many times it involves standing up for yourself and not letting someone you love abuse you. Saving your soul may mean ending your relationship. Thus the karmic lesson is learned. I believe in an evolved society where no one deserves abuse. If you steer clear of adverse Mars-Saturn contacts, along with the other listed malefic links, you can avoid abusive situations.

Unfavorable Mars-Saturn aspects, unless supported by a Jupiter aspect to Mars, may be destructive and, in the worse-case scenario, possibly lead to bodily harm. Favorable Mars-Saturn aspects can allow for a more constructive approach to relationship issues. (For more information refer to chapter 7, "Challenging/Malefic Combinations in Synastry.")

Mars-Pluto (Pluto-Ascendant)— Aggressive, Transforming, and Involved Experiences

There are no two planetary crossings that emanate such courageous, transforming qualities than Mars and Pluto. One is intensely dedicated and karmically driven toward an evolving goal that gradually changes one's life. In harmonious synastry, this aggressive drive is viewed as a powerful and sometimes overwhelming passion, especially when Venus is involved. The transformative, past-life influences of Pluto wish to take Mars to a new level of existence. Here, one's identity (Mars) is reshaped by Pluto. The passions of Mars are transformed and experienced on a deeper level (Pluto) so that the couple is changed emotionally for the sexual experience. To *feel* passion there has to be depth. The Pluto person will enhance the depth of intimacy in the Mars person. The assertive Mars person will arouse the Pluto person toward sexual involvement. Mars is intrigued with secretive Pluto and wishes to explore the unknown. Mutual, positive Mars-Pluto aspects will allow the couple to evolve sexually because of the emotional transformation that occurs while being intimate. The impact of Mars-Pluto influences generates a soulful experience that cannot be described, but only felt.

Due to past-life issues, difficult Mars-Pluto aspects can cause great resistance in a relationship. The couple may adopt a might-makes-right type of behavior pattern that brings unwanted stress. The Mars person may be demanding sexually with the Pluto person, who would rather be alone that night. The Pluto person may desire a sexually evolving rapport that the Mars person does not care for at the moment. Intimate conflicts arise that must be addressed. Pluto may manipulate the situation by enticing Mars to become involved, especially if jealousy is present. Mars may want to conquer Pluto's power to remain in control. A battlefield could easily develop if both people are not aware of their conscious (Mars) and subconscious (Pluto) desires that could transmute or destroy. A person born with Mars in square aspect to Pluto indicates that their sexual actions are aggressive and overly passionate, which may lead to some rough sex. Very karmic and abusive sexual situations may occur when Mars, Saturn, and Pluto are in adverse aspect to one another or even to planets in their respective signs, Aries, Capricorn, and Scorpio. If this combination is in your birth chart or your synastry with another, the possibility for abuse exists.

A person with Mars in sextile or trine aspect to Pluto in the birth chart indicates that the sexual actions are more refined. Here one goes beyond passion into the experience of two souls merging as one. *Transmuting our sexual desires that we might experience intimacy in its true form is the subconscious yearning of every human being.*

Uranus-Pluto—Involvement with the Unusual

We all encounter circumstances in life that seem to hold us back from realizing ourselves. Uranus-Pluto transits are harbingers of breaking out into a new lifestyle and direction. There is an intense drive to capitalize upon one's uniqueness and individuality.

Favorable Uranus-Pluto aspects in synastry support a special instinctive collaboration. Here, being in an extraordinary relationship means attracting someone into your life where there is a unique bond that transcends time. Through Uranus-Pluto influences, what unfolds is an unusual involvement where one feels intuitively committed to a person regardless of any barriers of age, distance, or cultural differences. A mutual like-mindedness and respect draws the couple together. A collective affinity (Pluto) is an experience that validates your importance (Uranus). The Pluto person intensely encourages the Uranus person to feel free in expressing their unique potential. The Uranus person brings new insights to the Pluto person's thought-out objectives. The couple will especially benefit where joint ventures are concerned. Since both planets invoke change of one kind or another, the idea is to be progressive with a shared vision.

We would hope not to find ourselves out of touch with our partner's inner desires. Yet, when Uranus and Pluto are in adverse aspect, an intense relationship may put undue pressure on the couple, thus making it very difficult to be in sync and agree on anything. Each person may have their own individualized ideas that clash with each other. Pluto will not appreciate the unexpected, erratic behavior of Uranus, whereas the hidden, manipulative motives of Pluto will aggravate the open, independent, and freedom-loving Uranus. If you wish to save this relationship, one of you will have to conform. Even so, you will find that attempting to compromise to bring unity to this relationship is a continuous problem. But try you must. Each person may feel the need to be their own individual. If this individuality can be mutually respected, there is some hope of reconciliation. Otherwise, both will strike out in their own direction. Since karma transcends time, Uranus-Pluto influences awaken the couple to a unique experience. The intuitive karmic connection draws them together for a spiritual reunion.

Neptune-Pluto—Intense Idealism

One of the more intense karmic connections I have seen involves Neptune-Pluto aspects. These outer planets coming together offer us an experience where we are guided into an unknown venture. In a relationship we feel the underlying impact, but are not clear as to its meaning. When in harmonious aspect, the depth of Pluto joins with the romanticism of Neptune, creating a meaningful yet mysterious bond between the couple. The depth of the connection somehow keeps the couple karmically intertwined. The romantic projection of Neptune may encounter an intimate rendezvous through Pluto. One's personal growth with Pluto finds limitless possibilities in Neptune. The couple have a shared vision of romance and of their future together. A subconscious exchange leads one to wonder about the bond that exists. Nevertheless, it also supports the continuance of the relationship, especially if there are joint creative goals.

The more difficult aspects with Neptune and Pluto bring great uncertainty into the relationship. The Pluto person feels adrift in a nebulous cloud that does not seem to encourage their best interests. The romantic gestures of Neptune are spurned by Pluto. Pluto's desire to understand and merge with the amorous illusions of Neptune are met with deception. Deeply rooted feelings of distrust may eventually dissolve this union unless a deep, spiritual approach is applied to one's goals. *What we learn of trust is to trust ourselves, especially when deception is ever lurking.*

15

♥ part of marriage
—another marriage indicator

The Part of Marriage was developed by Arab astrologers. This arabian part, which is considered to be a marriage indicator, is found through the placement of Venus and its position above or below the horizon. Favorable aspects to the Part of Marriage indicate a happy and successful marriage, especially if the sign in which it resides is positive. Unfavorable aspects to the Part of Marriage denote difficulty and strife.

The Part of Marriage is the same distance from the Descendant as Venus is from the Ascendant, yet located on the same side of the horizon line as Venus. The Part of Marriage is calculated by using the following formula:

The longitude of the Ascendant plus (+) the longitude of the Descendant, minus (-) the longitude of Venus, equals (=) the Part of Marriage.

For example, if Venus is 20° above the Ascendant, the Part of Marriage will be located 20° above the Descendant. If you find Venus 11° below the Descendant, the Part of Marriage will be 11° below the Ascendant. The placement of Venus indicates the placement of the Part of Marriage in relationship to the horizon. In time you will be able to spot the Part of Marriage with a visual assessment.

How a marriage will work out is described by aspects influencing the Part of Marriage. Harmonious influences will support the marriage and discordant influences will detract from the marriage. This describes the karmic repercussions that one has attracted in this lifetime. Significant aspects to the Part of Marriage not only predict a marriage's outcome in the natal chart, but may also be ascertained from the marriage chart itself. If you have a planet such as Saturn, Neptune, or Pluto afflicted and debilitated in aspect to the Part of Marriage or in the seventh house, the marriage could have very unfortunate results. Whereas a positive trine aspect from an unafflicted Saturn could offer long-term stability. An adverse Uranus aspect to the Part of Marriage could indicate an unexpected parting of the ways. Yet a favorable Neptune in Libra in trine aspect to the Part of Marriage generates a seemingly perfect couple.

Since the sign describes the experience, the Part of Marriage can be supported or diminished by the sign it occupies. If the Part of Marriage resides in Aries, there may be many more challenges than if it resides in Libra, a more congenial, romantic sign.

The Part of Marriage in Jacqueline Kennedy Onassis' astrology chart is in trine aspect to Jupiter in Gemini, which attracted prosperity and good fortune. We also find the Part of Marriage, although nicely placed in Libra, in semisquare aspect to Neptune in Virgo, in an exact semisextile aspect to Mars in Virgo, and in square aspect to Pluto in Cancer. These adverse influences created a very volatile situation involving deception, aggression, power, and the death of her husband, as history has shown.

The half a dozen marriages of Zsa Zsa Gabor is a reflection of her Part of Marriage in sesquiquadrate aspect to illusive Neptune in Cancer and in sextile aspect to a Sun-Uranus conjunction in the appropriate sign of freedom-loving Aquarius. Although Neptune in Cancer wanted to find a nurturing romantic ideal, Uranus pushed to break up old patterns, and Neptune's adverse angle consistently eluded Ms. Gabor from her long-term relationship goal. Her Part of Marriage in Sagittarius had a fortunate effect on men, attracting several marriage partners.

The overwhelmingly famous Paul McCartney seemed to only have eyes for one woman, his late wife Linda. His Part of Marriage is conjunct his Moon and in semisquare aspect to Jupiter exalted in Cancer, which is further proof that even Jupiter in a semisquare can bring luck or, in this case, the right woman. Neptune is also in semisquare aspect to his Leo Part of Marriage, which would describe the dissolution of his brief first marriage. Linda McCartney, however, was very Neptunian, being a creative, spiritual person who was also a photographer. Neptune rules over film. Even her family name, Eastman, was a pioneer in the film industry.

Earning the title of "The King," Elvis Presley found his true love, Priscilla, at an early age, she being even younger. His Part of Marriage in Aries is in sextile aspect to Saturn in Aquarius, but the stability that Saturn offered was undermined by Uranus conjunct and Pluto in exact square to his Part of Marriage. Such a volatile combination would break up any relationship. Uranus in Aries promoted a restless and independent attitude and Pluto in Cancer would eventually terminate the union. Only an evolved couple would be able to tackle these explosive variables.

16

♥ multiple marriages

When multiple marriages occur, we can attribute them to very specific influences that usually affect Venus, Mars, and the Descendant, the seventh-house cusp of relationships. More often than not, you will find a mutable (changeable) sign, Gemini, Virgo, Sagittarius, or Pisces, on the seventh-house cusp.

In the chart of Zsa Zsa Gabor, who was married several times, we find Pisces on the seventh-house cusp, along with a Mars-Uranus conjunction in Aquarius in semisquare aspect to the Pisces Descendant. The Sun, Moon, Venus, or Mars in aspect to Uranus will also create an unpredictable outcome when it comes to intimate relationships. If Uranus is in the seventh sector or in adverse aspect to any of the personal planets mentioned in the seventh sector, it will be quite difficult to lock-in a long-term commitment.

Mick Jagger has Uranus in Gemini in square aspect to Venus in Virgo, and Uranus opposes his seventh-house cusp, which is Sagittarius. His free spirit just can't seem to settle down with such erratic influences. Elizabeth Taylor, who has also had several marriages, has a Venus-Uranus conjunction that resides in the fourth house of domestic life, and Mars in Pisces is in semisquare aspect to the Venus-Uranus coupling. Gemini, a mutable sign, resides on her seventh-house cusp.

The eight marriages experienced by Mickey Rooney were a direct reflection of having Uranus in Pisces, in sesquiquadrate aspect to Venus and in square aspect to the seventh-house cusp, which just happens to be Gemini. Doris Day had four marriages due to Uranus in semisquare aspect to Venus, and Pisces on her seventh-house cusp. Her Aries Sun in the seventh-house sector in square aspect to Pluto caused her long-term alliances to expire only to encourage the process of regeneration. A stellium of planets occupying the seventh house may also indicate more than one marriage. The ninth house rules over the second marriage partner, the eleventh house rules over the third marriage partner, and so on.

A sudden parting in a relationship may be instigated by having Uranus situated in the seventh house, especially if this unpredictable planet is afflicted or in adverse aspect to the seventh-house cusp. A departure is even more likely when Venus is afflicted, especially by the outer planets. The occurrence of a divorce or separation is usually denoted when the Sun in a woman's chart, or the Moon in a man's chart, is aspected by a malefic influence. Saturn, Uranus, Neptune, and Pluto in adverse aspect to the Moon, especially in a man's chart, or in adverse aspect to the Sun, especially in a women's chart, will test your relationship to see if it's worthy of a lifelong commitment.

17

♥

sun/moon midpoint

Sun-Moon relationships are noted to be the best, especially when in favorable aspect, such as a conjunction or trine. If the Sun and Moon are not in aspect in your synastry, you will most likely find them in the Sun/Moon midpoint.

The midpoint of the luminaries of astrology indicates the potential of any future relationship. The Sun represents the male energies and the Moon represents the female energies. Male and female energies, regardless of sexual orientation, create an attraction that is hard to resist. Whenever your Sun/Moon midpoint aspects your partner's Sun or Moon, one feels drawn to the other, emanating a desire to be involved. This influence promises a long-term alliance, yet may not ensure sexual compatibility, which is related to Venus and Mars.

I have found both positive and adverse Sun/Moon midpoint aspects to the spouse's Sun or Moon in marriage charts, which substantiates the strength of the influence—just having them in aspect is what is important. Since attraction is so appropriately emanated from Sun-Moon aspects, we would expect these two planetary influences to join forces in enhancing fertility odds. Here again the luminaries promote conception and creation.

The Sun/Moon Increasing Fertility Odds

The studies on fertility deserve to be mentioned for the main reason that in some cases they worked, but not consistently. The studies involved matching up the time of a woman's biological ovulation cycle with a Sun/Moon cycle to become pregnant. This particular Sun/Moon cycle is derived from the fact that once a month a woman becomes more fertile when the Sun and Moon in transit form the same angle that occurred at her time of birth. More research however, needs to be done to further substantiate these findings.

Fertility is discouraged under adverse angles of Saturn, Uranus, Neptune, and Pluto to Venus, the planet of fertility. A woman's Saturn in aspect to a man's Mars blocks the conception process as well. Positive angles with Sun/Jupiter, Moon/Jupiter, Venus/Jupiter, and Venus/Uranus encourage pregnancy. (For more information on fertility problems, refer to the Mars/Saturn section in chapter 7, "Challenging/Malefic Planetary Combinations in Synastry.")

Although the studies involving a woman's ovulation cycle with the Sun/Moon cycle have been inconclusive, the Sun/Moon midpoint angle is still highly consistent in the attraction of relationships.

The Moon's North and South Nodes

The Moon's Nodes denote coming together, unions, groups, and connections. Wherever the Moon's Nodes, especially the North Node, fall in the composite chart for a couple, they will emphasize the direction that needs to be pursued by the two of them as well as the essential purpose of the union. In synastry, fated or karmic relationships are noted when the Sun, Moon, or Sun/Moon midpoint is in aspect to the Nodes, which represent the destiny—the past, present, and future of one's soul. The couple is fated to address a past-life intention that lends itself to the growth of their souls.

18

♥ corrected synastry

The potential difficulties indicated by certain adverse natal configurations can be alleviated if the planets involved are in favorable aspect in a couple's synastry, especially when beneficial combinations of the Love Relationship Formula are present. For example, if you were born with Mars square Venus, which represents difficulty in compromising in your relationships, and you find that you have Mars trine Venus in your combined compatibility, the positive dynamics between the two of you as a couple can help ease the personal limitation of the natal Mars square Venus. You may also discover that an adverse aspect such as Mars opposite Saturn in a couple's synastry is alleviated through a harmonious aspect in the composite chart, such as Mars trine Saturn. Positive configurations found in your natal chart will not be undermined by similar adverse aspects in synastry or a composite chart, but will help support the adversity. Check your natal chart for any adversity and see if any unfavorable combinations found are supported in your synastry as a couple.

19 ♥ aspects and orb

The Angles Describe What We Can Expect from Relationships

Math permeates our society, our life, and our earth. Everything that exists is based on a mathematical equation. Why? Because math is a form of perfection. Therefore, in discussing the Love Relationship Formula, the precision of the angles is important. However, for all of the angles to be totally precise you would have to be the ideal human being. This is where we allow for a certain orb from one point of an angle to the other point. This orb represents the flexibility that is a reflection of being human.

The distance between planetary angles emphasizes an influence. The basic orb used by most astrologers is 8 degrees. I prefer 6 degrees. The tighter the orb, the stronger the influence. A 1 to 2 degree orb is very significant, whereas an orb of more than 8 degrees loses its strength of impact. I have found, particularly in synastry, three other important orbs to consider.

1. Aspects to the Sun can be up to 8 degrees. I have found that aspects to the Sun of 10 degrees are too wide. I only allow for an 8 degree orb involving the Sun. Example: Venus at 1° Leo square Sun at 9° Taurus.

2. Planets or significant points of interest that are in the same sign are conjunct regardless of degree. A wide orb certainly will lose some strength, but the planets are still said to be interacting with one another in that specific sign. Example: Mars at 6° Sagittarius conjunct Jupiter at 20° Sagittarius (wide).

3. Planets or significant points of interest that are in opposition can have a wide orb from one exact opposite sign to the other exact opposite sign. Example: Mercury at 10° Aquarius opposite Pluto at 25° Leo (wide).

When a planet by degree interacts with another planet or significant astrological point, they form a geometry angle, such as 45 degrees, 60 degrees, 90 degrees, 135 degrees, 150 degrees, or 180 degrees, with space as its backdrop. These angles draw together planetary combinations that describe the image and personality of who you are and what you can expect from life. Harmonious angles, such as the sextile and trine, indicate what you may not have to work on in your relationship because the planetary influences are working in harmony with each other. The conjunction can be either harmonious or inharmonious depending on the planets involved.

You may have all of the Love Relationship Formula combinations, yet if some aspects are inharmonious, such as the semisquare, square, sesquiquadrate, inconjunct, or opposition, these angles represent the challenges that will surface in the relationship of the couple. This is what needs to be addressed and worked out together for a successful union.

Let's remember that adversity presents a challenge and is not to be looked upon as negative. Here the couple learns to balance the forces through the planetary aspects. Most aspects in astrology are not exact angles and/or are adverse angles because the human being still strives for perfection. The human being, however, is a combination of math/logic and emotion that is described by the flexibility and challenges of the angles.

Aspects

Conjunction (0–6 degrees)

When two planets or significant points of interest act together, influencing each other up to 6 degrees of orb, a conjunction exists. Up to 8 degrees is acceptable for the Sun. Depending on the dynamics of these two influences, the outcome may be positive or adverse. They must try to work as a team. If given the proper outlet, this effect can be channeled for the best results. Meeting someone under a conjunction may have a great deal of impact that could have a lasting effect if supportive influences are involved. In synastry, the planets or points of interest in aspect will have a strong impression on a couple.

Semisextile (30 degrees)

The connection of two planets or points of interest in a semisextile conveys a very subtle interaction of the cosmic influences involved. This persuasion, considered a soft aspect, is almost unnoticeable as it is so indirect. This inconspicuous angle will hardly affect any connection. The impact is felt more when the orb is within 1 degree.

Semisquare (45 degrees)

This angle is a minor adverse aspect that will create difficult circumstances that are dependent on the planets or significant points of interest involved. Pressure and confrontation will be experienced, as one is pushed to take action. Due to the challenges involved, this effect is not supportive of romantic meetings, but can create dynamics in a couple's synastry.

Sextile (60 degrees)

A compatible connection of two planetary forces that are usually in fire/air or earth/water signs, the sextile offers encouraging support from one influence to another. A romantic encounter will have a positive yet subtle influence under this aspect, which is supportive of any relationship.

Square (90 degrees)

This is the most adverse aspect in astrology. The angle denotes blocks to one's desires and highly volatile situations. The two cosmic influences are at odds with one another, provoking either an explosive conflict that needs to be addressed or producing a driving force to tackle the situation at hand. We need to remind ourselves that a crisis is also a rare opportunity. Square aspects can be very stimulating where a certain dynamic inspires a person to fulfill their potential. Depending on the influences involved, a strong romantic impact can be experienced with Venus and/or Mars. In most instances, a connection involving a square aspect will be challenging.

Trine (120 degrees)

This link promises success with a beneficial interaction. There is an ease of accomplishment that creates a favorable relationship between these cosmic points. The trine seeks harmony to bring more satisfaction into the scenario. This angle has a tendency toward laziness, expecting that everything will work out well. You may need to instill self-motivation to encourage some action. In most cases, a meeting under a trine influence will encourage a positive union and supports compatibility in synastry as well.

Sesquiquadrate (135 degrees)

When we combine the square and the semisquare, we form the sesquiquadrate angle. Under this influence you are compelled to take a stand, be decisive, and initiate a course of action. Even though you are driven, you will still meet up with resistance and challenges along the way. A romantic encounter under this influential angle denotes stress and is not considered to be enduring. In synastry, a couple will be challenged to direct the influence for the better.

Inconjunct/Quincunx (150 degrees)

The two planets involved in this particular aspect do not share the same element or quality, thus making it very difficult to communicate. The planets or points of interest engaged in this scenario will feel inclined to follow through, yet will switch gears before arriving at the end result. You will have to be flexible and make adjustments where they are needed. A person you meet under this effect will send mixed signals that may lead nowhere. Depending on the planets involved, this aspect will require attention to channel the influence for the best.

Opposition (180 degrees)

When two planets or cosmic points oppose each other, they are in conflict and choose not to compromise with each other. Each influence is determined to have its say, thus causing tremendous disagreement. Both sides need to find a way to cooperate to reach that middle ground. Although the opposition is considered the lesser of the hard angles, unless supported by favorable aspects, a romantic encounter affected by this aspect may relay too much tension to sustain a lasting partnership. In synastry, the influences need equal time and can create strong, romantic dynamics depending on the planets or points of interest involved.

part 4

the love
relationship
formula in
couples' charts

20

♥

famous
couples' charts

Compatibility Analysis of Paul Newman and Joanne Woodward

Paul Newman and Joanne Woodward have been married for over forty years. Their commitment has withstood the test of time and is a remarkable example of a long-term relationship. The rarity of finding the presence of mutual Sun-Moon conjunctions adds to the longevity of their union, as this important cosmic combination supports a lasting bond. Reciprocal Sun-Venus aspects bring love and appreciation for each other that encourage an affectionate tie. This well-established relationship is further enhanced by mutual Sun-Mars influences where the couple is motivated to take action, whether it be attending to domestic chores or enjoying a passionate evening together. Sun-Mars influences promote their success together, along with a strong competitive streak to see who wins first. Her Jupiter aspecting his Mars indicates she can persuade her man to do more for her, including arousing his romantic side. Not to mention her Uranus conjoining his Mars in Aries, which creates much sexual excitement.

But reciprocal Venus-Mars aspects are the drawing cards that fuel the romantic embers between them, which has led to the procreation of three children. Moon-Mars combinations may also heighten the passions if channeled properly. To add to the attraction, mutual Venus-Uranus aspects are present, causing this couple to find each other very appealing. To augment an already fine union, mutual Moon-Venus pairings instigate sensitivity to each other's feelings that show they care. Moon-Neptune combinations inspire a mutual emotional identity that makes them feel in sync and that took time to acquire after working through some tentative feelings. A greater understanding is reached as they are forced to understand each other's emotions under Moon-Pluto pairings that only deepen the emotional interaction. Mutual Moon-Jupiter aspects bring out a wonderful sense of humor as they thoroughly enjoy one another's company.

They are both highly encouraging of each other's ambitions in life with favorable, reciprocal Sun-Jupiter influences. He is able to bring out the best in her with his complimentary advances as his Jupiter aspects her Venus. Since his Saturn aspects her Venus as well, the Venus-Jupiter influences are able to balance out the rapport so she does not feel so suppressed by his Saturn influence. They are quite at home with each other under mutual Venus-Saturn aspects as Saturn finds comfort with Venus' warm embrace. This karmic connection makes them both feel at ease in each other's presence and may assure a lifelong commitment.

His Saturn aspecting her Sun and her Saturn aspecting his Moon also bring up some karmic issues that have put some pressure on this union. Nevertheless, this relationship is spiritualized by the auspicious Venus-Neptune pairings and intensified with a deep love through mutual Venus-Pluto aspects that instigate a compelling attraction for these two souls to unite. They have learned through Venus-Neptune that the truth counts and through Venus-Pluto that there is more unity in being agreeable. Under reciprocal Jupiter-Saturn aspects, a terrific friendship continues to link this couple together. However, any relationship is not without its difficulties, which may spring from reciprocal Mars-Saturn influences that will at times cause blocks to their desires or trouble in expressing differences. Luckily there are so many mutual Mercury influences, such as Mercury-Sun and Mercury-Jupiter, that the lines of communication are open to discuss whatever is necessary. Although mutual Mercury-Pluto aspects instigate deep, thorough conversation that succumbs to strong differences of opinion and Mercury-Neptune influences may cause nebulous yet creative dialogue, they are strengthened by the other Mercury aspects, especially to the Sun, Jupiter, and Saturn. They are able to give each other the space they need with reciprocal Sun-Uranus aspects, but maintain a wonderful, romantic, and compatible partnership. An exact conjunction of his Moon to her Sun/Moon midpoint supports a lasting connection. The Love Relationship Formula is in excellent display here with this honorable couple.

Paul Newman and Joanne Woodward, synastry aspects
(Love Relationship Formula aspects underlined)

Sun 6°02' Aquarius conjunct Moon 24°52' Aquarius (wide)

Moon 1°39' Pisces conjunct Sun 8°03' Pisces

Venus 14°24' Capricorn sextile Sun 8°03' Pisces

Sun 6°02' Aquarius semisquare Venus 13°05' Pisces (wide)

Sun 6°02' Aquarius conjunct Mars 16°02' Aquarius (wide)

Mars 23°38' Aries semisquare Sun 8°03' Pisces

Ascendant, a Mars Point, 13°05' Capricorn sextile Sun 8°03' Pisces

Sun 6°02' Aquarius trine Jupiter 7°33' Gemini

Jupiter 8°52' Capricorn sextile Sun 8°03' Pisces

Saturn 13°42' Scorpio trine Sun 8°03' Pisces

Sun 6°02' Aquarius sextile Uranus 9°30' Aries

Uranus 19°04' Pisces conjunct Sun 8°03' Pisces (wide)

Pluto 12°01' Cancer trine Sun 8°03' Pisces

Moon 1°39' Pisces conjunct Venus 13°05' Pisces (wide)

Venus 14°24' Capricorn semisquare Moon 24°52' Aquarius

Moon 1°39' Pisces semisquare Ascendant, a Mars Point, 11°50' Capricorn

Mars 23°38' Aries sextile Moon 24°52' Aquarius

Moon 1°39' Pisces square Jupiter 7°33' Gemini

Jupiter 8°52' Capricorn semisquare Moon 24°52' Aquarius

Moon 1°39' Pisces semisquare Saturn 9°40' Capricorn (wide)

Moon 1°39' Pisces oppose Neptune 2°03' Virgo

Neptune 21°38' Leo oppose Moon 24°52' Aquarius

Moon 1°39' Pisces sesquiquadrate Pluto 17°39' Cancer

Pluto 12°01' Cancer sesquiquadrate Moon 24°52' Aquarius

Mercury 13°19' Capricorn sextile Sun 8°03' Pisces

Sun 6°02' Aquarius conjunct Mercury 14°18' Aquarius (wide)

Mercury 13°19' Capricorn semisquare Moon 24°52' Aquarius

Mercury 13°19' Capricorn sextile Venus 13°05' Pisces

Venus 14°24' Capricorn semisextile Mercury 14°18' Aquarius

Mercury 13°19' Capricorn inconjunct Jupiter 7°33' Gemini

Jupiter 8°52' Capricorn semisextile Mercury 14°18' Aquarius

Mercury 13°19' Capricorn conjunct Saturn 9°40' Capricorn

Saturn 13°42' Scorpio square Mercury 14°18' Aquarius

Mercury 13°19' Capricorn square Uranus 9°30' Aries

Neptune 21°38' Leo oppose Mercury 14°18' Aquarius (wide)

Mercury 13°19' Capricorn sesquiquadrate Neptune 2°03' Virgo

Mercury 13°19' Capricorn oppose Pluto 17°39' Cancer

Pluto 12°01' Cancer inconjunct Mercury 14°18' Aquarius

<u>Venus 14°24' Capricorn sextile Venus 13°05' Pisces, Benefics in aspect</u>

<u>Venus 14°24' Capricorn conjunct Ascendant, a Mars Point, 11°50' Capricorn</u>

<u>Mars 23°38' Aries semisquare Venus 13°05' Pisces</u>

<u>Jupiter 8°52' Capricorn sextile Venus 13°05' Pisces</u>

<u>Descendant, a Venus Point, 13°05' Cancer semisextile Jupiter 7°33' Gemini</u>

<u>Venus 14°24' Capricorn conjunct Saturn 9°40' Capricorn</u>

<u>Saturn 13°42' Scorpio trine Venus 13°05' Pisces</u>

<u>Venus 14°24' Capricorn square Uranus 9°30' Aries</u>

<u>Uranus 19°04' Pisces conjunct Venus 13°05' Pisces</u>

Venus 14°24' Capricorn sesquiquadrate Neptune 2°03' Virgo

Neptune 21°38' Leo semisquare Descendant, a Venus Point, 11°50' Cancer

<u>Venus 14°24' Capricorn oppose Pluto 17°39' Cancer</u>

<u>Pluto 12°01' Cancer trine Venus 13°05' Pisces</u>

Ascendant, a Mars Point, 13°05' Capricorn conjunct Ascendant, a Mars Point, 11°50' Capricorn

<u>Mars 23°38' Aries semisquare Jupiter 7°33' Gemini</u>

Ascendant, a Mars Point, 13°05' Capricorn conjunct Saturn 9°40' Capricorn

Saturn 13°42' Scorpio square Mars 16°02' Aquarius

Saturn 13°42' Scorpio sextile Ascendant, a Mars Point, 11°50' Capricorn

Mars 23°38' Aries conjunct Uranus 9°30' Aries (wide)

<u>Jupiter 8°52' Capricorn conjunct Saturn 9°40' Capricorn</u>

<u>Saturn 13°42' Scorpio inconjunct Jupiter 7°33' Gemini</u>

Neptune 21°38' Leo sesquiquadrate Saturn 9°40' Capricorn

Saturn 13°42' Scorpio trine Pluto 17°39' Cancer

Pluto 12°01' Cancer oppose Saturn 9°40' Capricorn

Pluto 12°01' Cancer semisquare Neptune 2°03' Virgo

<u>Moon 1°39' Pisces conjunct Sun/Moon midpoint 1°27' Pisces</u>

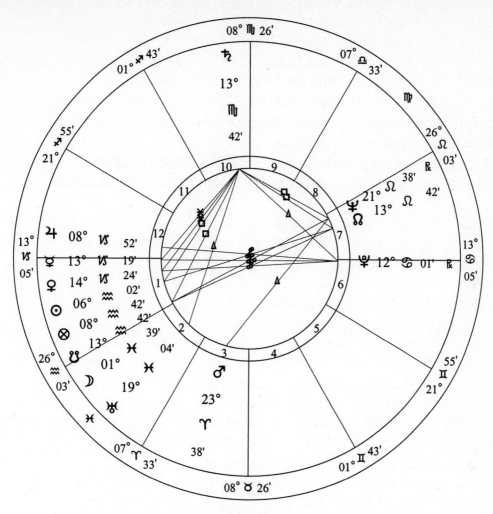

Paul Newman
January 26, 1925 / Cleveland, OH / 6:30 AM EST
Placidus Houses

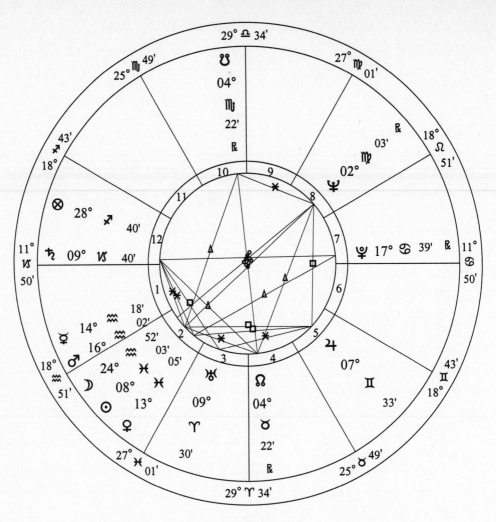

Joanne Woodward
February 27, 1930 / Thomasville, GA / 4:00 AM EST
Placidus Houses

Compatibility Analysis of John Lennon and Yoko Ono

John Lennon and Yoko Ono had a very controversial relationship. It is said that they had an incredible love for one another that we can now verify by their astrological compatibility. Their marriage of only eleven years may have lasted a lifetime, but it was cut short when Lennon was gunned down in front of his apartment building in New York City. When we evaluate their compatibility, it gives us every reason to believe that their love was genuine. Libra and Aquarius are well matched as they are both air signs. But the important link is his Moon (widely) conjunct her Sun, which has a lasting effect on the bond between them and indicates that he could rely on her, which would play out in their time together. Her Moon is also in favorable aspect to his Sun.

The love and respect they had for one another was instigated by mutual Sun-Venus aspects. What enhanced this love were reciprocal Venus-Mars aspects, which influenced the romantic dynamics, mutual Venus-Neptune aspects, which created a compassionate, spiritual bond, and joint Venus-Pluto influences, which instilled the merging of souls that they may understand love on a deeper level. Theirs was a bond of love that few may experience. They felt energized as well as competitive in each other's company due to reciprocal Sun-Mars influences, and her Jupiter aspecting his Sun showed support for his ambitions. She also offered her man tender-loving care with her Venus aspecting his Moon. Mutual Moon-Jupiter pairings helped ease the tensions and promoted an optimistic spirit, and shared Mercury-Jupiter aspects inspired excellent communication.

Shared Venus-Jupiter influences promoted a complimentary exchange that enhanced each other's talents. Although adverse Venus-Neptune aspects are present, they developed their higher spiritual side by respecting each other. His Neptune adversely influencing her Sun and Mercury may have caused some complications with her following through on some of her projects. Her Saturn aspecting his Sun and Moon has karmic implications, indicating that she felt responsible for him and that he had some lessons to learn from her. His Saturn aspecting her Venus and Mars still allowed him to feel very comfortable with her since he sensed that he must have known her before when they first met. Luckily both his Jupiter and Saturn influence her Venus, indicating that a complementary balance would ensue so he would not take her for granted. Nevertheless, he was able to call the shots in the relationship.

Although it is unusual to find her Saturn not in aspect to his Venus or his Descendant, her Saturn aspects his Jupiter, which establishes a good, long-term friendship, thus she felt secure with him. Conversation was inspired by Mercury, Venus, Mars, and Jupiter, and was realistic with mutual Mercury-Saturn pairings. They were able to motivate each other through Mars-Jupiter aspects to do errands or enjoy romance. They found each other appealing with reciprocal Venus-Uranus influences, and mutual Mars-Uranus, Mars-Neptune, and Mars-Pluto angles brought excitement, depth, and romanticism to the union. However, Mars-Uranus also created upset when they were out of sync with expressing their emotions and having a detached disposition. Adverse Mars-Pluto aspects needed to be channeled to avoid personal resistance from one another.

His Jupiter in trine aspect to her Mars inspired her to accomplish set goals. The mutual Jupiter-Neptune combinations persuaded them both to expand upon their ideals, which in this case is clearly writing, playing, and singing music. Reciprocal Sun-Uranus aspects encouraged both to be more progressive, as Sun-Pluto influences prompted deep-rooted changes that would affect their lives forever. They may have been an avant-garde couple, but their story of love cannot be denied.

John Lennon and Yoko Ono, synastry aspects
(Love Relationship Formula aspects underlined)
Sun 16°16' Libra trine Sun 29°23' Aquarius (wide)
<u>Moon 3°33' Aquarius conjunct Sun 29°23' Aquarius (wide)</u>
<u>Sun 16°16' Libra sextile Moon 11°08' Sagittarius</u>
<u>Sun 16°16' Libra sextile Venus 13°47' Aquarius</u>
<u>Venus 3°13' Virgo oppose Sun 29°23' Aquarius</u>
<u>Mars 2°40' Libra inconjunct Sun 29°23' Aquarius</u>
<u>Sun 16°16' Libra semisextile Mars 15°08' Virgo</u>
<u>Sun 16°16' Libra inconjunct Jupiter 20°42' Virgo</u>
Sun 16°16' Libra trine Saturn 9°44' Aquarius
Sun 16°16' Libra sextile Uranus 20°33' Aries
Uranus 25°33' Taurus square Sun 29°23' Aquarius
Neptune 26°02' Virgo inconjunct Sun 29°23' Aquarius
Sun 16°16' Libra square Pluto 21°38' Cancer
Pluto 4°11' Leo oppose Sun 29°23' Aquarius (wide)
<u>Moon 3°33' Aquarius conjunct Venus 13°47' Aquarius (wide)</u>
Moon 3°33' Aquarius sesquiquadrate Mars 15°08' Virgo
<u>Moon 3°33' Aquarius sesquiquadrate Jupiter 20°42' Virgo</u>

Jupiter 13°42' Taurus inconjunct Moon 11°08' Sagittarius

Moon 3°33' Aquarius conjunct Saturn 9°44' Aquarius

Mercury 8°33' Scorpio trine Mercury 7°53' Pisces

Mercury 8°33' Scorpio square Venus 13°47' Aquarius

Venus 3°13' Virgo oppose Mercury 7°53' Pisces

Mercury 8°33' Scorpio sextile Mars 15°08' Virgo (wide)

Mercury 8°33' Scorpio semisextile Ascendant, a Mars Point, 8°30' Libra

Ascendant, a Mars Point, 19°54' Aries semisquare Mercury 7°53' Pisces

Mercury 8°33' Scorpio semisquare Jupiter 20°42' Virgo

Jupiter 13°42' Taurus sextile Mercury 7°53' Pisces

Mercury 8°33' Scorpio square Saturn 9°44' Aquarius

Saturn 13°13' Taurus sextile Mercury 7°53' Pisces

Mercury 8°33' Scorpio sextile Neptune 9°05' Virgo

Neptune 26°02' Virgo oppose Mercury 7°53' Pisces (wide)

Pluto 4°11' Leo inconjunct Mercury 7°53' Pisces

Venus 3°13' Virgo conjunct Mars 15°08' Virgo (wide)

Mars 2°40' Libra sesquiquadrate Venus 13°47' Aquarius

Ascendant, a Mars Point, 19°54' Aries sextile Venus 13°47' Aquarius

Mars 2°40' Libra conjunct Ascendant, a Mars Point, 8°30' Libra

Venus 3°13' Virgo conjunct Jupiter 20°42' Virgo (wide)

Jupiter 13°42' Taurus square Venus 13°47' Aquarius

Saturn 13°13' Taurus square Venus 13°47' Aquarius

Venus 3°13' Virgo sesquiquadrate Uranus 20°33' Aries

Uranus 25°33' Taurus semisquare Descendant, a Venus Point, 8°30' Aries

Venus 3°13' Virgo conjunct Neptune 9°05' Virgo

Neptune 26°02' Virgo sesquiquadrate Venus 13°47' Aquarius

Venus 3°13' Virgo semisquare Pluto 21°38' Cancer

Pluto 4°11' Leo oppose Venus 13°47' Aquarius (wide)

Jupiter 13°42' Taurus trine Mars 15°08' Virgo

Ascendant, a Mars Point, 19°54' Aries inconjunct Jupiter 20°42' Virgo

Saturn 13°13' Taurus trine Mars 15°08' Virgo

Mars 2°40' Libra oppose Uranus 20°33' Aries (wide)

Uranus 25°33' Taurus sesquiquadrate Ascendant, a Mars Point, 8°30' Libra

Neptune 26°02' Virgo conjunct Mars 15°08' Virgo (wide)

Ascendant, a Mars Point, 19°54' Aries square Pluto 21°38' Cancer

Pluto 4°11' Leo semisquare Mars 15°08' Virgo

Jupiter 13°42' Taurus square Saturn 9°44' Aquarius

Pluto 4°11' Leo semisquare Jupiter 20°42' Virgo

Uranus 25°33' Taurus trine Jupiter 20°42' Virgo

Jupiter 13°42' Taurus trine Neptune 9°05' Virgo

Neptune 26°02' Virgo conjunct Jupiter 20°42' Virgo

Uranus 25°33' Taurus sextile Pluto 21°38' Cancer

Neptune 26°02' Virgo sextile Pluto 21°38' Cancer

Pluto 4°11' Leo inconjunct Neptune 9°05' Virgo

Sun/Moon midpoint 9°54' Sagittarius conjunct Moon 11°08' Sagittarius

Sun 16°16' Libra square Sun/Moon midpoint 20°23' Capricorn

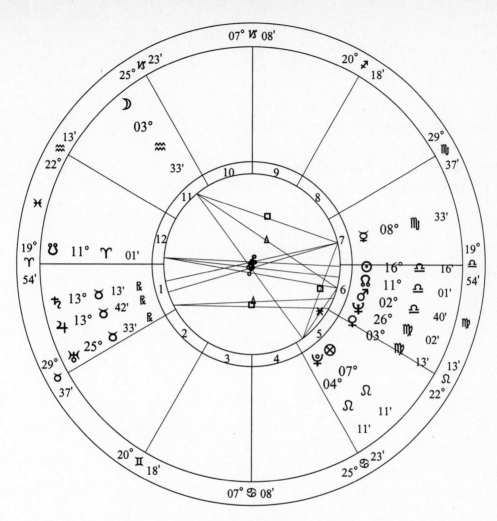

John Lennon
October 9, 1940 / Liverpool, England / 6:30 PM GMD
Placidus Houses

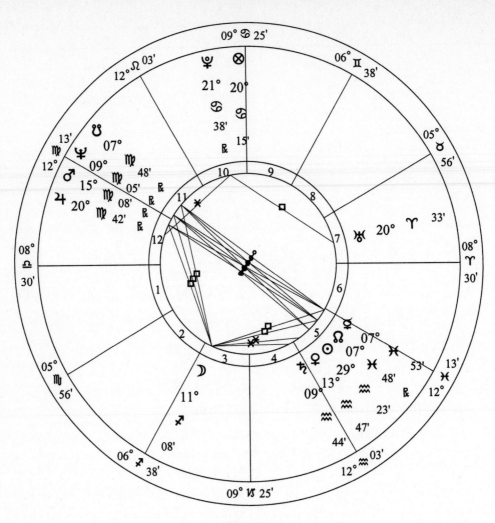

Yoko Ono
February 18, 1933 / Tokyo, Japan / 8:30 PM JST
Placidus Houses

21 ♥ Difficult couples' charts

Compatibility Analysis of "Gary" and "Sue"

You would think that this couple would be off to a good start in life. Their compatibility indicates mutual Sun-Jupiter and Venus-Jupiter contacts, along with his Venus conjunct her Sun. They would be supportive of one another's career goals and they would try to bring out the best in each other. Even a Venus-Mars conjunction in Cancer indicates a male/female attraction. This is further enhanced by his Venus in trine aspect to her Ascendant, a Mars Point. Mutual Mars-Uranus aspects add even more passion to this romantic connection. The benefics in aspect, Jupiter-Jupiter and Venus-Venus, are present, offering encouragement. The reciprocal Moon-Uranus aspects may promote emotional excitement, but also stress and detachment, which would play out.

The Sun-Moon midpoint aspects could be tighter in orb, but they are present, continuing to promote this relationship. There is also one discordant and one harmonious Sun-Moon aspect. Although Sun-Moon angles do endorse an attraction, a Venus-Uranus contact can be more magnetic. Here we find her Uranus in Cancer conjunct his

Venus, which indicates that she feels very drawn to him. She is also very sensitive to him and his needs, as her Venus is in wide conjunction to his Moon and Ascendant. He is very fond of her, as his Venus is conjunct her Sun in Cancer, but his attraction to her is limited and his emotional sensitivity toward her is lacking. Their Sun signs are very descriptive, too. She is a Cancer who nurtures and provides. He, on the other hand, is a Gemini who exercises a Mercurial approach and is looking for an intellectual challenge.

This couple, however, was very comfortable with each other with mutual Venus-Saturn contacts. But too much Saturn creates coldness and restraint. His Saturn, in particular, conjoining her Sun and in wide aspect to Mars and Uranus, as well as in semisquare aspect to her Venus and also in square aspect to her Neptune, limited her tremendously. He eventually would not cooperate, or show that he appreciated her efforts even if he did, and at times he was very critical of her actions. This was truly a reflection of his Saturn conjunct her Sun and semisquare her Venus. The burden became hers. She even looked after his teenage child. His Sun and Neptune in sextile to her Mercury assisted her in approaching him in a gentle manner, but there was no reciprocation. Even her Pluto in sextile to his Mercury tried to unravel the situation. His interaction was limited due to her Saturn in square aspect to his Mercury, signifying little if no communication at all. Her Saturn was also causing constraint in wide conjunction to his Moon and Ascendant. He clearly had difficulty expressing himself toward her. But his Pluto in conjunction to her Mercury indicated that he might be manipulating the situation, which would eventually become too taxing and suppressive for both of them.

There are no Moon-Jupiter contacts to alleviate the pressure and create more enjoyment, no Mercury-Jupiter aspects to improve the suffering communications, and no Jupiter-Saturn contacts to help build a friendship that shares the burden—three strikes against them. Although his Jupiter does semisextile her Ascendant, a Mars Point, and her Jupiter is inconjunct his Ascendant, the planetary pairing of Mars and Jupiter in aspect is missing. There are no Mars-Jupiter planetary contacts to bring more motivation and passion into this relationship, which is already lacking due to the mutual Mars-Saturn influences causing blocks to their desires and repressed anger.

She ended up becoming the aggressor in romance as well as the breadwinner, denoted by her Mars conjunct his Venus and in her eighth house, among other influences previously discussed. The financial situation was terrible, partially due to the fact that neither of their Mercurys were enhanced. She could not motivate him to change the circumstances, and he did not care to converse and address what was happening. This led to the deterioration of the bond between them. He became unsupportive and distant. She became drained and resentful, yet she tried not to show it. Although mutual Venus-Neptune aspects wanted a spiritual connection to unfold, because they are making adverse angles a level of dishonesty was clearly present. This relationship lasted for approximately five years. She finally decided to end it.

Gary and Sue, synastry aspects (Love Relationship Formula aspects underlined)

Moon 16°15' Virgo sextile Sun 20°01' Cancer

Sun 15°24' Gemini sesquiquadrate Moon 2°47' Scorpio

Venus 16°20' Cancer conjunct Sun 20°01' Cancer

Mars 22°26' Leo semisextile Sun 20°01' Cancer

Sun 15°24' Gemini sextile Jupiter 13°23' Aries

Jupiter 17°33' Libra square Sun 20°01' Cancer

Saturn 22°55' Cancer conjunct Sun 20°01' Cancer

Moon 16°15' Virgo conjunct Venus 4°04' Virgo (wide)

Moon 16°15' Virgo conjunct Saturn 27°12' Virgo (wide)

Moon 16°15' Virgo sextile Uranus 10°20' Cancer

Uranus 17°26' Gemini sesquiquadrate Moon 2°47' Scorpio

Sun 15°24' Gemini sextile Mercury 8°25' Leo (wide)

Mercury 23°02' Gemini sesquiquadrate Moon 2°47' Scorpio

Mercury 23°02' Gemini square Saturn 27°12' Virgo

Neptune 5°52' Libra sextile Mercury 8°25' Leo

Mercury 23°02' Gemini sextile Pluto 18°34' Leo

Pluto 9°53' Leo conjunct Mercury 8°25' Leo

Venus 16°20' Cancer semisquare Venus 4°04' Virgo, Benefics

Mars 22°26' Leo square Descendant, a Venus Point, 17°19' Taurus

Venus 16°20' Cancer conjunct Mars 6°12' Cancer (wide)

Ascendant, a Mars Point, 14°00' Virgo conjunct Venus 4°04' Virgo (wide)

Venus 16°20' Cancer trine Ascendant, a Mars Point, 17°19' Scorpio

Jupiter 17°33' Libra semisquare Venus 4°04' Virgo

Venus 16°20' Cancer square Jupiter 13°23' Aries

Jupiter 17°33' Libra oppose Jupiter 13°23' Aries, Benefics

Saturn 22°55' Cancer semisquare Venus 4°04' Virgo

Descendant, a Venus Point, 14°00' Pisces oppose Saturn 27°12' Virgo (wide)

Saturn 22°55' Cancer semisquare Venus 4°04' Virgo

Descendant, a Venus Point, 14°00' Pisces oppose Saturn 27°12' Virgo (wide)

Venus 16°20' Cancer conjunct Uranus 10°20' Cancer

Uranus 17°26' Gemini semisextile Descendant, a Venus Point, 17°19' Taurus

Venus 16°20' Cancer square Neptune 16°49' Libra

Neptune 5°52' Libra sesquiquadrate Descendant, a Venus Point, 17°19' Taurus

Saturn 22°55' Cancer trine Ascendant, a Mars Point, 17°19' Scorpio

Saturn 22°55' Cancer conjunct Mars 6°12' Cancer (wide)

Ascendant, a Mars Point, 14°00' Virgo conjunct Saturn 27°12' Virgo (wide)

Mars 22°26' Leo semisquare Uranus 10°20' Cancer

Uranus 17°26' Gemini inconjunct Ascendant, a Mars Point, 17°19' Scorpio

Neptune 5°52' Libra square Mars 6°12' Cancer

Mars 22°26' Leo conjunct Pluto 18°34' Leo

Saturn 22°55' Cancer conjunct Uranus 10°20' Cancer (wide)

Saturn 22°55' Cancer square Neptune 16°49' Libra

Uranus 17°26' Gemini sextile Jupiter 13°23' Aries

Jupiter 17°33' Libra conjunct Neptune 16°49' Libra

Jupiter 17°33' Libra sextile Pluto 18°34' Leo

Neptune 5°52' Libra square Uranus 10°20' Cancer

Uranus 17°26' Gemini sextile Pluto 18°34' Leo

Neptune 5°52' Libra semisquare Pluto 18°34' Leo

Sun/Moon midpoint at 0°12' Leo square Moon 2°47' Scorpio

Sun 15°24' Gemini square Sun/Moon midpoint at 11°24' Virgo

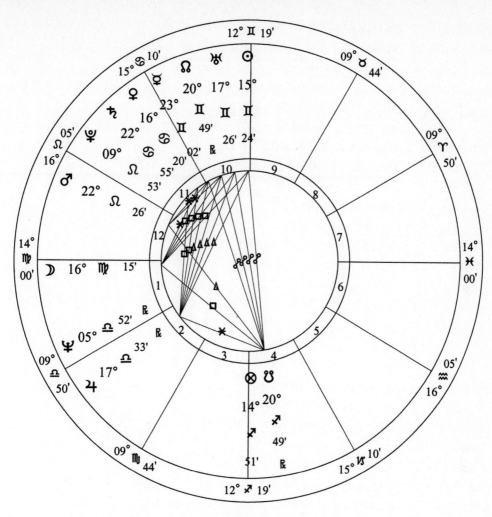

Gary
June 6, 1946 / Brinkley, AR / 11:50 AM CST
Placidus Houses

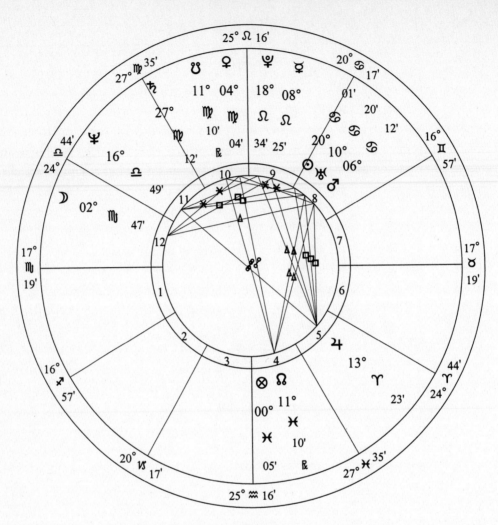

Sue
July 13, 1951 / Tokyo, Japan / 2:10 PM JST
Placidus Houses

Compatibility Analysis of "William" and "Ruth"

This couple felt an immediate attraction due to their mutual Venus-Uranus aspects. They fell in love, as reciprocal Sun-Venus contacts encouraged an affectionate exchange. The passion grew quickly with shared Sun-Mars aspects and even more supportive Moon-Mars influences. Mutual as well as hard Venus-Mars contacts created romantic dynamics, but also tension. Mutual Mars-Jupiter aspects also increased the romantic passion. Reciprocal and challenging Moon-Uranus aspects added excitement along with emotional erraticism and detachment. Unpredictable mood swings would eventually arouse great stress and possible emotional separation. In the beginning, she felt complimented by him (Venus-Jupiter). He had a way of bringing out her sense of humor (Moon-Jupiter). She supported his goals and believed in him with her Jupiter aspecting his Sun. He seemed to promise her more than he could deliver. Yet, she was sensitive to his needs as her Venus widely opposed his Moon, and he tried to be sensitive to hers as his Venus, in Aquarius mind you, was inconjunct her Moon. They also had a shared sense of identity with mutual Moon-Neptune aspects.

They decided to get married, even though they had only known each other for approximately four months. Since their relationship was long-distance, she moved to another country with the idea that he would eventually move back to the United States with her. There was a strong foundation of security due to her Saturn conjunct his Venus, the planet of comfort and love. His Saturn was sextile her Venus and was also in square aspect to her Ascendant, a Mars Point, and Descendant, a Venus Point, indicating that he felt totally comfortable and at ease with the relationship—maybe too comfortable. However, Venus-Saturn contacts tend to be very karmic. It was an experience that neither of them will ever forget. Anyone's Saturn in hard aspect to your Ascendant, along with Venus, may have the upper hand. He was in control and apparently liked it that way, too. This is a reflection of his Sun-Saturn conjunction and Saturn in semi-square aspect to his Venus.

It wasn't too long after they were married that major problems started to occur. Their communication broke down, he started controlling her by doing what he wanted, her self-esteem plummeted due to his demeaning comments, and this became a physically abusive relationship. What happened?

They were financially strapped and he did not seem motivated to change the situation. He began to take his frustration out on her. She became annoyed with him as well.

His Saturn in semisquare aspect to her Sun brought out criticism toward her and her goals, which never materialized as planned. Saturn in sesquiquadrate aspect to her Moon made it difficult for her to express herself because she was emotionally repressed. Saturn in semisquare aspect to her Mercury seriously blocked communications for her and made her fearful of saying something that might upset him. His Pluto and Neptune were in difficult aspect to her Mercury as well, indicating manipulative tactics by him and confusion and misunderstandings for both of them. Even though her Jupiter was in trine aspect to his Mercury, there was a language and cultural barrier that did not help matters.

Saturn in sextile aspect to her Venus and in square aspect to her Descendant, a Venus Point, can cause a man to take a women for granted, especially if he wants to control her. The physical abuse started when transiting Saturn in Pisces in 1994 and 1995 opposed his Mars, Uranus, and Pluto in Virgo, and conjoined his Sun, Mercury, and Saturn. Transiting Saturn in Pisces also conjoined her Mars and was in semisquare aspect to her Saturn. Since she was born under a Mars line with her Mars in the fourth house and with her Saturn in Aquarius in semisquare aspect to Mars, she needs to be very careful of violence erupting in the home. Her Sun and Mercury in Aries inconjunct Pluto, indicating resistance and aggressive tendencies, may have also contributed to the situation.

Other influences were triggered as well. Mars in Pisces exactly opposed Mars in Virgo. Her Saturn was in sesquiquadrate aspect to his Mars. His Saturn was in wide opposition to her Mars, and in square aspect to her Ascendant, a Mars Point. Mars-Saturn influences, if not channeled properly, can lead to aggravation, blocks to one's desires, and in extreme cases abuse. Also mutual Mars-Pluto influences intensified the conflict. He completely lost it. His actions destroyed the love between them. She sadly realized that it was not going to improve, and they divorced.

When a person starts abusing you, they feel that they can. They have convinced themselves that this is the way to handle the relationship, to keep it under control. One of the most painful situations in life is when you love someone and they verbally and/or physically abuse you. Because you love them, you continue to hope that they will change. They may only change when you decide to leave them. Too many Saturn contacts, especially with the personal planets and Mars in particular, along with communication difficulties, shattered this relationship.

William and Ruth, synastry aspects (Love Relationship Formula aspects underlined)

Sun 3°51' Pisces semisquare Sun 21°44' Aries

<u>Venus 21°42' Aquarius sextile Sun 21°44' Aries</u>

<u>Sun 3°51' Pisces sextile Venus 10°04' Taurus</u>

<u>Sun 3°51' Pisces conjunct Mars 24°06' Pisces (wide)</u>

<u>Mars 24°07' Virgo inconjunct Sun 21°44' Aries</u>

<u>Sun 3°51' Pisces conjunct Jupiter 3°35' Pisces</u>

Saturn 7°08' Pisces semisquare Sun 21°44' Aries

Moon 27°44' Scorpio trine Moon 25°07' Cancer

<u>Venus 21°42' Aquarius inconjunct Moon 25°07' Cancer</u>

Moon 27°44' Scorpio oppose Venus 10°04' Taurus (wide)

Moon 27°44' Scorpio trine Mars 24°06' Pisces

Mars 24°07' Virgo sextile Moon 25°07' Cancer

<u>Jupiter 19°08' Taurus sextile Moon 25°07' Cancer</u>

Saturn 7°08' Pisces sesquiquadrate Moon 25°07' Cancer

Moon 27°44' Scorpio square Uranus 26°37' Leo

Uranus 13°11' Virgo semisquare Moon 25°07' Cancer

Neptune 20°00' Scorpio trine Moon 25°07' Cancer

Moon 27°44' Scorpio conjunct Neptune 12°41' Scorpio (wide)

Sun 3°51' Pisces semisquare Mercury 17°24' Aries

Mercury 2°39' Pisces semisquare Mercury 17°24' Aries

<u>Mercury 2°39' Pisces conjunct Jupiter 3°35' Pisces</u>

Saturn 7°08' Pisces semisquare Mercury 17°24' Aries

Uranus 13°11' Virgo inconjunct Mercury 17°24' Aries

Neptune 20°00' Scorpio inconjunct Mercury 17°24' Aries

Pluto 15°19' Virgo inconjunct Mercury 17°24' Aries

<u>Mars 24°07' Virgo sesquiquadrate Venus 10°04' Taurus</u>

<u>Jupiter 19°08' Taurus conjunct Venus 10°04' Taurus (wide)</u>

<u>Descendant, a Venus Point, 2°10' Sagittarius square Jupiter 3°35' Pisces</u>

<u>Venus 21°42' Aquarius conjunct Saturn 10°08' Aquarius (wide)</u>

<u>Saturn 7°08' Pisces sextile Venus 10°04' Taurus</u>

<u>Venus 21°42' Aquarius oppose Uranus 26°37' Leo</u>

<u>Uranus 13°11' Virgo trine Venus 10°04' Taurus</u>

Pluto 15°19' Virgo trine Venus 10°04' Taurus
Mars 24°07' Virgo oppose Jupiter 3°35' Pisces (wide)
Jupiter 19°08' Taurus sextile Mars 24°06' Pisces
Mars 24°07' Virgo oppose Mars 24°06' Pisces
Saturn 7°08' Pisces square Ascendant, a Mars Point, 3°10' Sagittarius
Saturn 7°08' Pisces oppose Mars 24°06' Pisces (wide)
Mars 24°07' Virgo sesquiquadrate Saturn 10°08' Aquarius
Uranus 13°11' Virgo oppose Mars 24°06' Pisces (wide)
Mars 24°07' Virgo semisquare Neptune 12°41' Scorpio
Neptune 20°00' Scorpio trine Mars 24°06' Pisces
Mars 24°07' Virgo conjunct Pluto 7°51' Virgo (wide)
Pluto 15°19' Virgo oppose Mars 24°06' Pisces (wide)
Saturn 7°08' Pisces conjunct Jupiter 3°35' Pisces
Saturn 7°08' Pisces trine Neptune 12°41' Scorpio
Saturn 7°08' Pisces oppose Pluto 7°51' Virgo (wide)
Pluto 15°19' Virgo inconjunct Saturn 10°08' Aquarius
Jupiter 19°08' Taurus oppose Neptune 12°41' Scorpio
Uranus 13°11' Virgo oppose Jupiter 3°35' Pisces (wide)
Pluto 15°19' Virgo oppose Jupiter 3°35' Pisces (wide)

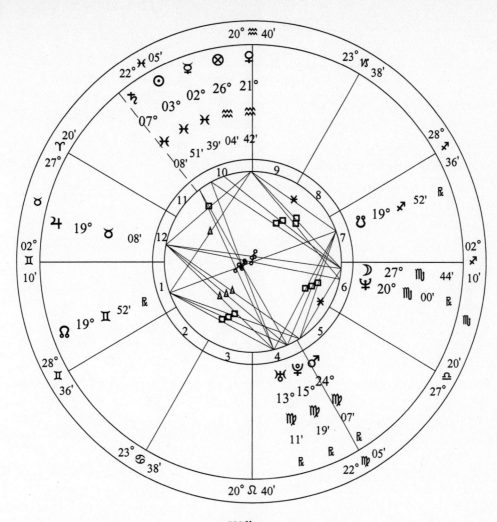

William
February 22, 1965 / Kingston, Jamaica / 11:30 AM EST
Placidus Houses

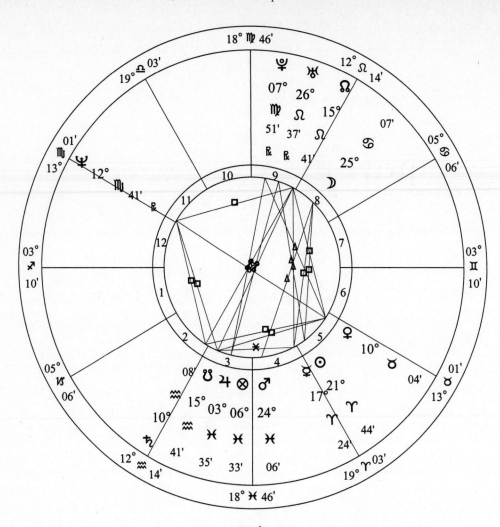

Ruth
April 11, 1962 / Philadelphia, PA / 10:00 PM EST
Placidus Houses

part 5

all about
the houses

♥ where should i go to meet someone?

As a counseling astrologer I was constantly asked, Where should I go to meet someone? The ruling planet of the seventh house holds great significance here as it describes by house and sign where you are most likely going to meet your partner. For instance, if you have Sagittarius on your seventh-house cusp and Jupiter resides in your sixth house, you will meet people who want to be in a relationship with you through your work environment. Aspects to seventh-house planets, in this case Jupiter, will be influential as well. For example, if the Sun in your third house of siblings is in trine aspect to Jupiter, the ruler of your seventh, a brother or sister could be instrumental in introducing you to a romantic prospect.

The Planet of Your Seventh House in Your First House

You may meet someone by pursuing your personal and physical interests. Nancy met her husband, Tom, in a Buddhist center while doing yoga and meditation, which was a daily ritual for her. She has Gemini on the seventh-house cusp and Mercury, which rules Gemini, in the first house, with Saturn in the ninth house of spiritual pursuits in trine aspect to Mercury.

The Planet of Your Seventh House in Your Second House

You may meet someone by enhancing your self-esteem and capitalizing upon your potentials and possessions. Holly met her husband, Bill, through a video dating service. Not only was the video all about her, but she was keen on selecting someone who was going to improve her image. She has Taurus on the seventh-house cusp and Venus, which rules Taurus, in the second house conjunct Mercury.

The Planet of Your Seventh House in Your Third House

You may meet someone through some form of educational activity, within your close community, through a sibling or cousin, or through traveling. Kathy met her husband, Rik, at her ballet school, which is very involved with the community. She has Taurus on the seventh-house cusp and Venus, which rules Taurus, in the third house.

The Planet of Your Seventh House in Your Fourth House

You may meet someone through the company of your parents or in a social setting in the home. Jan met her husband, David, at a party her parents gave in their condominium. She has Capricorn on the seventh-house cusp and Saturn, which rules Capricorn, in the fourth house.

The Planet of Your Seventh House in Your Fifth House

You may meet someone in a creative, romantic, leisurely, or recreational environment. Jim met his wife, Judy, at a tennis tournament. Even as a married couple they are both driven to play the game. He has Scorpio on the seventh-house cusp and Pluto, which rules Scorpio, in the fifth house.

The Planet of Your Seventh House in Your Sixth House

You may meet someone through work or environments that promote health and well-being. Nick met his wife, Mary, while working as a musician at a nightclub. Nick has Gemini on the seventh-house cusp and Mercury, which rules Gemini, in the sixth house in trine aspect to Neptune in the tenth house.

The Planet of Your Seventh House in Your Seventh House

You may meet someone through a close relation, business association, or a familiar couple. John met his wife, Lynn, at the home of a married couple he knows very well. He has Sagittarius on the seventh-house cusp and Jupiter, which rules Sagittarius, in the seventh house in trine aspect to Pluto in the fourth house of home.

The Planet of Your Seventh House in Your Eighth House

You may meet someone through financial institutions, such as banks or insurance companies, at monetary-strategy seminars, rejuvenation centers or spas, or through metaphysical or occult studies. Mary met her husband, Ron, who works in investing, at a bank. She has Cancer on the seventh-house cusp and the Moon, which rules Cancer, in the eighth house.

The Planet of Your Seventh House in Your Ninth House

You may meet someone through higher educational environments, religious/spiritual pursuits, traveling, advertising, publishing, the legal field, or long-distance communications media. Tim met his wife, Carol, at a graphic artist advertising firm. He has Leo on the seventh-house cusp and the Sun, which rules Leo, in the ninth house conjunct Venus and Jupiter.

The Planet of Your Seventh House in Your Tenth House

You may meet someone through the enhancement of your career and reputation. Nela met her husband, Dan, while attending to her career, which was managing one of her video/photography stores. She has Taurus on her seventh-house cusp and Venus, which rules Taurus, in her tenth house of career.

The Planet of Your Seventh House in Your Eleventh House

You may meet someone through a friend or group organization, or when pursuing your dreams. Debbie met her husband, John, through a group of close friends. She has Aquarius on the seventh-house cusp and Uranus, which rules Aquarius, in the eleventh house.

The Planet of Your Seventh House in Your Twelfth House

You may meet someone through being of service behind-the-scenes, attending to spiritual obligations, discovering hidden talents, self-analysis, hospitals, retreats, or anything that is secretive. Anne, a college student at the time, met her husband, Frank, while serving men food and drink at a USO party during World War II. She has Leo on her seventh-house cusp and the Sun, which rules Leo, in her twelfth house. Her Sun is also in opposition to Neptune in Leo, which rules dancing. It was the first dance that evening that took this couple to the altar.

23 ♥ The houses and house sector divisions

The Three House Sector Divisions

The twelve house sectors in astrology are divided into three categories called *angular, succedent,* and *cadent.* Each group has its own features.

The Angular Houses

The angular houses are the first, fourth, seventh, and tenth houses. These house sectors are known as power points since they form the cross that sustains the chart. The angular sectors depict worldly happenings and strengthen the character of the individual. They enforce the idea of interacting with others. Planets in these houses are referred to as being in the foreground. They hold a lot of weight and therefore can help or hinder an individual depending on the planets involved. Favorable influences to planets in an angular house describe a more fulfilled person. Unfavorable aspects denote a dominating, egotistical personality.

The Succedent Houses

The succedent houses are the second, fifth, eighth, and eleventh houses. These house sectors indicate where you hold steadfast to your goals to maintain self-perseverance. The succedent sectors instill determination to acquire results and attain more security. Planets in these houses are referred to as being in the middle ground and, although significant, tend to hold less weight.

Favorable aspects to planets in succedent houses denote one gravitating toward solidifying partnerships where there is much meaningful sharing. Unfavorable influences indicate an unstable direction in life, sometimes due to fickle romances.

The Cadent Houses

The cadent houses are the third, sixth, ninth and twelfth houses. These house sectors indicate that it's in your best interest to develop your mental skills so that you may adapt to ever-changing life experiences. The cadent sectors challenge you to confront a hidden persona and to find ways to interact with the world. Conceptual thinking does not need to be an isolated experience, but can be channeled by being of service to others. Planets in these houses are referred to as being in the background and are considered to be in a weak position, thus they may not be able to support or undermine you, depending on the influences involved.

Favorable aspects to planets in the cadent houses allow one's ideas to follow a course of action that supports intellectual exchanges. Unfavorable influences denote the tendency to hold on to stubborn opinions and not want to be flexible with one's plans.

Compatibility exists between the angular, succedent, and cadent houses as well. If the majority of a person's planets are in cadent houses, their thought-provoking energies may clash with someone who is action-oriented due to several planets in angular houses. If the majority of a person's planets are in succedent houses, they may find they are able to connect with either the angular personality or the cadent one, since the succedent personality wants to establish a partnership link.

The Houses

The houses are where the experience happens. Knowing what each house sector represents will give you a clearer understanding of the significance of a planetary placement in the chart.

The First House

The first house sector represents the self—your physicality, personality, appearance, and approach to your life goals. The manner in which you extend yourself will establish your identity. The Ascendant, or rising sign, which is the cusp of the first house, describes your projection out into the world. It is the mask you wear; the first impression you make on others.

The Second House

The second house sector represents earned income, values, possessions, and resources. Utilizing your potentials indicates how you will earn money and secure what you value. Establishing yourself financially is a reflection of your self-esteem. When we appreciate who we are by capitalizing upon our skills and talents, we are able to attract more into our lives. However, a true meaningful existence comes from developing spiritual and psychological resources.

The Third House

The third house sector represents communications, basic education, local environment, siblings, cousins, and brief trips. Gathering information and interacting with others will build upon your intellectual prowess. Relating to your brothers, sisters, cousins, and neighborhood will generate a community spirit of cooperation. Learning is encouraged as you obtain the facts that will secure your surroundings. Short journeys further your understanding.

The Fourth House

The fourth house sector represents the home, one's roots, emotional foundations, and one parent, usually the mother. All concerns about family living are indicated here, including real estate transactions. Psychological feelings may lead you to discover more about your heritage. One parent will be instrumental in shaping your emotional base. The fourth-house cusp describes your inner personality founded on early childhood experiences.

The Fifth House

The fifth house sector represents creative activities, romance, leisure life, speculative ventures, and offspring. Your creative experiences offer you an emotional outlet through which you may fully express yourself. The most significant aspect of creation is having children. What you create, be it art or children, is your legacy. There is opportunity to enhance romantic exchanges and relax in leisurely style. You will speculate on what life has to offer and where you might make an investment.

The Sixth House

The sixth house sector represents daily routine, work, service, and health and well-being. You will have to take on responsibilities and be of service to those in need. Although you have a daily agenda, you will learn how to make adjustments when and where they are required. Taking care of the basic needs of your physical, mental, and spiritual bodies will demand attention to maintain overall good health.

The Seventh House

The seventh house sector represents close relationships, marriage, and the public. You will develop the capacity to relate to those around you, especially on an equal basis in an intimate relationship. Looking for feedback, you will appreciate the idea of sharing. You must learn how to cooperate with your partner in order to maintain a peaceful balance in the union, knowing that every relationship requires some give and take. Your significant other may complement your life by entering into the institution of marriage with you.

The Eighth House

The eighth house sector represents regeneration, death/rebirth, sex, joint financial ventures, taxes, insurance, and inheritances. You are encouraged to draw upon your inner resources to undertake a personal transformation so that you may evolve to your highest potential. Old, worn-out issues are released so that you may experience a rebirth on an emotional, psychological, physical, or spiritual level. It is through partnerships that you will want to seek unity and therefore rid yourself of any conditions that limit your experience. Intense changes will always bring about an ending, but also a new beginning. The handling of money has much to do with life-and-death experiences and securing your status in society. Finances may be well invested to support your existence.

The Ninth House

The ninth house sector represents higher education, philosophy, spirituality, religion, foreign dealings, and long-distance communication and travel. There is an opportunity to expand your intellectual horizons, going beyond your close environment. You may indulge in traveling or involve yourself with spiritual or religious teachings. Wisdom is gained by opening your perspective to educational pursuits and establishing your philosophy about life.

The Tenth House

The tenth house sector represents your career, reputation, social status, and one parent, usually the father. You will find your place in the world by establishing your reputation and career position. It is only through achievement that you can reach success with your chosen ambition, securing yourself in a more prominent status. Your professional image may be defined by others as you build a more successful foundation through your social involvements. One parent will be instrumental in forming your career.

The Eleventh House

The eleventh house sector represents friends, groups, organizations, and future hopes and dreams. Looking ahead you will want to define your ideals so that you can attain your prospective goals. Selective choices will have to be made among future possibilities in order to realize your dreams. Your reward will be as brilliant as your everyday achievements. Friends and organizations that share your vision will offer their support. You may attract groups with similar progressive ideals that develop an awareness for humanity.

The Twelfth House

The twelfth house sector represents self-analysis, hidden abilities, secrets, transcending past issues, hospitals, and behind-the-scenes involvements. Our unconscious experiences from the past lie buried deep within our psyche. Unraveling these karmic issues will require a psychological transformation that will allow you to realize your potential. Karmic retribution involves spiritual debts and, once resolved, spiritual rewards. Here you meet with challenges that test your faith in yourself. As you rise above past conditions that have plagued you, you can attend to spiritual obligations that free your soul.

24 ♥ planets in the seventh house of relationships

What Type of Mate Will You Choose?

Since the seventh house represents our personal relationships, the type of partner you will attract is derived from an analysis of the planets in your seventh house. You will be inclined to choose a partner who in some manner exemplifies the qualities of the planet(s) residing in your seventh house, along with the sign on your seventh-house cusp. Whatever house sector the planet that rules the seventh-house cusp is found in will add to this scenario. Any aspects from other planets to planet(s) in your seventh house or the ruling planet of the seventh-house cusp will also influence this interpretation. Transiting planets may affect the outcome as well.

Sun in the Seventh House

Minor Influence with Leo on the Seventh-House Cusp

Marriage, committed relationships, and partnerships are the center of attention with the Sun in the seventh house. You are inclined to find a mate whom you can depend on and admire. Pride will cause you to be selective in choosing a marriage partner. You are hopeful that your partner will promote your own strengths where you both feel empowered as a couple. A desire for social prestige may cause you to delay marriage. You need to be careful in seeking out a dominant spouse. You may look for a father figure, someone you can lean on if necessary. If the Sun is afflicted, you may attract an arrogant, selfish, and dictatorial individual. Adverse Pluto aspects instill jealousy and manipulation. Adverse Neptune aspects bring deception. When Jupiter or Venus are in positive aspect to the Sun, there is opportunity for a successful marriage.

Moon in the Seventh House

Minor Influence with Cancer on the Seventh-House Cusp

You may experience ambivalent feelings when choosing a partner since you are easily influenced by your romantic prospects. Yet, there is a strong emotional need for a mate that will compel you to seek out that special connection. Once found, cooperating with your partner will help you avoid mood swings that may cause you to feel vulnerable. There is a tendency to rely on others too much, especially for emotional support, which could develop into a co-dependent situation that challenges your relationship. You may need to guard against attracting partners who play on your sentiments and manipulate you emotionally. For men, there is a desire to have a "mother figure" who nurtures and protects them.

If the Moon is afflicted, the couple will encounter difficult situations that test their emotional limits. An over-active Moon could indicate more than one marriage. Since the Moon is domesticated, it would be best to consider establishing a home environment. Exercising mutual sensitivity will create deeper bonds.

Mercury in the Seventh House

Minor Influence with Gemini or Virgo on the Seventh-House Cusp

Desiring mental satisfaction, a great deal of thought is applied to establishing a relationship that fulfills an intellectual need. Thus, you will seek out a partner who appeals to you intellectually, bringing out your communicative abilities. A person who expresses interesting concepts will encourage you to develop your own intellectual potential. You are easily bored with people who are not mentally stimulating. You will lose interest unless they are able to inspire a gratifying communicative exchange.

Positive aspects to Mercury indicate an intriguing, witty intelligence in a mate, along with excellent speaking skills and social etiquette. Adverse influences indicate arguments, or at least a clashing of opinions. Aim toward cultivating an open exchange of ideas. Your partner may be involved with literary pursuits, education, sales, or some form of communications media.

Venus in the Seventh House
Minor Influence with Taurus or Libra on the Seventh-House Cusp
Since Venus rules the seventh house, there is a need to bring balance into a relationship by sharing one's ideas and experiences to accomplish this one-on-one exchange. You are eager to be received well by those around you as you attract affectionate exchanges. You may need to temper your desire for too much affection, as this will put pressure on your mate. Wanting to achieve the perfect marriage may be an unrealistic goal. Nevertheless, you will appreciate your relationship. You wish to have a partner who finds pleasure in a harmonious lifestyle, surrounded by quality and beauty. Your partner's physical appearance will be important to you. A mutual affectionate exchange needs to be adopted to balance your expectations of each other. Indulging in sensuous delights can be thoroughly enjoyed, but depending on your partner to ease every unsettling circumstance is too demanding. A joint effort will create a more amicable environment where both of you benefit.

If Venus is in favorable aspect, a promising marital situation will be the result. Your partner may also be blessed with good fortune, monetarily and socially.

Adverse aspects to Venus may undermine your relationship, causing disappointment and loss. Saturn afflicting Venus will cause insecurities and delays. Neptune afflicting Venus will attract deceptive conditions. All discordant aspects need to be monitored to achieve true relationship development.

Mars in the Seventh House

Minor Influence with Aries on the Seventh-House Cusp

Mars conquers and rules when it resides in the sector of relationships. Chances are your partner will like to call the shots and dominate the relationship. This placement will bring about combative situations where one person is antagonized and feels defensive. As social relations are very active, you will find a partner who is worldly and not afraid of competition, and who will challenge you to compete as well. This behavior may bring out the worst in your relationship, unless you learn to adjust to such aggressive behavior. Your relationship to your partner may seem unexciting without a forceful, argumentative engagement. Mars enjoys confrontation and likes to win, so don't expect a compromising attitude. Your partner may be connected with the police or the armed forces, or may be an athlete or a pioneer conquering new territory. For women, you will want a mate who is willing to fight for you, or a man, bound by tradition, who takes the lead. For men, you will attract a woman who is direct, controlling, takes the initiative, and is able to handle both domestic and work responsibilities. Romance can be very passionate as your partner will not settle for anything else but intense desire. Ardent attractions will prompt you to get involved at a young age. There is a desire to marry early, especially if the aspects to Mars are favorable.

When Mars is afflicted, strife and hostility could be the result with a partner. Tempers tend to flare, as Mars wishes to control and dominate, even resorting to violent behavior if necessary. Aggressive actions will not deliver wanted results. You may have to change your war-like strategy to a more compromising one in order to come out winning.

Jupiter in the Seventh House

Minor Influence with Sagittarius on the Seventh-House Cusp

Jupiter's benefic influence promises a happy and successful relationship or marriage, unless afflicted by adverse aspects. You will attract a partner who expands your horizons. This inspiration will only improve your relationship. You may develop a whole new philosophy about life as you are encouraged through your partner to extend yourself socially, and to enjoy other cultures and life experiences. You may depend on your partner to provide you with avenues that build confidence and purpose.

When both partners have Jupiter in the house of Venus, the couple benefits tremendously because they are able to bring out the best in each other. Your mate may be involved with the law, philosophy, teaching, sales, promotional enterprises, foreign dealings, or travel.

Adverse aspects to Jupiter will be challenging. Hardships are incurred when Saturn influences Jupiter. A marriage later in life is possible. An afflicted Jupiter denotes a partner who is self-indulgent, opinionated, lazy, extravagant, and dishonest. Discordant Neptune aspects attract what seems to be a dream relationship, only to end in deceit and betrayal. Since Jupiter's influence is so resilient, even after a nasty break-up you will find the courage to seek out another relationship. Although you may need to curb high expectations and a tendency toward over-indulgence, you naturally bring out the best in others, emphasizing their generosity and friendliness.

Saturn in the Seventh House

Minor Influence with Capricorn on the Seventh-House Cusp

You will approach relationships with a serious, calculating attitude, recognizing that you gain by being responsible toward your partner. You desire a mate who gives you a sense of purpose and encourages a dutiful disposition. A mature partner will be appealing to you, as this type of person represents stability and the opportunity to achieve success. Yet, you may be reluctant to accept the responsibilities of a long-term relationship. Fears and insecurities about commitment may cause delays in marriage. You may have concerns that a controlling partner may take advantage of you. Until you feel secure with yourself, a permanent relationship should be carefully considered. Women may tend to look for and marry a "father figure," someone to guide them through life. If discipline is lacking, such paternal stability can be extremely helpful. Saturn wants us to be more reliable, to face up to the realities in our life that will secure a solid foundation. Exercising complete faith and loyalty toward your partner is what is required to maintain a long-lasting relationship.

Being that the seventh house is also the area of open enemies, avoiding your obligations may bring an unwanted reprisal from your partner. If you neglect your partner's needs and happiness, you may be neglecting your own as well. Saturn in the house of Venus represents a karmic debt owed to your partner. Any form of abuse, however, is not to be tolerated.

An afflicted Saturn indicates an unhappy marriage, yet you may feel inclined to stay in the relationship, as Saturn seeks stability here. This union may come with restrictions from a controlling partner, who may also be cold, critical, and uncommunicative.

Favorable aspects to Saturn may attract a partner who is industrious, faithful, dependable, conscientious, and seemingly unaffectionate but responsible. Although your partner may be uncommunicative at times, he or she will provide a solid, hard-working base that you can rely on. Appreciating your partner will bring more stability and understanding to your relationship.

Uranus in the Seventh House

Minor Influence with Aquarius on the Seventh-House Cusp

You will have an unconventional approach to your relationships where marriage may be idealistic or unusual, with platonic overtones. Your partner may be younger or older than you, from a different ethnic group or cultural background, or of the same sex. Everything that departs from tradition is considered to be Uranian. A lot of space or breathing room may be necessary in your relationship so both of you are able to realize your individuality. Being apart for long periods of time or living in separate residences are two possibilities. On occasion, the accelerated personal growth of one party outshines their partner and a drifting apart occurs. Uranus in the seventh house is associated with divorce, but if the union is exciting and original enough, the couple will enjoy their time together. Any new developments in the relationship should be taken nonchalantly.

Under positive aspects you will most likely choose a partner who has a unique approach to life and wishes to maintain a separate identity. Their inventive, creative, and original approach will inspire you to further your own uniqueness, as well as contribute to the relationship itself. The personal magnetism of your partner is quite appealing, along with their brilliant mentality, sometimes bordering on genius. Subconsciously, you may be looking for a partner who can be a dynamic catalyst, challenging you to break with tradition.

Adverse aspects to Uranus may reveal a restless disposition and fanaticism in your mate that requires patience and understanding. If you are not willing to give your mate sufficient freedom, tensions may ensue that cause discord in your relationship. Your inclination to find excitement in romantic alliances will stimulate you to experience love affairs that sour your commitment. If your mate is unfaithful, you may need to question why you selected a dishonest partner. The conventional marriage will be tested with Uranus residing in the sector of relationships. To uphold this union you may need to be understanding of your partner's eccentric, progressive ideas and to give them the freedom they need to be themselves. Loving someone does not mean binding them to an agreement, but allowing them to discover their potential.

Neptune in the Seventh House
Minor Influence with Pisces on the Seventh-House Cusp
Yearning for your "soulmate," you seek the ideal marriage. But you are likely to be disappointed since the perfect relationship does not exist. To bring your vision into manifestation, you need to be realistic about feeling entitled to have the ideal union. In order to attract what you wish for, you must believe it is right for you to have. A partner with integrity will fulfill your need for a spiritual connection.

Pursuing a partner you idolize but who cannot be there for you is a lost cause. Your partner may be unattainable due to their affluence, status, religion, or nationality.

You are inclined to establish a partnership centered on being overly sympathetic or full of admiration. In either case, you could become a victim. Showing compassion from a spiritual perspective allows you to maintain your power so that the other person does not take advantage of your good nature. Overglamorizing your partner will one day lead to a rude awakening. You will realize the type of partner you attracted was not at all what you had imagined. You may need to be more selective in choosing a partner where there is mutual respect and loving understanding.

Under favorable aspects, a creative individual will inspire you to new heights. Your mate could be a poet, an entertainer, an artist, a spiritual or religious person, or someone who is involved with film or television. Platonic partnerships tend to go smoothly.

An afflicted Neptune in the sector of relationships brings major disappointments and loss in intimate partnerships. One is completely fooled by their partner's demeanor. Deception in marriage can be the result of being with an alcoholic, drug addict, homosexual, or downright liar. A self-deceptive tendency will continue to attract unstable situations. Your involvement with unstable, indolent mates may leave you feeling drained. Always remember, when taking care of someone who is in ill health, needy, or disabled, don't forget to be there for yourself. One must be realistic to attract a solid partnership.

Curbing the urge to become involved with vague romantic attractions that never reach the ideal is necessary if you hope to attract a substantial relationship.

Pluto in the Seventh House

Minor Influence with Scorpio on the Seventh-House Cusp

There may be a subconscious desire to comprehend the depth of your being. To understand your deepest resources, you may seek out an overpowering partner. Although your partner will challenge you, they will unleash the strength you need to transcend past issues, especially those issues that continue to plague you. You wish for a strong, dominating mate, one you can admire, yet you are resentful when their fortitude overwhelms you and you are unable to handle the repercussions. You will discover profound insights that supersede a superficial persona. You will gain tremendously from the wisdom acquired.

Since Pluto deals with extremes, you are either intensely committed or not committed at all. Favorable aspects to Pluto encourage a long-term commitment, where your partner promotes personal growth. Fated meetings are inspired that bring a deeper sense of purpose into the relationship. Your partner will project a strong, self-sufficient image that helps further your own metamorphosis.

When Pluto is affected by unfavorable aspects and placement, intense problems in the relationship surface that will require the effort of both partners to transcend. If you are not willing to change along with your partner, then you may be alienated from them until you learn to resolve your deep-rooted issues. Pluto in the seventh house of Venus forces you to find a meaningful purpose in having a relationship so that you might be changed forever. Unfinished business from a past life may need to be addressed. Shocking situations may occur because of your partner's sarcastic attitude and complete disregard for your feelings. You may be the one left with mounting responsibilities after your partner has disappeared. Facing a precipice after a marriage has fallen apart is not uncommon. When you learn to understand your inner self, you can remain detached and straightforward about your life, not allowing your partner's will to entice you into questionable affairs that undermine your integrity. Concentrating on your personal evolution will promote regeneration so that you may discover for yourself what your true, subconscious motives are. In this manner you are able to perpetuate a lasting relationship.

♥

25

THE LOVE
RELATIONSHIP
FORMULA
THROUGH
THE HOUSES

The Love Relationship Formula can also be interpreted by placing the planets of one person's chart into the houses of the partner's natal chart. Since each house sector is represented by a certain planet, placing a planet by sign and degree in a house sector either positively emphasizes that influence or detracts from it. If your mate's Jupiter falls in your second house of values and self-esteem, the house of Venus, your earning potential and self-esteem will be enhanced by your partner. Your partner's planets falling in a certain house sector does not take the place of the stronger dynamic of your partner's planet(s) aspecting a planet in your chart (synastry), but adds to it. Adverse aspects occurring in your partner's chart to a natal planet will undermine the planet's influence when placed in your chart. Transits, progressions, and solar arc directions to your partner's planets may also affect this interpretation.

Sun in the First House

Your partner's Sun falling in or aspecting your first house will bring forth a higher vitality, motivating you to excel and compete. The emphasis is on the needs of the self. You will have an opportunity to release your inhibitions and aggressively pursue your desires. Your solar partner is able to respect and appreciate who you are, as they see themselves through you. This is especially true if the Sun is conjunct the Ascendant, as the Ascendant is a mirror image of the projection of your personality. If a man's Sun falls in the first house, near a woman's Ascendant, he will feel comfortable expressing himself effectively in the male role. She will encourage him to take the lead, appreciating his importance and acknowledging him with high regard. He will feel accepted in being able to project himself naturally toward his lady friend. A woman's Sun in the man's first house would have a similar effect. When the Sun is in adverse aspect, major differences may arise where the Sun person attempts to win over their partner with a charming manner, or the complete reverse, dominating their partner, to no avail.

The Sun in the house of Mars, a pairing in the Love Relationship Formula, inspires confidence, along with warmth and affection. One's passions are aroused with this placement as well. A partner's image is enhanced, benefiting the couple as a whole. Your solar partner will supply the support and morale, yet expects some recognition as the Sun does seek attention here. You reap the glory, yet in turn have admiration for your solar partner. Sharing in the enjoyment of displaying your highly regarded, beautiful relationship will benefit both you and your partner.

Sun in the Second House

When your partner's Sun falls in or aspects your second house, there is a concentrated focus on the accumulation and capitalization of your resources, financial and personal. Skills and talents are brought to light to improve your monetary status. Your solar mate attracts opportunity that benefits you, even if it involves providing the financial backing. Monetary security can be attained through reliable guidance.

Under adverse aspects, monetary difficulty may be present. Your partner may also have too many expectations of your potential, including financial independence. A generous nature will need to be acknowledged to continue congenial ties. Your solar mate feels that they have earned the recognition. Bestowing kindness for services rendered will placate any needs. Unless it is under adverse aspect, the Sun in the house of Venus, which is part of the Love Relationship Formula, wishes to compliment their partner by showing respect and affection, emphasizing their good traits, including physical attraction. By encouraging your potentials, your self-esteem will increase and in turn generate monetary gain that provides mutual benefit.

Sun in the Third House

When your partner's Sun falls in or aspects your third house, there is an emphasis on interacting in your environment, especially where new information is gathered. You are mentally stimulated, learning, formulating, and exchanging ideas that open up your perspective and allow you to appreciate the art of conversing. Your solar mate encourages you to express your point of view and will listen attentively. This mental exchange promotes camaraderie.

Although your partner will expect you to be able to tackle any problem, determine an agenda, or make plans for traveling, they will provide the intellectual insight to help you do so successfully. A platonic brotherly or sisterly companionship is highlighted rather than a marital situation of husband and wife.

Sun in the Fourth House

When your partner's Sun falls in or aspects your fourth house, especially in conjunction to the *Imum Coeli,* you may find an inner comfort through your solar partner's ability to build up your self-confidence. Your mate allows you to literally feel at home here. This is the house of the Moon, which tends to rely on the Sun. A Sun/Moon coupling is a strong match in the Love Relationship Formula.

Your partner may have a tendency to take on a parental role with you, as you are intuitively looking for guidance. Bringing out the potential in the home, they present an extraordinary collection of interior living ideas that you will find appealing. Although your solar mate may have certain standards, you will subconsciously go along with them to emulate the example.

Adverse aspects to the Sun may bring emotional issues that test your confidence and cause an unsettledness in the home. Your solar partner may not offer the leadership you are seeking or be a domestic wizard. You may find yourself relying on your own inner strength to steer you through challenges on the home front.

Sun in the Fifth House

When your partner's Sun falls in or aspects your fifth house, you are encouraged to enjoy creativity, romance, recreational activities, and speculative ventures to the fullest. Your involvement will only increase your pleasure with your solar partner. You will feel more at ease, putting your worries aside to appreciate leisure life and the world of entertainment. Romantic activities are enhanced as your solar partner delights in your affectionate exchanges.

Your partner will promote any creative or recreational pursuits, knowing that you will find more fulfillment through participation. Your involvement with children may be more pronounced, and if other astrological factors agree, raising your offspring will be a welcomed experience.

Sun in the Sixth House

When your partner's Sun falls in or aspects your sixth house, they can be of great assistance to you, serving your needs. Since your solar partner appreciates your services as well, they will also want you to return the favor. If you are not functioning up to par, suggestions on how to improve your output will be discussed, and you will value your partner's support to maximize your efforts.

Having the Sun in the sixth house is a very platonic position where there is, generally speaking, no emotional involvement. It can indicate a relationship between employer and employee that ends up being temporary. Needs attract relationships, and if there is a need that is being accommodated by a work situation, then the union may continue, yet is still deemed to be short-term. Your solar partner will have expectations and wish to be compensated for services rendered.

Adverse aspects to the Sun will cause difficult situations to appear on the job. If your health practitioner's afflicted Sun falls in your sixth house, you may be misdiagnosed. Finding a doctor whose Sun supports your sixth house of health is worth the effort. Your partner may be the cause of added stress to your daily routine. Both of you will benefit from attending to your health and well-being.

Sun in the Seventh House

When a person's Sun falls in or aspects your seventh house, especially in conjunction to the Descendant, it indicates a very karmic relationship, especially when it is mutual. Although the person may feel the karma, they may want to hide, too, so as to hopefully avoid it. But karma needs to be confronted. Under favorable aspects to your partner's

Sun, a significant relationship can be developed that leads to a commitment. Your solar partner emphasizes the better traits of the relationship, promoting a diplomatic balance based on respect. Your weak points may be exposed only to be strengthened by the support of your solar mate. This connection marks the ideal partner, one who is always acting in your best interests. The Sun in the house of Venus, a powerful connection in the Love Relationship Formula, will motivate you toward fulfilling worldly ambitions and exploring what can be achieved in relating to others. Romantically, you will be selective in appeasing your tastes and desires. You will emanate an affectionate nature toward your solar partner, revealing your true feelings.

Adverse aspects to the Sun could lead to a rivalry, where your partner turns out to be a worthy adversary. You may feel vulnerable that your once-loving confidante may reveal your personal flaws to their benefit. Eliciting the cooperation of a disgruntled solar mate will require an affectionate manner. Unconditional love works wonders.

Sun in the Eighth House

When your partner's Sun falls in or aspects your eighth house, you are encouraged to make a metamorphic change in your life. You are destined to be reborn by relinquishing old patterns that will be addressed by your solar mate. Much thought will be given to past loves, life-and-death issues, and monetary handlings. You will discover with added insights that you can now face these problems once and for all.

Since the eighth house deals with fated relationships, you will feel the need to pay back some karmic debt to your partner. According to the aspects to the Sun, this may bring freedom to these two souls or instigate further complications in working this obligation out. Either way, there is much to be learned and gained regardless of the outcome.

An afflicted Sun denotes a very critical solar mate, where you will have to stand your ground and display your strengths to handle a possibly undermining situation. The Sun person is not tolerant of a weak character. Winning your solar partner over will require that you respect yourself and show the confidence to prove it. Unless you empower yourself, you will be met with disapproval and degradation that may destroy your self-esteem and desire for personal growth. Intimate exchanges are limited and sometimes denied to further demean you.

Favorable aspects to the Sun support rebirth experiences that add to your evolvement. Your solar mate is inclined to assist you financially, offering good advice that benefits you in the long run. Joint monetary ventures are promising as long as there are no afflictions to the Sun. Soulmate connections can produce a strong sexual attraction that is enhanced by harmonious influences to the Sun. Harnessing a deep mutual respect will allow your relationship to transcend any setbacks that may arise, intensifying the bond between you.

Sun in the Ninth House

When your partner's Sun falls in or aspects your ninth house, your life direction will change as you embrace a new philosophy that becomes your own. Broadening your horizons through higher education, spirituality, or travel is inspiring. This is a significant placement for being guided by the guru. Your solar partner may instill in you their own beliefs that will only enhance the mental exchange between you both. The Sun in the house of Jupiter, a combination in the Love Relationship Formula, will enlighten the intellectual rapport and offer expansive opportunities for growth.

Under adverse aspect, the Sun person may expect you to comprehend and accept their concepts without rebuttal. Beware of the religious fanatic who attempts to entice you into a cult. More often than not, misunderstandings occur, along with a clashing of opinions.

Travel may be a theme in the relationship, especially if you met this way. You may expand your horizons as you are exposed to other cultures by your solar partner. Under favorable aspects to the Sun, a subjective understanding will be communicated that benefits both parties. Fulfillment is attained by moving beyond the confines of your surroundings and pursuing higher ideals.

Sun in the Tenth House

When your partner's Sun falls in or aspects your tenth house, especially in conjunction to the Midheaven, your career goals are promoted to enhance your success. Your solar mate will also want to further your reputation by upgrading your job title, thus improving your status in life. If your solar partner is in an influential position, you may be introduced to a privileged echelon that supports your advancement. Your partner may feel responsible for helping you achieve a higher rank. Once a position of importance is attained, you will be required to maintain your placement.

Adverse aspects to the Sun may hinder you from making progress in your career. Your reputation could be soured by a solar partner who wants all of the attention and is looking out for their own best interests.

Harmonious aspects to the Sun create tremendous ambition, where you will seek the approval of your superiors to secure your work position. Prestigious connections will be made that augment your social standing.

Sun in the Eleventh House

When your partner's Sun falls in or aspects your eleventh house, you are encouraged to relate to groups so that friendships are enhanced and wished-for goals are achieved. Your partner may inspire you as well as assist you in realizing your goals by providing you with the information you need to express your vision. Friendships and group affiliations established through your solar spouse may offer you the support you are looking for to achieve your aims.

Unfavorable aspects to the Sun could prevent you from attaining success with your ambitions. Friends may seem unreliable, vanishing just when you need them.

When the Sun is under favorable influences, your goals are easily accomplished. Your partner is seen as a caring companion who offers wise advice. Because of your spouse's leadership ability, you are inclined to follow their lead, especially in group situations. They will provide sound guidance in the management of your affairs. Honoring the companionship that develops over time will produce mutual respect. You can depend on your solar mate to be both a trustworthy friend and lover.

Sun in the Twelfth House

When your partner's Sun falls in or aspects your twelfth house, you will become more aware of a need for privacy, self-analysis, and the transcending of past experiences. Your partner will encourage you to see that working behind the scenes is necessary to achieve not only worldly objectives but also personal objectives. Great spiritual depth is attained as you explore the hidden areas of your life.

Under harmonious aspects, you may find that your solar mate is a knowledgeable advisor, allowing you to unload your burdensome issues while offering you sound counsel. Being that you are able to confide in your partner, you are willing to share your deepest secrets. You are confident in your ability to transcend personal limitations and further your potentials in life.

Adverse aspects to the Sun indicate that your mate can become your covert enemy, taking advantage of any secrets you would rather not have exposed. Not only will their advice cause setbacks, but you may be persuaded to become involved with clandestine, unethical dealings.

Although your solar partner is capable of helping you see your subconscious problems, it is in your best interests to make an effort to transcend any limitations that may have held you back from achieving your fullest potential. You are also prompted to seek out your highest ideals, as the Sun resides in the house of Neptune.

Moon in the First House

When the Moon of your partner falls in or aspects your first house, especially in conjunction to the Ascendant, an emotional bond is established between the couple. Both will feel at home with each other. You are willing to compromise to maintain a sensitive balance in the relationship. This familial behavior is recognized by your lunar mate as part of their own patterns, creating a mutual approach to goals. When a similar disposition exists, it adds to the compatibility.

Favorable influences to the Moon will cause your partner to persuade you to express your sensitivity, through their demonstrative manner. Emotional ideas are the seeds that you could turn into meaningful projects. Your partner will want to nurture and protect you when you are ready to launch any worldly venture.

Unfavorable aspects to the Moon will provoke your partner to become quite moody and uncooperative. Worry and depression may set in that could affect your health. Your mate may be overly concerned about your problems and want to take measures to alleviate them.

Since your lunar mate will be able to understand the inner workings of their partner, it will be easier to arouse a compassionate response that is reciprocated. In addition to an emotional interest, your desire in your mate will instigate a passionate, physical attraction, as the Moon resides in the house of Mars. Considering your partner's feelings, you will need to change your approach to accommodate their psychological awareness.

Moon in the Second House

When your partner's Moon falls in or aspects your second house, there is an emotional focus on meaningful values and financial holdings. Your lunar mate will take an interest in advising you on how to capitalize upon your resources. The Moon is exalted here in the sign of Taurus, an economically productive sign that likes to see results. Your partner's intuitive ability will be accurate when selecting investments to increase your gains. The Moon in the house of Venus, a pairing in the Love Relationship Formula, promotes feeling, kindness, and generosity, where one takes pleasure in giving. Venus becomes quite fond of their lunar mate in this regard.

Adverse aspects to the Moon denote complications with a chosen financial strategy. Your earnings may fluctuate under the guidance of your partner, causing much stress. You may be criticized for your lack of efficiency. Your lunar mate may experience mood swings that are not easily quelled until you are generous in return.

Harmonious aspects to the Moon promote an innate understanding that allows you to give unconditionally. You are taught what has value, as you yearn for a meaningful connection with the partner whom you hold in deep regard. A bond of thankfulness may be formed with those for whom you feel a strong affection.

Moon in the Third House

When your partner's Moon falls in or aspects your third house, they are inclined to promote your communicative potentials, which will enhance the rapport between you. Your partner will be intrigued by your mental abilities, including problem-solving techniques. Your mate will be actively involved in imparting a flow of ideas, along with pertinent information that improves your own conceptual understanding. When your intellectual prowess is augmented, both parties gain.

Discordant aspects to the Moon may make it difficult to comprehend one's point of view. Your lunar mate may become emotional and touchy when you fail to be a good listener and do not care to converse. Whatever ideas you do choose to express may not be heard due to your partner's moody disposition or total lack of interest.

Harmonious aspects to the Moon favor educational interests, where you are mentally stimulated to expand your cerebral point of view. Your mate's objective will be to open up your mind to new concepts and help you converse more effectively. If your partner is looked upon as a mentor, this placement is excellent for increasing the rapport between teacher and student. What can be gained through traveling may also be introduced by your lunar partner. Brief trips to connect with siblings or relatives are encouraged.

Learning to appreciate what your partner has to say will expand your intellectual horizons. An instinctual feel of how to relate to your partner will cause the communicative exchange to flourish, cultivating a strong friendship.

Moon in the Fourth House

When your partner's Moon falls in or aspects your fourth house, especially in conjunction to the *Imum Coeli,* you will feel a close affinity to your lunar mate. Since the Moon naturally resides in the fourth sector, there is a mutual sensation of empathy toward each other that makes you feel right at home. This powerful emotional link will allow your partner to anticipate your every response.

Adverse aspects to the Moon may cause your lunar partner to smother you with too much nurturing, thus oppressing your efforts. Domestic upheavals are common as emotional stress becomes excessive. Your partner may feel overly confined by pressures at home. They may also want to avoid making any property investments that make them feel trapped. Frequent changes of residence are common.

Under favorable aspects, your partner may prefer the role of mother, wanting to protect, nurture, and counsel you. A reciprocal, instinctive bond will bring about a greater understanding between you that may be communicated nonverbally. Suggestions on how to improve domestic affairs, such as sharpening one's culinary skills or addressing household chores, will be openly discussed. Developing a deeper awareness of your intuitive environment will only improve the emotional connection between you and your mate.

Moon in the Fifth House

When your partner's Moon falls in or aspects your fifth house, you are encouraged to pursue your creative talents with your instinctual guidance. There will be support from your partner as they will intuitively know how best to advise you, finding pleasure in your quest for personal fulfillment. As a couple you will enjoy the feelings that are emanated during romantic and leisurely get-togethers, and you may demonstrate a strong commitment by sharing in the raising of children. The Moon in the house of the Sun, a combination in the Love Relationship Formula, indicates a long-lasting union.

Favorable aspects turn your lunar mate into your best fan, someone who will support your talents and encourage a more dramatic presentation. They will offer insights that benefit speculative gains as well.

Unfavorable aspects to the Moon can limit your creative expression. Romantic and leisurely endeavors may be inconsistent. Your partner's moody temperament may make life disagreeable at times.

You will become aware of the need to project yourself in a more creative manner that will be accepted by your audience. Demonstrating what you truly feel will touch the hearts of many.

Moon in the Sixth House

When your partner's Moon falls in or aspects your sixth house, they will offer you insight into improving conditions with health matters and on the job. You will appreciate how your partner seems to know just what to say or do to help perfect your daily routine.

Inharmonious aspects to the Moon may cause a stressful environment on the job, not to mention the subsequent ill effects on your health. Your partner's temperamental disposition may create irritable circumstances for both of you. They may become a hindrance to your job advancement, although they claim to be your equal in handling matters.

Under harmonious aspects, your physical well-being can be upgraded with the help of your lunar mate. This is similar to a doctor taking a sympathetic interest in his patient. Instinctual suggestions on how to refine your job situation further your daily progress. Serving the needs of others will allow your lunar mate to be a Good Samaritan.

There is much to be learned in being of service to others and not being concerned about what one is receiving in return.

Moon in the Seventh House

When your partner's Moon falls in or aspects your seventh house, especially in conjunction to the Descendant, there is an opportunity to create a strong emotional bond within the relationship. Your partner will instinctively desire a harmonious balance that engenders a more congenial exchange. Complimenting your persona will be important to your mate. The sensitive awareness of your lunar mate will promote a favorable reputation with others, and they may even act as a mediator, negotiating in your best interests.

Under adverse influences, your partner will not tolerate any condescending remarks, but prefer equal status. A touchy disposition may delay any cooperation.

Positive influences to the Moon in the house of Venus, an important combination in the Love Relationship Formula, give your lunar mate the opportunity to broaden your social circle. Their innate understanding will lead you to connections upon which you can capitalize. You will embrace the emotional link established between the two of you, knowing that the feelings that are appreciated and respected will only escalate into a spiritual love.

You will find yourself wanting to compromise with your partner, as a shared collaboration is better than none. The fond caress of a couple demonstrates the caring attitude that one develops over time with this lunar placement.

Moon in the Eighth House

When your partner's Moon falls in or aspects your eighth house, there is an emotional intensity connected with partnerships that may even relate back to a previous life. The Moon in the house of Pluto indicates extremes where you and your lunar mate are either seriously involved in a commitment or not. According to what transpired in your relationship in a past life, you may have a mutual exchange of ardent intimacy or a sense of alienation from your mate. You have an opportunity to awaken your mate's memory and point out how they can benefit now from what was experienced then, whether it was good or bad. The intuitive insights gathered from your partner may help guide you as a couple toward a more evolved commitment.

Discordant aspects to the Moon may cause you to decline from entering into a romantic relationship with your mate. Joint financial ventures may not succeed as planned. Disagreements over how to handle monetary dealings, including any inheritances, may strain the rapport between you. Your partner may not find you trustworthy, creating quite a dilemma for both of you to resolve. They may become emotionally confused, dwelling on the negatives of the union.

Harmonious aspects generate gains through joint financial enterprises where payoffs are used to improve the couple's life together. Your partner is keen on you developing your personal growth, that you might feel reborn. Intimate relations are deeply moving, where you both experience a transcendence together.

You need to take into consideration the fact that evolvement involves the feelings of your partner, and that respecting those feelings will instigate a lasting relationship.

Moon in the Ninth House

When your partner's Moon falls in or aspects your ninth house, you will be intuitively guided by your lunar mate to expand your horizons through educational pursuits and travel, and through experiencing other cultures. Your mate may feel they comprehend your beliefs and philosophy about life, but may want to add to your ideas to reshape your theories. Their intention is to improve upon the intellectual exchange to benefit the relationship. Traveling to foreign countries is highly encouraged, as your lunar mate, with their dreamy imagination, will want to explore all facets of the world.

Afflictions to the Moon indicate a lack of understanding of your beliefs, be it religious or spiritual, or of your philosophical outlook on life. Educational goals may be limited or not pursued at all, denying you the opportunity to better your standard of living. The mental rapport that you and your partner desire may be unsatisfying and disagreeable.

The Moon in the house of Jupiter is a pairing in the Love Relationship Formula. Favorable influences give your lunar mate an innate ability to expand your philosophical horizons, thus benefiting both of you. The discovery of what can be learned from different cultural backgrounds will enhance your sympathetic understanding of the world around you. This emotional perceptiveness will enrich your intellectual connection.

Appreciating your partner's viewpoint will allow you to be more sensitive to humanity. The result is a shared, higher-minded affinity that enriches you both.

Moon in the Tenth House

When your partner's Moon falls in or aspects your tenth house, especially in conjunction to the Midheaven, they will rely on the intuitive wit that you possess and be extremely supportive of your ambitions. Your partner's belief in you will help you achieve success. Inspired by your lunar mate, you are more determined to go that extra mile to attract the recognition you desire. Your mate may offer suggestions on how to bring out your dormant skills and talents, protecting your reputation at all costs.

Under adverse aspects, your career may be thwarted by your partner advising you incorrectly, detracting from your talents. Your dislike of your mate's damaging efforts will build resentment that may cause them to malign your reputation. The mishandling of their own affairs may become a draining burden for you.

Positive aspects to the Moon will enhance your career position. You are destined to come before the public as you are instinctively guided by your lunar mate. Respect from others will come easily with your partner's assistance.

You will gain by showing respect for the people who help you, for success in life also depends on the support we receive from those around us.

Moon in the Eleventh House

When your partner's Moon falls in or aspects your eleventh house, a strong friendship may develop as your partner is intuitively drawn to you. Your mate will encourage your ideals and may even share in the pursuit of them. As a couple you will gain from group associations such as a club or guild.

Under afflicted aspects, your lunar mate's mood swings may strain friendly ties. As they reveal a selfish neediness, group affiliations are denied.

When harmonious aspects are present, a bond of companionship is developed that enriches a long-term relationship. Organizations with similar ideals are enjoyed together. Displaying a sensitive awareness will cultivate friendships with your lover and those around you.

Moon in the Twelfth House

When your partner's Moon falls in or aspects your twelfth house, they will instinctively understand your secrets and be able to delve into buried issues that seek to be resolved. The Moon in the house of Neptune creates a compassionate awareness where your partner will want to nurture and protect you from any harm.

Discordant influences to the Moon may cause your partner to take advantage of you, exposing your weak points, which could be quite embarrassing. They may even become your secret enemy.

If harmonious influences are present, your lunar mate will be a sympathetic counselor, allowing you to feel comfortable confiding in them. Although your partner's interest is to help you, some deep issues may require your own self-analysis.

It is only through the passage of time that your partner can assist you in transcending past limitations. Trusting another is a confidence that needs to be earned.

Mercury in the First House

When your partner's Mercury falls in or aspects your first house, especially in conjunction to the Ascendant, you are inspired to partake in a stimulating intellectual exchange. Thus, conversation with your Mercurial partner is appealing.

If Mercury is afflicted, the mental rapport is on different wavelengths, where you cannot seem to find any common ground on which to work issues out. Misunderstandings may be the result. Repetitious discussion can be draining. Patience is required to develop a better communicative manner.

Under favorable influences, your Mercurial mate will augment the exchange of ideas, creating intriguing conversation. You are motivated to participate, knowing there is great knowledge to be acquired.

The intellectual rapport that your partner instigates will not only continue to enhance your relationship, but open up your perspective on how enlightening it can be to share new concepts.

Mercury in the Second House

When your partner's Mercury falls in or aspects your second house, they may be helpful in reorganizing your monetary situation to be more efficient. Any inadequacies will be addressed. Thoughtful suggestions will be given to improve your financial investments and returns.

Any unfavorable aspects to Mercury will cause difficulty in working out an economic plan. Your partner's ideas may be too risky, increasing your spending or perpetuating a loss of revenue.

Favorable influences indicate that your Mercurial mate will inspire you to develop financial strategies that upgrade your earnings. Because of their assessment, your income will be more than sufficient. Ideas on how to further one's monetary earnings can always be appreciated. However, the final decision is yours.

Mercury in the Third House

When your partner's Mercury falls in or aspects your third house, you are motivated to share in the intellectual exchange of ideas and opinions. Your Mercurial mate will feel at ease maintaining an open dialogue with you.

If Mercury is badly aspected, restricted communications lead to misunderstandings that are difficult to resolve. Your ideas may clash with your partner, causing arguments.

Under well-aspected influences, knowledge is acquired through the discussion of new and interesting concepts. Ideas flow easily, engendering a successful rapport. Your partner may put you in touch with the neighborhood and siblings alike. Traveling plans are encouraged.

We are constantly learning through our interaction with one other. It's advantageous to aim toward a communicative exchange that benefits you and your partner.

Mercury in the Fourth House

When your partner's Mercury falls in or aspects your fourth house, especially in conjunction to the *Imum Coeli,* your partner will want to understand your deeper emotional foundations. This is usually derived from your link with your family and what was experienced. Open expression will be encouraged by your Mercurial mate, giving you an outlet to demonstrate how you feel. Your mate will also be keen on organizing domestic affairs. Being able to move about when needed or travel out of town can be incorporated into your daily agenda.

If there are afflictions to Mercury, you may be restricted from expressing how you feel. Your partner may manipulate your schedule to agree with their own itinerary.

Under positive aspects, your emotional issues are discussed and understood. You will be instinctively aware of your partner's ideas and how they can improve your domestic or personal issues. The household runs smoothly with the assistance of your partner.

Mercury in the Fifth House

When your partner's Mercury falls in or aspects your fifth house, you are persuaded by your partner to pursue creative aspirations, hobbies, or recreational activities. They will inspire you to find fulfillment with your objectives. Romantic conversation is highlighted, which at some point in time will help if the discussion of having children arises.

Under adverse aspects, your partner may hamper your creative accomplishments. An overly critical approach may discourage your efforts.

Harmonious influences denote that your Mercurial mate's ideas will spark your imagination and excite you with new possibilities. Ideas on any speculative venture are thoroughly discussed. Creative ambitions are furthered and brought into manifestation by applying carefully thought-out, intellectual insights to your plan.

Mercury in the Sixth House

When your partner's Mercury falls in or aspects your sixth house, they will be able to offer you good advice on improving your health through diet or exercise, along with suggestions on maintaining quality health. In this manner you will be better prepared to handle daily stress. Your partner will also provide you with insights on being more efficient on the job.

If discordant influences to Mercury are present, job production is hindered by misinformation from your partner. Be careful not to get involved with a misleading health plan that does not bring results.

With favorable aspects, you look forward to the counsel of your partner on physical fitness. You will also appreciate the work strategies that are designed by your Mercurial mate to make your job easier. Developing positive health habits and job productivity will only benefit you in the years to come.

Mercury in the Seventh House

When your partner's Mercury falls in or aspects your seventh house, especially in conjunction to the Descendant, you will share your viewpoint about your relationship with your partner. You will find your Mercurial mate open-minded and willing to listen to and embrace your perspective. Smooth communications not only improve your rapport, but enhance romance as well. A cooperative attitude motivates your partner to broaden your social circle. Developing such connections may also lead to lucrative gains.

Adverse aspects to Mercury sour the communications between you. Your partner may be adamant about airing their opinions. You will have trouble finding ways to relate to your mate.

Well-aspected influences will support the intellectual bond, allowing you to interact on a cooperative level, free to express your point of view. Your partner will wish to compliment you with their concepts so that you can share and improve upon your own ideas. Appreciating what your mate has to say will enhance the social link between you.

Mercury in the Eighth House

When your partner's Mercury falls in or aspects your eighth house, they may have an understanding of your deeper self and therefore be instrumental in giving you ideas on initiating your personal transformation. Your Mercurial partner will also impart sound advice on financial investments.

A badly aspected Mercury indicates that you need to be cautious of risky joint investments with your partner, as financial fraud is likely. Manipulative tactics could be used against you. Personal growth is limited.

Harmonious aspects offers you insight on promoting your evolvement. You may trust your partner's guidance to better yourself personally as well as monetarily.

It is only through probing the deeper mind that we can understand our true selves with the good intentions of our mate.

Mercury in the Ninth House

When your partner's Mercury falls in or aspects your ninth house, you will be more inclined to relate to your partner on a higher intellectual level, although discussing everyday events may be a part of the conversation. When traveling together, you will be exposed to exciting new sights that may change your outlook.

Unfavorable aspects indicate that you may be at odds when conversing with your Mercurial partner. Differences of opinion may lead to arguments.

Under favorable influences, Mercury in the house of Jupiter, a combination in the Love Relationship Formula, will promote the expansion of your mental horizons. Excellent one-on-one communication is developed involving one's beliefs and philosophy about life. Your view of life will be enriched through your partner's cerebral inspiration.

Mercury in the Tenth House

When your partner's Mercury falls in or aspects your tenth house, especially in conjunction to the Midheaven, they will provide logical advice on your career as well as appreciate your efforts in achieving set goals. Your partner will be interested in furthering your reputation and will interact with others in hopes of enhancing your persona.

Discordant influences to Mercury indicate that your partner may misguide you, hurting your career and reputation. Their critical approach may deter you from making any progress.

Under positive aspects, your Mercurial partner enjoys telling others of your accomplishments, hoping to advance your social standing. They may want you to be aware of the particulars and polish up your fine points to achieve success.

Your partner, wanting to act in your best interests, will create a platform where you both can discuss the manifestation of your career.

Mercury in the Eleventh House

When your partner's Mercury falls in or aspects your eleventh house, they will be able to appreciate the pursuit of your ideal goals. Your partner will connect you with those who share similar interests. Since you find conversation with your mate very appealing, you hope to strike up a friendship as well.

Inharmonious aspects may cause your partner to distort the facts about you, putting you in a precarious situation with your social circle. You cannot fully rely on the advice received from your mate.

Under harmonious influences, your Mercurial partner, after evaluating your potentials, will indicate where you can make improvements to attain the success you desire. Interaction within your group affiliations will make you feel more secure about your objectives. Developing a friendship with your romantic partner will always support you into the future.

Mercury in the Twelfth House

When your partner's Mercury falls in or aspects your twelfth house, you are encouraged to deal with hidden problems that may be hindering your progress in life. Your partner may act as a therapist, offering good counsel to unravel those issues. Your mate wishes to understand your transformation and provide support where it is needed.

If there are adverse aspects to Mercury, you are not inclined to take the advice of your Mercurial partner. Your mate is inclined to spread gossip about you, humiliating you behind-the-scenes.

Under positive influences, your partner's guidance in furthering your personal growth is welcomed. Your partner's ability to peer into your deeper self and point out your weaknesses will assist you in your metamorphic change.

Venus in the First House

When your partner's Venus falls in or aspects your first house, especially in conjunction to the Ascendant, the social/romantic sparks fly. Venus in the house of Mars, a powerful duo in the Love Relationship Formula, will motivate you to turn on the charm and be yourself. Your partner will find you quite captivating and want to compliment you both personally and romantically.

If afflicted, your Venusian partner may become overly possessive or jealous. You may not be so open to their warm affection. Confrontational situations may arise that lead to arguments. Yet, the romantic link may still be present amidst the hot/cold rapport. Although this affectionate placement is strong, there is also a chance of rejection with seriously adverse influences.

Harmonious aspects to Venus will persuade your partner to show their love and admiration for you. Flattering comments will promote both you and the relationship.

Loving someone is complimenting them. When you compliment your partner, you compliment yourself. This loving exchange is meant to build a stronger bond so that continues to enhance your relationship into the future.

Venus in the Second House

When your partner's Venus falls in or aspects your second house, your earning potential is strengthened as your partner promotes the use of your skills and talents. Your mate has your best interests at heart. Compliments and respect will befall you, bringing out your finer qualities so that you may take advantage of them. Capitalizing upon all of your resources, not just monetary resources, can bring more meaning into your existence.

Adverse aspects to Venus could jeopardize any financial opportunities. At your partner's request you may become involved with risky ventures, overspending, or handling money recklessly, which should be avoided. Personally, because of neglect, you may experience a lack of appreciation or low self-esteem.

Any favorable aspects with Venus in the house of Venus, representing benefics in aspect, will support your efforts in utilizing your potentials. The appreciation of love as well as spiritual and artistic values is enhanced that you might gain in your development as a human being.

Venus in the Third House

When your partner's Venus falls in or aspects your third house, a smooth communicative rapport is developed that enhances the bond between you. Your Venusian partner's warm reception will motivate you to express your thoughts and feelings in a pleasing manner. Being your charming self, you will take advantage of the many ideas that intellectually inspire you. Your partner will also share their compromising perspective.

Unfavorable aspects to Venus block the natural course of conversation. Your partner may have an uncooperative attitude that leads to a strained rapport.

Favorable influences indicate an effortless rapport where both of you share your ideas to benefit each other. A mutual understanding instigates a harmonious exchange.

Venus in the Fourth House

When your partner's Venus falls in or aspects your fourth house, especially in conjunction to the *Imum Coeli,* your mate emanates a feeling of warmth and comfort in the home. You are persuaded to beautify your home, creating an appealing environment. The two of you are quite cozy in your peaceful surroundings. Your mate may also assist you with property investments, which fare well with this placement.

If any afflictions to Venus exist, a disagreeable home environment is the result. An uncooperative mate will have you taking flight to avoid conflicts.

Under positive aspects, your feelings are sensitized, allowing you to fully appreciate the company of your Venusian partner. You can relax and be yourself knowing that you can rely on your partner's sympathetic understanding.

Since Venus is in the house of the Moon, an important combination in the Love Relationship Formula, your relationship will thrive with mutual caring and approval.

Venus in the Fifth House

When your partner's Venus falls in or aspects your fifth house, you are convinced to enjoy leisure life to its fullest. Venus in the house of the Sun, a significant combination in the Love Relationship Formula, partakes in appreciating the social and sensuous pleasures that life has to offer. Your mate is romantically enticing and you will always enjoy their company. Your creative abilities will interest your partner and you are encouraged to pursue them, expressing their dramatic appeal. A specific talent may be brought to the light for more exposure. This can be a great placement if your partner happens to be your agent, representing you.

Stressful aspects to Venus make it difficult for you to benefit from the world of relaxation and entertainment. Creative ambitions may be limited by your mate. Romance is seen as more serious than exciting.

When harmonious influences are present, you can rely on truly enjoying the simple pleasures of life, showing love and appreciation for what your Venusian partner has to offer.

Venus in the Sixth House

When your partner's Venus falls in or aspects your sixth house, they will want to serve and comfort you so that your daily work routine functions smoothly. Your partner is inclined to accommodate your needs to relieve stress and promote health and well-being.

The presence of adverse aspects to Venus may cause your mate to be uncooperative in serving your needs. Pressure may mount, making it difficult to accomplish daily goals.

When Venus is well aspected, your partner is pleased to be of assistance to you. They will have the ability to alleviate your worries, but you will also care for your partner's concerns if needed.

Venus in the Seventh House

When your partner's Venus falls in or aspects your seventh house, especially in conjunction to the Descendant, you are inclined to establish a harmonious one-on-one exchange. Venus in its ruling house, representing benefics in aspect, prompts you and your mate to find pleasure in a mutually cooperative relationship. Still, your partner may need to assess the romantic potential before entering into a solid commitment.

When Venus is afflicted, disagreeable tendencies make life difficult for both of you. You may find yourself placating your mate to keep the peace.

Positive influences enhance compatibility when Venus is in the house of Venus, where both of you strive toward a successful union. If other factors agree, a congenial, lasting relationship is the result.

Venus in the Eighth House

When your partner's Venus falls in or aspects your eighth house, your feelings will be deeply aroused by your partner, instigating a personal transformation to occur. You may feel a stronger awareness toward your Venusian partner as well, where your sensitivity may either be intense or nonexistent. You may need to search for the truth behind such reactions. Venus in the house of Pluto, an important duo in the Love Relationship Formula, perpetuates a powerful, magnetic attraction that deepens with intimacy and supports a long-term union.

Under adverse aspects, your partner may become obsessed with you and make demands. You may become overwhelmed and not be able to cope with your mate.

When Venus is well aspected, your partner may be captivated by your mysterious allure. Your evolvement through a sexual exchange, however, is necessary if your union is to have more meaning than just being physical. Other connections demonstrating appreciation and respect must be present for a serious commitment to occur.

Venus in the Ninth House

When your partner's Venus falls in or aspects your ninth house, you will establish a congenial rapport with your partner that improves the flow of ideas. You are encouraged to have a more relaxed manner in planning your direction in life. You will accomplish more when applying an easygoing approach toward educational goals. Your Venusian partner will show you how to travel in comfort to make the most of any trip.

Discordant influences perpetuate a disagreeable manner where your partner is uncooperative in supporting your ideas. Your mate's philosophy is enforced, without consideration.

Under positive aspects, you are intrigued with your partner's beliefs and philosophy about life, wanting to emulate their example. An understanding rapport attracts an agreeable environment where everyone is friendly.

Venus in the Tenth House

When your partner's Venus falls in or aspects your tenth house, especially in conjunction to the Midheaven, they will help you attract career opportunities. Your partner will appreciate the direction of your ambitions, providing you with the encouragement to succeed. Venus in the house of Saturn, a combination in the Love Relationship Formula, allows your partner to value your career interests and assist you in stabilizing your monetary position, which will provide you with comfort and security. As you work toward your goals, you will earn a reputation of respect from those around you.

Unfavorable influences may delay or block you from achieving your goals. Your partner may undermine your efforts by discouraging your aspirations. If you are conniving, you may take advantage of your mate's generosity.

Under favorable aspects, your Venusian partner is sure to value your career choice, thus increasing your productivity and self-worth.

Venus in the Eleventh House

When your partner's Venus falls in or aspects your eleventh house, they will introduce you to a circle of friends who sincerely support your ideals. Your Venusian partner will appreciate your sought-after aims and help you realize your dreams.

If there are any afflictions to Venus, your partner may interfere with your friendships, even possibly becoming jealous. Your mate may take advantage of your amicable connections, acting in their own best interests. They will not be able to fully appreciate your skills and talents or the pursuit of your ideals.

Under positive influences, an appealing friendship develops that will engender a mutually respectful approach in attaining both your hopes and ambitions.

Venus in the Twelfth House

When your partner's Venus falls in or aspects your twelfth house, they will be able to comfort you with your problems and offer advice. Your Venusian partner is capable of understanding your inner needs and is sensitive to alleviating burdensome issues in your life, not wanting to upset you any further. They will want to familiarize you with hidden topics such as the occult or exploring the mysteries in life. Your mate is interested in your higher well-being and will link you up with a spiritual mentor who can help transcend personal limitations.

When Venus is aspected by discordant influences, your partner may be concerned about satisfying their own needs and taking advantage of your weaknesses at the same time. You will want to look elsewhere for reassuring counsel.

Venus in the house of Neptune emphasizes a spiritual connection where both of you may feel a strong empathy. Harmonious aspects to Venus will calm your private concerns and allow you the chance to ease out of personal restrictions through a more compassionate approach.

Mars in the First House

When your partner's Mars falls in or aspects your first house, especially in conjunction to the Ascendant, you are highly motivated to be independent and pursue your desires. Your Martian partner will stand firm and be an advocate in your defense if needed. Yet, they will demand that you be brave and daring as well. You will both develop a similar assertive approach to your aims, expecting to excel from your accomplishments. You will become an equal, competing on the same level, and be able to form a successful, occupational partnership.

Adverse aspects to Mars will instigate arguments where your partner may want to dominate. Your mate will have high expectations that stress you out and drive you to accomplish set goals too quickly. An aggressive stance will only put you on the defensive, making it complicated to come to any kind of agreement. If your partner wants to win, they need to consider succeeding together.

When Mars is in its ruling house conjoining the Ascendant and positive influences are present, the romantic passions are more pronounced than ever. A powerful physical attraction will enhance a long-term union.

Mars in the Second House

When your partner's Mars falls in or aspects your second house, you are driven by your mate to improve your earning potential and acquire more financial resources. They will want you to utilize your skills and talents to gain monetarily.

If any afflictions exist, your partner may persuade you to squander your money. You will have opposing views on any monetary dealings, yet your Martian partner may show signs of jealousy toward your economic growth. Your mate will expect you to be financially independent and not interfere with their own earnings.

Under favorable aspects, your partner will motivate you to capitalize upon your resources and succeed financially. Besides supporting lucrative gains, Mars in the house of Venus, a significant connection in the Love Relationship Formula, will enhance your self-esteem with romantic passions as well. You are also motivated to pursue your worthiness by capitalizing upon your potentials. Your success enhances your appearance.

Mars in the Third House

When your partner's Mars falls in or aspects your third house, they will motivate you to express your ideas and opinions so that you may benefit socially. You will find your partner quick-witted and intellectually stimulating. Challenging debates may ensue that entice you to get involved. Your Martian mate may expect you to courageously say what's on your mind even if it causes conflict with others.

Inauspicious influences will cause your partner to aggressively disagree when conversing with you, not wanting to comprehend your opinion. Nasty arguments could lead to animosity.

When auspicious aspects are present, you learn not to be swayed by another's point of view, so that you base your own ideas on the information that you have derived. Your partner's insistence on opening up your mental perspective may lead to greater intellectual accomplishments.

Mars in the Fourth House

When your partner's Mars falls in or aspects your fourth house, especially in conjunction to the *Imum Coeli,* they will bring an active influence into the domestic scene that encourages you to attend to chores and repairs. You will appreciate your partner, inspiring a busy attitude. Since Mars is in the house of the Moon, your emotions will be aroused, allowing you to relate to and express your inner feelings. Hopefully this will happen in a positive way, prompting you to like your partner's motivation as opposed to disliking it. Nevertheless, passions will run high with this placement.

Under discordant influences, your partner may turn out to be a source of aggravation, becoming an extra responsibility in the home. You may detest their presence there.

Supportive influences allow much to be accomplished in the home. Your Martian mate will want you to assume an independent stance when it comes to domestic dealings. You are motivated to express your feelings, which will lead to a passionate exchange.

Mars in the Fifth House

When your partner's Mars falls in or aspects your fifth house, you are excited to engage in creative activities and discover your potential. Your Martian mate will inspire you to participate in experiencing more of the pleasures of life. Romance will be pursued to the fullest with Mars in the house of the Sun, a strong duo in the Love Relationship Formula. Your partner will bring out the passion in you, and persuade you to develop a take-charge attitude.

If there are any afflictions to Mars, both of you may want to be the aggressor, especially in sexual relations, which can lead to quarrels. Your partner may need to tone down their creative expectations of you.

A powerful romantic connection will develop under favorable influences that intensifies the passionate bond. To enhance this amorous link, respect and appreciation need to be present.

Mars in the Sixth House

When your partner's Mars falls in or aspects your sixth house, you will be motivated by your mate to tackle your daily routine and get the job done. Your partner will offer suggestions as to how to improve your efficiency and will even be of service to you if necessary to further your productivity. You will be persuaded by your mate to address health matters.

Under adverse aspects, your Martian partner will cause upsets about finishing a job by making unnecessary demands. They think that they can do the work better and faster, which creates much aggravation and stress for you.

Your partner will keep you quite busy when favorable aspects exist, wanting you to serve the welfare of others as they would. Attending to your health and well-being will enable you to give your all to any job situation.

Mars in the Seventh House

When your partner's Mars falls in or aspects your seventh house, especially in conjunction to the Descendant, you are challenged to direct this force into motivating outlets for your relationship as you deal with the pros and the cons. You will need to find a balance in giving and receiving. You will be tested on just how well you can cooperate and keep unity within the relationship. The passions run high when Mars is in the house of Venus, a dynamic coupling in the Love Relationship Formula. The energies of desire and love come together to enhance a lasting union.

If there are afflictions to Mars, your partner may create much disagreement between you both, where neither of you is inclined to cooperate to work out issues. Unanticipated arguments may occur for no reason at all. Your mate will want you to join into any conflict in their defense. Try to support your partner's side of the story before resisting.

Your Martian partner will stimulate you to express your best, under positive aspects, building a more confident self-esteem. Your feelings and sex drive are activated for mutual intimacy.

Mars in the Eighth House

When your partner's Mars falls in or aspects your eighth house, you are convinced by your mate to delve into your inner being and address the areas that need to be transformed. You may at first feel uncomfortable about focusing on these areas, yet this is what is required if you hope to attain a personal rebirth. Your mate may want to understand some of your deep, subconscious motivations to know what they will encounter in a long-term union. You are swayed by your partner to capitalize upon your investments and upgrade your financial handlings where needed. Joint monetary ventures bring gains as long as your strategy is carefully planned out.

Under adverse influences, your Martian partner may not be able to make any headway with you in understanding deeper issues. Both of you will feel frustrated by this experience, causing the relationship to falter unless other supportive influences compensate for the adversity.

Under favorable influences, your partner can be a catalyst to your personal growth, offering spontaneous pieces of information that you can relate to and apply. Mars in the house of Pluto intensifies transcending experiences and one's sex drive where as a couple you may be transformed through an intimate exchange.

Mars in the Ninth House

When your partner's Mars falls in or aspects your ninth house, you are intellectually stimulated by your mate to formulate new ideas and philosophies to assist you in expressing yourself. At your partner's request, you are encouraged to travel to broaden your outlook. In assimilating new information, you are challenged to speak your mind, not backing down from any opposition. Your partner will rely on your mental resourcefulness, expecting you to possess knowledge of every subject. Your mate will want you to be a good listener while they verbalize what has been decided upon prior to the conversation.

Discordant influences indicate differing beliefs and philosophies that erode the communications between you. Arguments may ensue.

Under harmonious influences, vigorous communicative exchanges are highlighted that expand your perspective. Your Martian partner will insist that you pursue educational goals that will assure your future success.

Mars in the Tenth House

When your partner's Mars falls in or aspects your tenth house, especially in conjunction to the Midheaven, your partner will be adamant about you being driven toward your career goals and rising to the top. Living up to your reputation, your persevering attitude is admirable. Although your partner may challenge your efforts, their intentions are to bring out your finer qualities so that you might truly succeed. Your partner's encouragement will always be there as long as you are making an effort.

When unfavorable aspects to Mars are present, your partner may take advantage of you to achieve an influential position, possibly hurting your reputation at the same time. Your mate may also be overbearing toward you reaching a successful title, forcing you to compete at your own expense. Your rise to the top may be a bitter one.

Favorable influences will allow you, under your partner's guidance, to achieve your ambitions. Mars is exalted in the tenth house of Capricorn, indicating great accomplishment with the positive reinforcement of your partner.

Mars in the Eleventh House

When your partner's Mars falls in or aspects your eleventh house, they will be actively involved in the pursuit of your hopes and dreams. You are eager to accomplish your sought-after goals with the inspiration of your partner behind you. Besides being your lover, your Martian mate wants to be your friend.

If there are any afflictions to Mars, your partner may disrupt ongoing friendships and display jealousy toward them. Your enthusiasm for your ambitious aims may be short-lived as your mate makes outrageous demands and derails your achievements.

Favorable influences allow you to pursue your idyllic vision and bring it to manifestation. Your partner may become your best friend, offering strong support and dedication toward the one they love.

Mars in the Twelfth House

When your partner's Mars falls in or aspects your twelfth house, you are prompted to delve into the mysteries of life, including your own. Your partner will challenge you to learn to understand any hidden areas of yourself. Weaknesses will be revealed and transcended. Any dishonesty will be exposed, causing your partner to lose trust in you. You may question their motives as well. Through your partner's determination, you will ascertain that honesty with yourself and others is the best policy.

Adverse aspects to Mars may also cause your partner to take advantage of your weak points, where they could easily become your secret enemy. Your mate may become upset with you for not making an effort to sort out psychological issues.

Under positive aspects, your partner is compelled to bring your weaknesses to the surface where they can be confronted and addressed. You will only benefit from such a direct approach by developing more self-confidence to defend vulnerable areas and overcome any personal limitations.

Jupiter in the First House

When your partner's Jupiter falls in or aspects your first house, especially in conjunction to the Ascendant, you are encouraged to expand upon your personality and good humor since you may feel relaxed and optimistic about the future. You will honor and not take advantage of your partner's generous nature, knowing that they prefer to be a benevolent giver. Whatever you ask for, your Jupiterian partner will most likely be there to provide. Jupiter in the house of Mars, one of the important combinations in the Love Relationship Formula, will heighten the romantic passions as it energizes the relationship. Lovemaking is superb. As a couple, you will feel active and enjoy each other's company.

Under discordant influences, your partner my cause you to be overindulgent or reckless. Be careful of biting off more than you can chew. Even though your partner is charitable, you should avoid taking advantage of their kindness.

If Jupiter is well aspected, you and your partner will be filled with enthusiasm and be very productive. Expansive opportunities find you. A competitive zest for life is augmented by a passionate, romantic drive that is exciting and complimentary.

Jupiter in the Second House

When your partner's Jupiter falls in or aspects your second house, you will be complimented by your partner to succeed on a personal and financial level. They will be a catalyst in expanding your resources to improve your monetary status. Your Jupiterian partner will show appreciation for your skills and talents, thus improving your self-esteem. Jupiter in the house of Venus, a highly significant duo in the Love Relationship

Formula, indicates that your partner is acting in your best interests, happily inclined to always admire you.

When inauspicious aspects are present, your partner may advise you to overspend or become involved with risky monetary dealings. Favors may come with a price tag.

Under advantageous influences to Jupiter, your partner will provide for you financially if needed and you will feel obligated to do the same. Investments could reap lucrative gains. Your partner is inclined to cherish you with compliments and goodwill that further your image.

Jupiter in the Third House

When your partner's Jupiter falls in or aspects your third house, conversation is intellectually stimulating. You will feel enthusiastic about communicating your thoughts, building a wonderful rapport that can last for hours. You never fail to enjoy each other's company. Your Jupiterian partner will encourage you to pursue avenues of learning and new traveling experiences.

Adverse aspects to Jupiter may cause your partner to dominate the conversation, at times mentally exhausting you. Nevertheless, you will feel motivated to express your ideas and opinions.

When Jupiter is well aspected, your partner is interested in expanding your knowledge. Jupiter in the house of Mercury, an important pair in the Love Relationship Formula, inspires excellent communication where both parties benefit.

Jupiter in the Fourth House

When your partner's Jupiter falls in or aspects your fourth house, especially in conjunction to the *Imum Coeli,* you will want to enhance the ambiance in your home so that you may fully enjoy your relationship there. Your partner will know how to ease any stress, emphasizing a content and relaxed atmosphere. Your mate will inspire home improvements that will increase the value of your property. You will be inclined to explore your roots and develop greater insight on your past.

If any unfavorable aspects exist, the home scenario may seem too busy, not allowing you a chance to unwind when that may be just what you need.

When Jupiter is well aspected, your partner will alleviate any pressure so you experience more joy. Jupiter in the house of the Moon, an uplifting duo in the Love Relationship Formula, increases your personal happiness in a relationship.

Jupiter in the Fifth House

When your partner's Jupiter falls in or aspects your fifth house, they have faith in your creative pursuits and will inspire you to develop your talents. Your partner will show you an easier way to attain your objectives, and you will be grateful for their presence. As you are exposed to new opportunities, you will be confident about taking any risks, knowing you have the support of your Jupiterian mate behind you. You will thoroughly enjoy their company, delighting in leisure life and the world of entertainment. Romance is highlighted and pursued with enthusiasm as the two of you dance the night away. Your partner will also be supportive of procreation, besides displaying generosity and appreciation toward any existing children.

If there are any afflictions to Jupiter, risky, speculative ventures need to be avoided, whether concerning intimate involvements or creative goals. Plans need to be in place for you to reap results. Too much of the good life or overindulgence in gambling will be troublesome.

When auspicious aspects are present, Jupiter in the house of the Sun, a powerful combination in the Love Relationship Formula, encourages a romantically enriching experience that enhances long-term possibilities.

Jupiter in the Sixth House

When your partner's Jupiter falls in or aspects your sixth house, you are inclined to expand your work capabilities in the area of service. You are encouraged to look after the welfare of others, yet also be concerned about improving your own well-being. Your partner will introduce you to more efficient ways of addressing your daily routine and being productive on the job to help you excel to be your best. You are open to new ways of approaching your goals and are grateful for their support.

Discordant influences to Jupiter may cause your partner to overwhelm you with their own work methods.

Under harmonious aspects, your partner will provide you with the backing you may need to elevate your job status. Your Jupiterian mate's desire to expand your health outlook will benefit your output and your life. Although Jupiter is residing in another house of Mercury, a combination in the Love Relationship Formula, this area represents one's daily routine, health, and well-being as opposed to communication, which relates to the third house. Therefore, there is only subtle support with Jupiter in this placement concerning relationship development.

Jupiter in the Seventh House

When your partner's Jupiter falls in or aspects your seventh house, especially in conjunction to the Descendant, you are both inclined to focus on developing a successful, committed relationship, often involving marriage. The admiration that your partner shows is fully appreciated by you. Due to mutual cooperation it's a pleasure to be in each other's company. Your partner may want to broaden your social circle, including prestigious individuals.

Adverse influences to Jupiter compel your partner to display too much praise for you, thus making you feel uncomfortable, or not enough praise where your mate is unable to follow through on promises. Because of your partner's wishes, you could find yourself in a situation that is beyond your capability, to your embarrassment.

Under positive influences, Jupiter in the house of Venus is a benevolent combination in the Love Relationship Formula that attracts romantic success in a lasting union.

Jupiter in the Eighth House

When your partner's Jupiter falls in or aspects your eighth house, you may become involved with joint ventures with your partner that expand your financial possibilities. Your mate's investment tips bring lucrative returns.

At the request of your partner, a complete change is what is needed to release limitations and capitalize upon your strengths. Personal and sexual regeneration occurs where you experience a rebirth that improves the intimate relations between you and your mate. A deeper, physical bond, which is part of the attraction, will continue to grow.

If there are any afflictions to Jupiter, your partner may drain your financial assets. Their idea of how you should change yourself will not be well received.

When favorable aspects exist, your Jupiterian partner will encourage a major transformation that allows you to become in touch with your true self and appreciate your good qualities. As your mate enhances your self-awareness, you are able to bring out your best.

Jupiter in the Ninth House

When your partner's Jupiter falls in or aspects the ninth house, its ruling position, expansive opportunities enlighten your personal, spiritual, social, and physical experience. You will find your partner's enthusiasm to communicate ideas and opinions mentally intriguing. You may develop a newly found confidence in your life direction as your philosophy and outlook inspire hope. Since Jupiter represents the teacher and the priest, as well as the guru, you will discover insights that may change your beliefs. Your partner will persuade you to further your education, travel, and accumulate as much knowledge as you can to enlarge your experience in this lifetime.

When discordant aspects are present, your Jupiterian mate may expect you to gather information and be your own teacher when you thought you could depend on them for guidance. The advice received may not be appropriate for you.

Under positive aspects, your partner may rely on their own wisdom to enlarge your perspective. Jupiter in the house of Jupiter, representing benefics in aspect, attests to great mental growth that has the capacity to change your life forever.

Jupiter in the Tenth House

When your partner's Jupiter falls in or aspects your tenth house, especially in conjunction to the Midheaven, you will be inspired to pursue your career ambitions and attain a rewarding position. Your partner is happy to assist you in building your occupational reputation. You will be introduced to prestigious individuals who can improve your status. Since your mate believes in your career direction and wants you to have faith in yourself, you are confident you will succeed. Your partner may display a fatherly approach in supporting your goals.

With unfavorable influences, you may have grandiose ideas of what you are capable of accomplishing due to your partner's persuasion.

When Jupiter in the house of Saturn, a pairing in the Love Relationship Formula, is well aspected, you may have high expectations of formulating a prosperous career that brings you the fulfillment and social status you desire.

Jupiter in the Eleventh House

When your partner's Jupiter falls in or aspects your eleventh house, you will expand your social circle. The enthusiasm generated toward group involvements is reciprocated. Your significant other will become your best friend and will appreciate your idyllic aims, besides supporting the attainment of your hopes and dreams. Expanding upon your aspirations is the priority.

If Jupiter is afflicted, you may take advantage of your partner's goodwill. Being overly confident may disturb the progress you have made.

Under harmonious influences, you will expand upon your ideals, knowing that your partner and friends will cheer you on as you reach for the stars.

Jupiter in the Twelfth House

When your partner's Jupiter falls in or aspects your twelfth house, you have an opportunity to successfully transcend personal shortcomings that have limited your experience. Your partner's benevolent nature will assist you and protect you in understanding your hidden self. Working behind-the-scenes, your mate will renew your confidence and be a rock of Gibraltar in resolving personal problems. Such reassurance by your partner will allow you to comfortably delve into any mysteries that need to be understood. Exploring the unexplained in life, such as the occult, will be encouraged.

Under discordant influences, your partner may not keep your secrets private, being somewhat vulnerable to inquiring minds. You may need to defend yourself from scandalous activities.

If Jupiter is well aspected, you will feel at ease in sharing confidences with your mate, knowing that they have your best interests at heart. As you release your fears, you will be open to undergoing a complete metamorphosis.

Saturn in the First House

When your partner's Saturn falls in or aspects your first house, especially in conjunction to the Ascendant, you will find your partner relying on you to come through and support their needs. This dependency may cause you to feel more and more responsible for your Saturnian partner. You may feel as though you are paying back some type of karmic debt. Although your partner will appreciate what you do, they will still make demands of you, at times pushing you to the limit. Your Saturnian partner may actually be trying to bring out a more realistic view of your personality to help you acquire a better perspective of yourself. Due to the karmic implications, this placement indicates a lasting relationship as long as Saturn is not seriously afflicted.

When inauspicious aspects are present, you will feel overwhelmed with the responsibility of taking care of your partner. There may be times when you need to be tolerant because your partner is in serious need of your assistance. For example, your mate may experience a job loss and then need to depend on you financially, or there may be a physical setback that you have to contend with until circumstances change. Unless you are able to inject some sense of cheerfulness into the union, you may feel the heavy pressures of Saturn continue to challenge you.

Under auspicious influences, you may feel obligated to promote your partner by doing important deeds through which they will profit significantly. In turn, your partner may delineate a realistic approach to assist you in the accomplishment of your own aims with their accumulated insights.

Regardless, you must guard against being controlled by your partner, as they will have a strong tendency to project their fears and insecurities onto you, thus making your life miserable. If you feel you are the only one pulling the weight in the relationship, then you must work feverishly to modify the conditions before a pattern sets in; otherwise consider it over. Saturn in the house of Mars also opposes a Venus point when in opposition to the Descendant. Saturn prefers to control, yet Mars seeks comfort through Venus. Controlling someone can lead to very abusive and destructive actions. You will be able to provide for and love your partner much more if they learn to channel the Saturn influence for constructive gain. Your partner needs to curb their habit of projecting fear onto you and be concerned about forming a solid relationship based on mutual respect.

Saturn in the Second House

When your partner's Saturn falls in or aspects your second house, they will teach you how to increase your earnings and resources by applying a more realistic approach. You will discard the nonessentials and preserve that which is necessary. Your Saturnian partner will persuade you to be financially responsible so that you only take calculated risks and thus protect your assets. Sound investments will prosper.

Under afflicted aspects, you may need to avoid your partner's advice, as they may not possess the financial wherewithal to improve your economic status. Your partner's floundering monetary situation underscores their flawed counsel. You may find yourself assisting your Saturnian mate financially when they come up short. Since Saturn may suppress Venus, your self-esteem may be lowered due to your partner's lack of appreciation for you. Because Saturn makes us earn our way, you need to address depreciation that takes away from the individual that you are, personally and monetarily.

When there are favorable influences, Saturn in the house of Venus, a coupling in the Love Relationship Formula, attracts financial stability through your partner, as they are instrumental in helping you save money and making safe yet lucrative investments. In return, your partner will feel safe and sound with you, as you are capable of providing food, shelter, and comfort. Your partner will encourage you to work hard, knowing that applying yourself in this manner will have a positive effect on your self-esteem. Securing your earnings and your image will build a solid foundation that lasts a lifetime.

Saturn in the Third House

When your partner's Saturn falls in or aspects your third house, you may address the areas of communication and learning in a serious, disciplined manner. Your partner will teach you strategies to firmly express yourself. If you are willing to learn, much can be attained. Critical thinking will enable you to concentrate on the important issues so you develop a focused way of communicating. Trivial topics will be bypassed in favor of more in-depth, comprehensive subjects.

If Saturn is afflicted, your partner may limit your ability to communicate effectively. Conversation may be frustrating and boring, lacking any kind of excitement. Your mate may cause the rapport with your neighbors to sour as well. Any advice on furthering your education may not suit your purposes. Travel plans may be difficult to formulate and you may experience setbacks or delays. Even attending to errands for your partner will be tedious.

When Saturn is well aspected, thought-provoking, meaningful subject matter inspires conversation between you. Your partner will be able to guide you intellectually to make the most of your communicative capabilities.

Saturn in the Fourth House

When your partner's Saturn falls in or aspects your fourth house, especially in conjunction with the *Imum Coeli,* they will want you to examine your emotions from a realistic perspective. Hence, you will have a more serious outlook on life because you are seeing situations with clarity. Your partner may want to assume a dependable parental role in the household. They will also expect you to be responsible with domestic affairs.

Under adverse aspects, Saturn in the house of the Moon will put pressure on both of you to be extra responsible in the home environment. Your partner will feel it is their strict obligation, and you will feel the need to be dutiful and support your partner's efforts. Over time, a depressing situation may be the result, but there is no end in sight as this has now turned into a co-dependent relationship. The Saturn person's fears and insecurities are looking for comfort through the sensitivity of the Moon, yet have to work so hard to acquire such contentment that it may not be worth it.

Only positive aspects will save this situation, where you implement a practical and truthful approach so that you both benefit.

Saturn in the Fifth House

When your partner's Saturn falls in or aspects your fifth house, you will develop a serious attitude about romance with your partner since they may not be so receptive to your advances. Your Saturnian partner may spurn your creative aims, pointing out that it's not practical to pursue such activities. Although your partner may be critical of your artistic pursuits, wanting you to be realistic, you may have too great of expectations for them to be realized and appreciated by your mate. It is not necessary to win your partner's approval to achieve your goals. However, assuming a responsible position in taking care of children may be required.

Under discordant influences, you may try even harder to dramatically express your creativity just to prove your partner wrong. But this strategy may not change their demeaning attitude; in fact, your actions may encourage indifference. Romantic expression may be completely denied. Eventually you may feel as though you cannot thoroughly enjoy life with your partner.

If Saturn is well aspected, a realistic approach to your creative ambitions will serve its purpose as you slowly succeed with your planned efforts. You may be concerned with securing a long-term alliance.

Saturn in the Sixth House

When your partner's Saturn falls in or aspects your sixth house, you will feel obligated to be of service to your partner's needs. Albeit your partner is interested in improving your productivity, they will expect you to be dependable and look out for their welfare also. They will be adamant about following a strict daily agenda.

When Saturn is afflicted, your partner will constantly analyze your output and will find flaws in your performance that you will not appreciate. As your mate may hinder your progress, your health may suffer due to such tension.

If harmonious influences are present, your Saturnian mate will demand that you develop a strong work ethic that increases your efficiency. You are practical about implementing a structured itinerary, knowing you will acquire solid results.

Your quality of life is determined by a disciplined approach to your well-being that not only augments your effectiveness, but adds many years of good health.

Saturn in the Seventh House

When your partner's Saturn falls in or aspects your seventh house, especially in conjunction to the Ascendant, you and your mate have an opportunity to establish a long-lasting relationship. Saturn in the house of Venus, an important combination in the Love Relationship Formula, allows your partner to find great comfort in the union. Since this is a very karmic placement, indicating that you were once soulmates in a previous life, your Saturnian mate will experience a familiar, reassuring connection with you. However, your partner may test you to see if you meet their expectations. Although you will find this to be a tedious process, it could lead to a lifelong union.

If Saturn is afflicted, you will become very annoyed with your partner's testing methods. They may be too critical of you, undermining your confidence and self-esteem. You may feel that whatever you do, it's not enough for them. Your partner's intentions may be to control you by making you question your self-worth so that you feel you deserve little in return. This type of behavior is abusive and should be avoided.

Favorable influences signify your partner's dependability and will motivate you to show loyalty as well. When there is mutual reliability, a permanent relationship may develop that will endure life's tribulations.

Saturn exalted in Libra, the sign of relationships, perpetuates the importance of embracing stability to enhance a long-term union. It is only when one demonstrates respect and appreciation toward their partner that significant advances are made in a lasting relationship.

Saturn in the Eighth House

When your partner's Saturn falls in or aspects your eighth house, they will make you more conscious of the need to address your weaknesses and experience a transformation. But achieving this goal will not be easy as you will feel uncomfortable when your partner makes you aware of your shortcomings. In time you are more willing to look at your issues realistically and acknowledge that your partner could actually be acting in your best interests. Still, your Saturnian partner may want to take their time in establishing a relationship with you.

Adverse aspects will hinder your personal development and cause frustration between you both, especially in intimate moments. Your partner may not find you so trustworthy and question your motives. You may realize that their suspicious actions are a strong deterrent to furthering the relationship and cause you to retaliate. Any business partnership may seriously limit your success. Joint financial ventures should be avoided since accumulated debt could be the result. You may have to face adversity together with the hope that the tie will grow stronger for the experience. If this relationship is going to continue, you will have to compensate by contending with your mate's insecurity. Unfortunately, this does not indicate a cheerful union.

When Saturn is well aspected, there is an opportunity to stabilize the partnership, realizing that in working together on personal issues it might improve long-term prospects. Some hardships may have to be endured, but if you are on the same team, slowly but surely you can win. You need to aim toward establishing a solid partnership, one you can rely on, to secure a future tie.

Saturn in the Ninth House

When your partner's Saturn falls in or aspects your ninth house, they will want you to be practical about planning your direction in life along with considering a solid education. Your partner will act as your mentor as well, offering realistic guidance that has you reshaping your personal philosophy, as well as your spiritual or religious beliefs. Your Saturnian mate will insist on effective, direct communication that impresses your listener. You will gain from a serious attitude that strengthens your conviction in acquiring your objectives.

Discordant influences to Saturn will cause the two of you to have differing opinions. Your philosophies and religious beliefs may clash, causing much dissension. Since you are not in agreement, it will be difficult to make plans for the future. You will feel frustrated in not being able to carry on a progressive conversation with your partner. Travel plans may be hindered or discouraged, limiting your mobility.

Harmonious aspects depict a planned strategy that enables you to accomplish your goals. As you restructure your beliefs and philosophies, life takes on a realistic perspective that allows you to broaden your cultural horizons.

Saturn in the Tenth House

When your partner's Saturn falls in or aspects your tenth house, especially in conjunction to the Midheaven, they will want you to formulate a realistic view of your career as you diligently apply yourself in achieving your goals. Although your partner, through a parental approach, may delay your success with their strategy, you will benefit in the long run as you are better prepared to manage your position. Your partner's critical assessment of you is only meant to further your self-development. You will learn how discipline will make you more effective on the job and earn the respect of your co-workers and superiors alike.

Difficult influences will stall your efforts to succeed. Your mate will discourage your career ambitions, creating much anxiety between you. They may disrupt your means of establishing a good, solid reputation, possibly undermining your position at work.

When Saturn is well aspected, you gratefully accept the responsibilities that come with the job, knowing that what is earned can never be taken away. Saturn in its ruling house will bring the career stability you are looking for, and strengthen your work ethic. Your mate will support you in building a solid reputation that will carry you through the years.

Saturn in the Eleventh House

When your partner's Saturn falls in or aspects your eleventh house, they will support you in the achievement of your goals, especially if they are within your reach. Your partner will offer you sound guidance, outlining a strategy as to how to attain these sought-after desires. But you will be expected to discipline yourself by working diligently to be successful. You may develop a strong friendship that you can rely on into the future. However, your Saturnian partner will on occasion create hardships through their untimely demands. You will both benefit from having a compromising attitude and appreciating the significant bond between you.

When Saturn is afflicted, your partner will be overly critical of you in the pursuit of your ideals and limit your accomplishments. The attention your mate needs will put restraints on your social circle. As you develop an aversion toward your partner, you will not want their companionship. It may be more trouble than it's worth.

Under auspicious influences, you want to seize the moment in realizing your ambitious ideals. Your partner will be extremely helpful in assisting you toward the fulfillment of this objective. There is no greater reward than when you are required to call upon yourself in every way to achieve your finest aspirations.

Saturn in the Twelfth House

When your partner's Saturn falls in or aspects your twelfth house, you are encouraged to face up to your fears and insecurities so that you may cultivate a stronger emotional foundation from within. But if your partner constantly points out your weaknesses, you may become resentful. Your mate needs to find a helpful way of addressing your problems so as not to undermine your self-confidence.

Under adverse influences, you may feel forced by your partner to deal with your shortcomings, when you are not ready to confront them. This conflict will only further your insecurity as you will feel vulnerable in handling such pressure. In a nefarious scenario, your partner may become a secret enemy, willing to drastically alter your life for the worse.

When Saturn is well aspected, constructive approaches in dealing with your weaknesses will allow you to build a tremendous source of inner strength. You will be comfortable in relying on your Saturnian mate for practical advice that alleviates your fears. This may be reciprocated as your partner may also need to depend on you for help in difficult times. The stability provided to you can be given in return.

Uranus in the First House

When your partner's Uranus falls in or aspects your first house, especially in conjunction to the Ascendant, you are inspired to tap into your individuality and expose your unique self. You will feel enlightened for the experience of discovering more about yourself in an exhilarating manner. Your partner will greatly intrigue you as you both enjoy each other's stimulating company. Uranus in the house of Mars will create a strong attraction, besides arousing exciting passions. Although your partner may want to be the aggressor, both of you will feel the desire to initiate romance. Your mate may also encourage you to modify your persona, with the intention of revealing a new image.

Discordant aspects to Uranus indicate there may be struggles over who should take the lead. Still, you will find your partner forcing you to make drastic changes that you will object to adamantly. Their lifestyle may not agree with you. Arguments may ensue as neither of you want to compromise on the issue. If this behavior continues, your partner may suddenly leave your life as you will not abide by their compelling ways.

You are destined to experience completely new circumstances that will change your approach to life when Uranus is well aspected. The fascinating dynamics that you share will always remain. To progress in life, you need to be open to self-discovery, for a revitalized union will be the result.

Uranus in the Second House

When your partner's Uranus falls in or aspects your second house, you are encouraged to look for new possibilities to improve your income. Exploring your skills and talents may reveal some new avenues of employment. Since Uranus is known for its unpredictable nature, a watchful eye must be kept on all financial dealings.

Unfavorable aspects denote erratic monetary swings that will create stress between you and your mate. You, especially, may be the one left holding the bill.

Under positive influences, your partner will be a source of inspiration, believing in your potentials. You will capitalize upon original ideas that increase your revenue. Since

Uranus in the house of Venus is a pairing in the Love Relationship Formula, a personal attraction may develop over the enhancement of your earnings. Improvements toward your image will create a more exciting persona.

Uranus in the Third House

When your partner's Uranus falls in or aspects your third house, you are mentally stimulated to express yourself due to the enthusiasm conjured up by your partner. They will excite you into learning and gathering new information that inspires your intellectual growth. You may alter your perspective in lieu of innovative concepts that you find intriguing. Your partner will instigate changes in your environment that enliven your daily errands. Since travel is highlighted, this is an activity that can be enjoyed together. You may visit thrilling new places.

When Uranus is afflicted, your partner's ideas may drastically clash with your own. Their concepts may be so outrageous that you are inclined to reject any suggestions. Nevertheless, you will be encouraged to open your mind to another's unusual views.

Under harmonious influences, you may benefit from unconventional methods of learning that will enlighten your understanding. An exciting intellectual rapport will create an exhilarating attraction as you thoroughly relish each other's company. Uranus in the house of Mercury allows you to look at life from different perspectives so that you and your relationship may truly benefit.

Uranus in the Fourth House

When your partner's Uranus falls in or aspects your fourth house, especially in conjunction to the *Imum Coeli,* you may experience a great deal of restlessness in the home as your partner will cause you to feel uncomfortable in your own domestic environment. Your mate may inspire spontaneous actions and want you to upgrade your living situation by adding a computer, cell phone, or innovative equipment. Such an impulsive lifestyle may have you coming and going, yet there will never be a dull moment at home. Your Uranian partner may prompt you to look into your family history so you can make new discoveries about your roots.

Unfavorable aspects will cause much distress in the household. Your partner may have an erratic schedule that upsets your normal routine. Their ideas on how to improve the living space may be too unconventional for your tastes, thus provoking turbulence. It will require great patience to handle sudden disruptions that destabilize your equilibrium. Constant moving may also be a source of agitation.

When favorable aspects to Uranus exist, you and your partner can apply innovative ideas to the home that create a more progressive and interesting environment.

Uranus in the Fifth House

When your partner's Uranus falls in or aspects your fifth house, they may stimulate your creativity in a dramatic manner. You will find original ways to express your talents. Your partner's motivation will direct you toward new and exciting opportunities. Leisure life will be enjoyed from a new perspective. Romantic adventures are thrilling and inviting. Your partner's intriguing hobbies are fun.

If Uranus is afflicted, your partner is disruptive to your creative pursuits. Their impersonal actions will discourage your provocative desires. Romantic escapades may turn sour and possibly lead to a separation.

When positive influences are present, romantic exchanges are highlighted where new experiences instigate excitement for both of you. Your artistic prowess is enhanced by your Uranian partner's inspiration. Being your unique self, you discover your true creative essence.

Uranus in the Sixth House

When your partner's Uranus falls in or aspects your sixth house, you are encouraged to seek alternative health regimens to improve your physical well-being. A New Age diet plan or stress-relieving techniques such as acupuncture or therapeutic massage will be revitalizing. Upgrading your vitality will allow you to be more productive at work. Your partner will also want to persuade you to implement progressive methods on the job to make your work that much easier to accomplish. After applying these innovative techniques, you will agree that your methods were outdated. You may take on a renewed interest in being of service to others, where you and your partner may discover a unique way to further their welfare.

When Uranus is in adverse aspect, your partner will cause disruption on the job that is not easily settled. They may think they know it all and may be critical of your work strategy. Nervous tension may escalate into a turbulent situation. You may be concerned about your partner's health as well.

Under harmonious aspects to Uranus, you will want to be more effective on the job and, at your partner's request, upgrade your work strategy. A progressive attitude is rejuvenating and improves your well-being. You will always benefit from implementing a plan that leads to better work and health conditions.

Uranus in the Seventh House

When your partner's Uranus falls in or aspects your seventh house, especially in conjunction to the Descendant, you may feel compelled to look at your relationship from a whole new perspective. Although unsettling, you will make adjustments that are accommodating for each other. In selective cases, a forced separation due to traveling could create some distance. A sudden attraction can be overwhelming and needs to be carefully evaluated, as a sudden departure could be the result if there is not enough intrigue to keep your partner interested in you. Through your partner, you could establish a whole new social circle that includes some unconventional associations.

Discordant influences indicate that you would be wise to avoid a romantic alliance due to the fact that you could be easily fascinated by your partner only to have them suddenly disappear without a trace. This attraction gone awry would be extremely tumultuous, making it difficult for you to recover from such a shocking disclosure.

Only under auspicious aspects is this Uranian influence to be trusted. The changes you make within yourself will be reflected back onto your relationship to compliment the union. As Uranus falls in the house of Venus, a combination in the the Love Relationship Formula, a powerful attraction will bring continued excitement into the relationship. Other elements of the Love Relationship Formula need to be present to support this dynamic appeal.

Uranus in the Eighth House

When your partner's Uranus falls in or aspects your eighth house, they will enlighten you to discover more about yourself through experiencing a major metamorphosis. You will be exposed to the occult and death/rebirth issues that awaken you to the possibilities of transcendence. The avenues pursued that allow you to rejuvenate yourself will be rewarding. Joint finances are progressive as long as you keep your wits about you.

You will need to guard yourself when inharmonious influences are present, as erratic situations will unfold that are monetarily disruptive. Following the financial advice of your mate is not recommended. Although you will be inclined by your partner's persuasion to involve yourself with a transcendental experience, their plan on how to proceed does not agree with you.

Only under positive aspects to Uranus should new investment opportunities be pursued. Most partnership dealings are favored and will have an original twist. Your partner will appreciate your instilled quest to find the truth about yourself.

Uranus in the Ninth House

When your partner's Uranus falls in or aspects your ninth house, you are challenged to alter your views on life. Your beliefs and philosophy will be enlightened with a whole new perspective through the persuasion of your partner. Expansive thoughts will stimulate your mind, possibly changing your outlook forever.

When Uranus is afflicted, the direction of your life may drastically change. You will be confronted by your partner with radical ideas that may be too bizarre for your tastes. Your mate's beliefs may seriously differ from your own, causing much trepidation.

When Uranus is well aspected, your partner will inspire you to take an interest in foreign dealings and possibly travel abroad. You will form new opinions about your beliefs. Life will take on an entirely new meaning as you implement original concepts into your philosophy. The wisdom gained is intellectual insight that will always perpetuate a broader understanding of your life experience.

Uranus in the Tenth House

When your partner's Uranus falls in or aspects your tenth house, especially in conjunction to the Midheaven, your career ambitions may suddenly change for the better as your partner provides you with opportunities to achieve success. You may reevaluate your own position and look for original avenues that accelerate your progress.

Under adverse aspects to Uranus, your partner will be disruptive to your career goals and reputation. They may not offer the proper occupational guidance, possibly steering you in an unpredictable direction.

When auspicious influences exist, you may attract a unique career position through your partner's assistance. A cultivated awareness allows you to be flexible and adapt to changing situations on the job. Since your social circle is intrigued by you, you sport a good reputation.

Uranus in the Eleventh House

When your partner's Uranus falls in or aspects your eleventh house, you are inspired to pursue your sought-after ideals. Your partner will provide you with connections to organizations, societies, clubs, or charities that you appreciate being involved with on a regular basis. Since Uranus rules the eleventh house, it stimulates the growth of friendships where new and interesting associations will develop.

Unfavorable influences will not allow a good friendship to manifest between you and your mate, or others in your surroundings. You may experience an unpredictable future in your partner's presence, and not be sure which path to follow to reach your dreams.

Under favorable aspects, your partner may want to enlighten you to a new, humanitarian way of living. As you attain the goals you desire, exciting friendships grow and prosper.

Uranus in the Twelfth House

When your partner's Uranus falls in or aspects your twelfth house, they will provide you with new ways of unraveling subconscious issues that cause you to discover more about yourself. You will be able to solve deep-rooted problems that have hindered you for years. You may find that in changing your emotional outlook, you and your partner will benefit. You may trust your Uranian mate with their unusual antidotes to improve any psychological condition.

Discordant influences indicate that your partner's approach to deeper issues generates tremendous stress. They may demand radical changes that leave you in turmoil. You will wonder if your partner is becoming your enemy by the erratic tactics seemingly designed to undermine you.

When Uranus is well aspected, hidden talents are discovered that inspire your confidence. You will feel relieved and exhilarated by the personal gains made in addressing deep-seated issues. Finally, your unique self can be realized to the fullest.

Neptune in the First House

When your partner's Neptune falls in or aspects your first house, especially in conjunction to the Ascendant, you will emanate a mysterious aura when you are in the company of your partner that others find quite alluring. Although your partner will support the projection of a compassionate attitude to those around you, you may need to protect yourself from being taken in by their sympathies. Cultivating an understanding manner, your Neptunian mate may be sensitive enough to appreciate your dreams and fantasies. They will quickly learn to relate to you on an emotional/spiritual level that defies definition. A relaxed atmosphere will exist when you are in each other's company.

When Neptune is afflicted, the person you thought you could rely on eludes you. Since you are not able to see each other for who you really are, your relationship gradually dissipates and you are very disappointed. If your partner is inclined to misrepresent you, beware of the repercussions.

Positive influences to Neptune indicate you will learn that in giving there is much to be gained, even in the pursuit of your desired ideals. Your partner will proclaim that a compassionate understanding allows you to embrace all of life so that your spiritual essence may be found.

Neptune in the Second House

When your partner's Neptune falls in or aspects your second house, you are prompted to use your imagination to create new sources of income. Your partner will encourage you to consider avenues that help the less fortunate, but have limited funding. Although your mate's intentions are good, you may want to be extra cautious in following any financial advice, as it may be shrouded with deception. You may find money slipping through your fingers, yet your Neptunian partner doesn't seem to be concerned. What works for your partner may not always be economically reliable for you.

Under adverse aspects, you would be wise to ignore the monetary counsel of your mate, as they sport rose-colored glasses that envision delusions of grandeur. An impractical budget will see you going in the red. What appears to be a lucrative investment will not work out as planned. Disappearing acts belong in the circus, not in your bank account. You are better off following your own advice. Beware of your partner wanting to exploit your generosity.

Even under harmonious aspects you are still vulnerable to your partner taking advantage of you. Your mate's motives need to be questioned to see if they are acting in your best interests and inspiring new earning potential.

Neptune in the Third House

When your partner's Neptune falls in or aspects your third house, you will be inclined to go beyond everyday reality and develop your intuition when interacting with your mate or those around you. You will find yourself learning through osmosis and, at the request of your partner, cultivating your imagination to assist you in expressing your ideas. Glamorizing your educational aims will make them more interesting than before.

Discordant aspects to Neptune in the house of Mercury depict a complete breakdown in communications. You are two ships passing in the night, as nebulous ideas never seem to reach each other. Major misunderstandings will be the unfortunate result. If you cannot communicate with your partner, you do not have much of a relationship. The wrong information will also stymie learning experiences and traveling plans.

When Neptune is well aspected, you will embellish your communicative thoughts, expressing yourself in a colorful manner. Using your vivid imagination will enable you to be entertaining in the company of others. Your Neptunian partner will persuade you with fascinating traveling adventures that refresh your mind and spirit.

Neptune in the Fourth House

When you partner's Neptune falls in or aspects your fourth house, especially in conjunction to the *Imum Coeli*, there will be a mutual empathy where you both will be able to relate to each other's emotions and habitual patterns. Nevertheless, your mate may at times play on your sympathies, wanting all of your tender-loving care. A spiritual link may develop that brings out your compassionate nature. Issues involving your upbringing will be addressed in a sensitive manner to help you heal vulnerable areas.

When Neptune is afflicted, you will feel obligated to support your partner's every need, leaving you drained. No matter what you do, your partner may not trust you, which could lead to the deterioration of your relationship. Joint property dealings may be mismanaged leading to disappointment and possible financial loss. Your Neptunian mate may engage in scandalous real estate deals that you find appalling. Keep a careful eye on inheritances, which could be easily undermined without your knowledge.

Under favorable aspects, you will establish a feeling of mutual identity that is long lasting. As your compassion is aroused, you both benefit from sharing the sensitivity surrounding your emotional foundations.

Neptune in the Fifth House

When your partner's Neptune falls in or aspects your fifth house, they will impress upon you the need to bring out your creative prowess so that you may use your imagination to the fullest. Any ingenious talents may be cultivated. Your partner will inspire you to enjoy the glamorous world of entertainment, taking pleasure in the romantic delights that life has to offer. Remember, showing a compassionate nature involves making sacrifices that may lead to true love.

Inharmonious influences denote a painful dissolution of a union that once seemed ideal. Having starry-eyed relationships will only lead to a broken heart. Try resisting your Neptunian mate's enticement to escort you down a crooked road. You may have difficulty aspiring toward illusive, creative goals that your partner insists you can achieve.

When Neptune is well aspected, artistically and romantically you are keen on pursuing your heart's desire. A heavenly romance may develop that is full of fun and wonder. Loving unconditionally has its own reward.

Neptune in the Sixth House

When your partner's Neptune falls in or aspects your sixth house, they will be a source of inspiration to you in living up to your ideals on the job. You are more inclined to look for the "blind spots" that limit your productivity. Your partner will be understanding with your problems and may encourage a relaxed, meditative approach toward your work goals. Still, they may cause confusion with your previously set agenda, which is draining. You may lose track of your priorities, thus dismantling progress that has already been made.

When Neptune is badly aspected, your partner's vague, careless advice on how to address your daily routine is very disconcerting and undermines your stability on the job. They may misdiagnose health issues, instigating even more setbacks. It may be such that you have to sacrifice taking care of your partner's welfare.

Positive aspects indicate that the healing effects of Neptune will improve your overall well-being. These influences generate a calming effect on you where you are more capable of seeking and attaining your work ideals. Nevertheless, your Neptunian mate's involvement may interfere with your progress at times. You will appreciate their support, but following your own counsel will attract better results.

Neptune in the Seventh House

When your partner's Neptune falls in or aspects your seventh house, especially in conjunction to the Descendant, you may feel you have found the perfect partner. But your starry-eyed perceptions may elude you into believing that this is the ideal mate when maybe he or she is not. When it comes to love, our imagination can easily play tricks on us. This spiritual influence may describe a platonic relationship. Your partner's association in your social surroundings will enhance the feeling of having close connections with others.

When misleading influences denote that you are under the illusion your true love will last forever, you are swept off your feet into heavenly abandonment only to return to earth with a seriously disappointing thud. A romantic travesty has overcome you, leaving you in the depths of despair. Deception in love gets even the best of us. But, as they say, "What you lose in the world will not be a loss to your soul."*

When auspicious aspects are present, you will have a compassionate understanding of your Neptunian partner's needs, which will generate better communications. But, this spiritual link is something that can only be felt, not described. How you now perceive love will change your entire outlook. Neptune in the house of Venus depicts a heavenly romance that is the soul connection you desire.

---

* Paramahansa Yogananda from *Spiritual Diary* (Los Angeles, CA: Self-Realization Fellowship, 1982).

Neptune in the Eighth House

When your partner's Neptune falls in or aspects your eighth house, you may feel the spiritual need to experience a personal transformation, yet lack the focus to attain this goal. Gradually you will be able to channel this influence and realize that a meditative retreat may provide you with the means to change your inner being. Still, you may encounter a vague understanding with your partner that makes you feel uncertain about your relationship with them. Finances need to be carefully guarded. Any joint bank accounts may see the quick dissemination of funds.

Under adverse aspects, your inheritance may be laced with fraud. Personal and financial joint ventures are slated to fail. What you start may seem to dissolve without you ever knowing it. Therefore partnerships are not guaranteed to grow and prosper. Intimacy never seems to evolve to a higher plane, but descends to unsatisfied desires. You may have to face fears of the unknown, possibly involving death-and-rebirth experiences or even the occult. You are facing a tremendous challenge to find your way and perhaps learn when not to rely on your Neptunian partner.

When harmonious aspects are affecting Neptune, a wonderful spiritual bond could be the result. You are able to tap into the deeper realms of consciousness with your mate. Sexuality is experienced on a more compassionate level that may even be dream-like. Your partner puts you at ease with your metamorphosis, knowing that in purifying your being you will transcend to your highest self.

Neptune in the Ninth House

When your partner's Neptune falls in or aspects your ninth house, you are persuaded to open up your mind to otherworldly avenues of communication. Implementing a spiritual practice may change your whole philosophy about life. A more compassionate approach to your beliefs allows you to honor and broaden your understanding of other religious doctrines. Cultivating an interest in unusual avenues of learning, you may find that being creative brings out the intellectual genius in you.

Discordant aspects may cause your Neptunian mate to mislead you in the assimilation of intriguing ideas. You may be led into religions or philosophies that do not agree with your beliefs. Phony concepts will disrupt your direction, making you feel disillusioned about learning in any capacity. Travel plans are not to be trusted. Since nebulous communications foreshadow the union, you will encounter major misunderstandings.

When Neptune is well aspected, your partner's imagination will redefine your own outlook and stimulate you to travel to see new, colorful sights. Your mate will motivate you to gather knowledge from many different sources so that you can reach new horizons and develop faith in a higher cause. Sometimes we must go beyond ourselves to have a more meaningful existence.

Neptune in the Tenth House

When your partner's Neptune falls in or aspects your tenth house, especially in conjunction to your Midheaven, they are convinced that you can reach the ideal goals that you set for yourself. Although it's nice to have the support of someone who believes in you, your illusive aspirations may at times seem unattainable no matter how much effort is applied. You may become discouraged trying to emulate the success of your partner, not realizing that their ambitions are not comparable to yours. If your aims are to ever be achieved, you must have faith in their materialization.

Unfavorable aspects to Neptune may completely undermine your efforts to triumph in a prosperous career. You may have to make sacrifices for your partner that distract you from your own career goals. Due to your mate's dishonest actions, your reputation may be unknowingly fraught with disgrace. If your Neptunian partner shows signs of unreliability, they could have other motives.

When favorable aspects exist, your partner will provide you with the means to make your career aspirations come true. You are confident that the aims you have set for yourself can be realized. When you accomplish a goal that requires total devotion, you know that you have fulfilled a great purpose in life.

Neptune in the Eleventh House

When your partner's Neptune falls in or aspects your eleventh house, you are inspired to develop a spiritual friendship with your mate. You envision your soulmate possessing a compassionate understanding that surpasses the eyes of time. Your Neptunian partner may be able to provide you with the resources that help you manifest your fondest hopes and dreams. A geographical barrier may exist that allows you the space to flow with this relationship and be creative on your own. Different backgrounds may cause a division that will require a sensitive approach to rekindle the bond.

When inauspicious aspects are present, you may be required to make sacrifices where your sympathetic gestures are needed, possibly due to ill health. Your partner's presence in your life may confuse your ideals and interfere with your friendships. It may seem that your mate is not acting in your best interests.

Under auspicious aspects to Neptune, your partner is a desirable friend who supports your idyllic pursuits. They have the ability to put you in touch with groups that reflect your aims. Showing empathy in developing friendships in life will be one of your greatest accomplishments; the other is a sincere dedication to your ideals that allows your dreams and wishes to come true.

Neptune in the Twelfth House

When your partner's Neptune falls in or aspects your twelfth house, you will be more at ease working with underlying psychological issues that need to be addressed. Your partner will approach you with compassionate counsel, knowing that this is the best way to handle sensitive problems. They may help you open your heart to be more sympathetic to those around you. You are also inclined to show empathy toward your Neptunian mate.

Under badly aspected influences, your partner may cause you to feel very confused about how to manage any personal difficulties. You may exercise escapist tactics to avoid what you need to face. Personal weaknesses may cause self-defeating tendencies. Pursuing unexplained phenomena or creative activities may be largely disappointing as plans go awry. Secrets may somehow be revealed to the public through your partner's detrimental intentions.

When Neptune is well aspected, there could be a shared interest in the unknown, including mysteries and the occult. Developing any hidden talents will boost your confidence and be the right form of therapy for you. Your partner will be instrumental in bringing out your generous concern for the welfare of others. They want you to shelter yourself as well from those who would divulge your deepest secrets.

To grow spiritually one has to be giving but also perceptively cunning, knowing only to release information that others cannot take advantage of in some manner.

Pluto in the First House

When your partner's Pluto falls in or aspects your first house, especially in conjunction with the Ascendant, they may become intensely attracted to you and driven to uncover the real personality that lies beneath. Your partner will want you to develop an awareness of your unconscious motives so that you learn to redirect your energies to accomplish more in life. Because of your Plutonian partner's persuasion, you will experience a personal transformation that will allow you to feel entirely rejuvenated. As a couple, you may become more aware of your mortality as a near-death experience changes your view about life and the afterlife.

When Pluto is afflicted, your partner may manipulate you with a mesmerizing effect into following their lead. Nevertheless, much animosity will arise when you point out your mate's psychological problems and they project this issue right back onto you, making it your fault.

This karmic link describes a deeper bond established in a prior lifetime. Although you are destined to work out your karma on a profound level that surpasses time, this could be for constructive or destructive reasons depending on other intersecting influences. Positive aspects will support you in discovering hidden elements within yourself that are in need of transcendence, thus driving you toward a meaningful outcome.

Pluto in the Second House

When your partner's Pluto falls in or aspects your second house, you are prompted to come to a deeper understanding concerning money and values. Your whole attitude may change as you recognize what is important and what isn't. Your partner will instigate a more meaningful approach in capitalizing upon your skills and talents. They will want you to recognize what the underlying motive is behind earning money and accumulating possessions. Questioning your ideas and intentions toward establishing security will bring a clearer perspective on finances as well as on the significance of your existence. Pluto in the house of Venus, a strong combination in the Love Relationship Formula, intends to awaken you to what is meaningful so that you may value your relationship completely.

When unfavorable aspects exist, you are slated to experience economic difficulty. Although your partner will want to be involved with your financial situation, they may force you to take financial risks or pursue a monetary strategy that is not appropriate for you. As lucrative gains are not to be found, financial loses will cause dissension between the two of you.

Favorable aspects to Pluto indicate that your partner will be a great source in generating wealth. Materialistic rewards, although supportive to one's lifestyle, never take the place of the true, meaningful riches that life has to offer.

Pluto in the Third House

When your partner's Pluto falls in or aspects your third house, you will explore the world of ideas and recognize that the vat of life's knowledge is ever filling. Your partner will strongly influence your opinions, questioning your every thought so that you may find deeper meaning in relating to those in your surroundings. Both of you will benefit from such an in-depth exchange. As you modify your manner of thinking, you will demonstrate a powerful persona when communicating to others.

Discordant aspects may cause your partner to coerce you into following their pattern of thinking. They may want to manipulate you in conversation, causing you to feel uncomfortable interacting on a social level. Regardless of your opinion, your partner may want to determine your mode of education.

Under harmonious aspects, you will apply depth of understanding to your thoughts and way of communicating. Your mate's persuasion to probe your intellectual abilities will only add to your wisdom.

Pluto in the Fourth House

When your partner's Pluto falls in or aspects your fourth house, especially in conjunction to the *Imum Coeli,* they will stir up your emotional and habitual patterns so that you might develop a deeper understanding of your inner being. You will form strong feelings toward your partner that augment the bond between you. As your awareness increases, you may sense a past-life connection that touches upon your psychological essence in such a manner that you are amazed at the effect your mate has on you.

When Pluto is badly aspected, your partner may bring to the surface emotional issues you would rather not deal with at this time. You may feel repulsed at your mate's extreme behavior. Domestic conflicts may arise that involve other relatives. An underlying pressure emanating from your partner will challenge your stability at home.

When Pluto is well aspected, you are stimulated by your partner to understand and transcend your instinctive and responsive experiences to add to your emotional and psychological growth. One's true essence is exposed through the process of change.

Pluto in the Fifth House

When your partner's Pluto falls in or aspects your fifth house, they will bring to the surface any dormant talents so that you will enjoy becoming involved with and expressing yourself in a dramatic manner. Whether they be creative or recreational talents, you will still feel compelled to excel in this capacity. You will be inclined to engage in leisure life as well, increasing the romantic time spent together. You may have a propensity to attract love-affair situations even in the company of your mate. Prior romances may appear that demand your involvement. You may need to explore your deeper motives for experiencing an affair with someone other than your significant other. In understanding why you are susceptible to enticement, you will modify your approach to romantic ties.

Inauspicious influences to Pluto denote that your partner may manipulate love to satisfy their own desires. You may feel unwanted pressure to pursue creative avenues that do not agree with you. Your partner may not be interested in collaborating when it comes to leisurely activities or the raising of children.

Under auspicious aspects, your Plutonian partner will have an influential effect on you that changes your disposition toward romance, leisure life, and children. You will find deeper meaning in spending time together and sharing in life's pleasantries.

Pluto in the Sixth House

When your partner's Pluto falls in or aspects your sixth house, you are persuaded to embark on a mission to help others. But you may first need to attend to your partner, who will be expecting your services. Your work routine will be scrutinized by your mate, who will want you to function in a well-organized manner on the job. They will be adamant about you changing your routine and implementing more concentration, knowing that this will improve your output.

Under adverse aspects, your partner may be overly critical of your efficiency on the job. You may find yourself in a subordinate position where you are constantly meeting the needs of others, but there is no concern for your needs. This intense pressure may affect your overall health. Deep-rooted conditions may not be easily treated. You will need to compensate by fortifying your diet and physical fitness so that you may be better able to tolerate such stress.

When Pluto is harmoniously aspected, you will become involved with upgrading your health and well-being, satisfying your nutritional intake, which will justify your good health. Your partner's persuasion will convince you to modify your work routine, which will bring you the job results you desire.

In looking out for the welfare of others, you will develop a grateful attitude for the experience of helping someone in need.

Pluto in the Seventh House

When your partner's Pluto falls in or aspects your seventh house, especially in conjunction to the Descendant, they will be intensely drawn to you, desiring a deep, lasting commitment and expecting complete loyalty from you as well. You will be challenged in learning how to cooperate in a long-term relationship. Your partner will reveal your attitude toward relationships, which will indicate some needed changes. Once certain areas of your mindset are modified, you can enter into a totally satisfying union with your mate.

When Pluto is afflicted, your partner will become very possessive with you, wanting to alienate you from any social contacts and monopolize your time and attention. You will bring up issues that disturb your partner's psychological well-being, where they may lash out at you, demonstrating hostility. You will need to protect yourself from fatal attractions or stalkers who are compelled to be with you.

Pluto in the house of Venus, a vital link in the Love Relationship Formula, makes this connection a very karmic one that aims toward renewing the depth of love that the couple has experienced in another lifetime. Good aspects to Pluto intensify the longevity of the commitment, where you both will seek a more meaningful experience of love.

Pluto in the Eighth House

When your partner's Pluto falls in or aspects your eighth house, they will convince you to confront your deep-rooted psychological issues. You may feel very uncomfortable about tackling these subconscious conditions, which may cause upset between you and your partner. Gradually you will realize that in experiencing a total transformation, you will be better able to connect with your partner on an emotional, spiritual, sexual, and intellectual level. Facing these psychological issues will take courage, but you have everything to gain. As you empower yourself through this rebirth experience, the confidence you acquire will prepare you for another step in your evolvement in life—one your partner may envy.

Unfavorable aspects to Pluto will make it difficult for you to experience a personal transformation, as your partner does not want to cooperate in any manner. You may find yourself burning out from this union, which seems too intense to survive. It would not be wise for you to become involved with joint monetary ventures since they are likely to be manipulated by your Plutonian partner. Beware that your partner may be interested in capitalizing upon your personal strengths. Quests to unravel the occult would prove to be questionable and in some cases harmful.

Pluto in its ruling house under favorable aspects indicates your partner will insist on offering you help in releasing psychological repressions. Once purged, you will be a freer soul, wanting to immerse yourself in personal growth experiences. You will be exposed to the probability of reincarnation, which will affect your outlook on life. A close bond will be established through satisfying intimate moments that will support a long-term union. Your metamorphic change may make all things possible.

Pluto in the Ninth House

When your partner's Pluto falls in or aspects your ninth house, you are swayed by your partner to change your beliefs, philosophy, and outlook on your existence. You may be challenged to explore your own concepts and spiritual or religious values, finally concluding that you may need to totally alter your viewpoint. Understanding what lies behind a certain attitude or motivation will bring greater clarity.

When Pluto is badly aspected, your partner will try to persuade you to follow their beliefs and philosophy, which will cause major disagreements between you.

When Pluto is well aspected, you have an opportunity to examine your beliefs and perspective on life, discarding worn-out concepts and broadening your outlook, which may include traveling to foreign countries and experiencing other cultures. You may discover an unlimited interest in reaching for new possibilities that bring a profound experience.

Pluto in the Tenth House

When your partner's Pluto falls in or aspects your tenth house, especially in conjunction to the Midheaven, they will be highly influential in the pursuit of your career goals, wanting to propel you into the limelight so that you may improve your status. You may feel driven to succeed no matter what the cost, realizing that to acquire a position of power you must have a great strategy combined with a hard-working attitude. A stronger awareness will allow you to understand your subconscious motivations to achieve your ambitions. Since your reputation is at stake, hopefully you will demonstrate honorable actions. If you want to receive respect from others, you must maintain your integrity even in the midst of power plays.

Under discordant aspects, your partner may manipulate you for their own ambitious gain, or your partner could be envious of your success. Your reputation could be damaged as your Plutonian mate may be dedicated to undermining your position.

Harmonious aspects will fortify your career outlook where you are determined to succeed. Victory will require a clear conscience, as you aim toward attaining a position of power, moving in for the right reasons and not the wrong ones.

Pluto in the Eleventh House

When your partner's Pluto falls in or aspects your eleventh house, you are inclined to redefine your hopes and dreams so that you are better able to fulfill them. As you grasp a thorough understanding of what's behind your approach to your sought-after aims, you are more prepared to succeed. Your partner will connect you with groups, clubs, or organizations that share similar ideals to assist you in achieving your ambitions.

When inauspicious influences are present, your Plutonian partner may coerce you into pursuing the wrong ideals, which may turn out to be their dream. Your partner may also display signs of jealousy, which may ruin your friendship and undermine your social circle.

Under auspicious aspects, you will establish a strong friendship with your significant other that could last through the years. You are encouraged to form deep connections with others as well. Now you have a special opportunity to pursue your dreams to the peak of fulfillment. Once you're involved, there's no turning back.

Pluto in the Twelfth House

When your partner's Pluto falls in or aspects your twelfth house, they will cause personal issues to surface that you would rather ignore. Yet, if you can find the courage to address these problems that shake your confidence, you may once and for all release these repressive conditions that have blocked you for years. Your partner may provide you with intense counsel to resolve what is burdening you, and also encourage you to help the sick and underprivileged. When we become involved with someone, the union always seems to bring up what we need to confront. All relationships have a tendency to expose our weaknesses, some that we never knew we had.

If unfavorable influences are affecting Pluto, you may feel vulnerable that your partner will easily manipulate you since they know your shortcomings and may wish to take advantage of them. Your partner may be enticed into becoming your secret enemy just to see how far they can go without letting you know. You are not only forced to deal with your psychological issues, which may have everything to do with why you attracted this person into your life in the first place, but also faced with dealing with a corrupt relationship. Your partner may try to lure you into underground enterprises that would deface your integrity. If you are constantly on guard, you may be able to avoid such negative situations.

Favorable aspects will allow you the opportunity to transcend repressed conditions that have made your life unhappy. Subconscious motivations reveal a lot about who we are. In understanding these hidden problems, you have a real chance of finding your true self.

part 6

timing is everything

26

♥ when to attract
the right partner
using the love
relationship formula

When you are looking for that wonderful relationship, *timing is everything!* Favorable meeting times, as predicted by the heavens, will enhance your chances of connecting with that special someone. In predicting romantic relationships, fate and karma play an important role. In terms of relationships, fate means that you are destined to meet a special someone. Karma indicates what kind of person you might meet considering how well you have balanced your own personal karma. What also comes into play is your belief system. You must believe that you deserve to be with Mr. or Ms. Right. So let's say your fate has been decided and it is established that you will meet a significant other. Don't question whether or not you will, just think that your destiny is such that you will experience this important meeting. *If you know it's possible, then it's just a matter of when.* And "when" is dependent upon the astrology involved in the Love Relationship Formula to attract the best soulmate you deserve.

We come to this planet to learn about loving others as well as ourselves. Many times loving and respecting ourselves is overlooked. However, it is only when we love and appreciate ourselves that we have a chance to find true love—the love we desire.

People say they are looking for love, yet they can't seem to find a relationship. And I can clearly see why. They are programmed to believe that they never will.

Give yourself a chance! Changing your thinking can help change your life. If you want to be in a relationship, you have to think about it, and more importantly, you have to believe it will happen!

> *"What you believe in you serve and are served by."**
> —Rev. Catherine Ponder

When we meet someone new, that meeting is the birth of the relationship. And with timing, you have a good idea of what to expect. The transits, progressions, and solar arc directions that are in aspect at that time will surely affect the outcome of this relationship. *Utilizing the astrological connections involved in the Love Relationship Formula, along with an understanding of your belief system and karma, will bring the greatest results. It is important to remember that you can meet someone under positive planetary influences, but the Love Relationship Formula must be intact in order for the relationship to prosper.* Keep in mind that the transits, progressions, and solar arc directions make aspects to the natal chart as well as aspects among themselves.

Venus Transits/Progressions/Solar Arc Directions

Venus Conjunct Sun—Social Exchanges, Love and Affection

Minor Influence with Sun Conjunct Descendant

The Sun shining on Venus will emphasize affectionate encounters with those around you. It will also motivate you to turn on the charm as you enjoy the pleasantries that exist in the moment. Bringing beauty into your environment will attract approval from others. Accentuating your Venusian assets, you are bound to win the favor of your social circle. Others are agreeable and willing to please. Loved ones will appreciate your

---

* Ponder, Catherine, *The Dynamic Laws of Healing* (1966; revised, Camarillo, CA: DeVorss Publications, 1985).

company. In compatibility and with progressions, this influence is much more pronounced than the subtle effect that emanates from the transits themselves. In fact, when progressed Venus goes over the natal Sun or is in conjunction in an angular house in a Solar Return, one can expect to meet up with a congenial partner possibly suited for marriage. Positive Sun-Venus aspects are a vital part of the Love Relationship Formula.

Venus Trine/Sextile Sun—Favorable Social Exchanges, Love and Affection
Minor Influence with Sun Trine/Sextile Descendant

The affections of Venus are highlighted by the Sun, as your charming self attracts pleasant and agreeable social encounters your way. A relaxed attitude will allow you to enjoy the company of those around you. Loved ones feel content in your presence. A harmonious environment will continue to enhance the social decorum. Your efforts to create a beautiful environment win compliments and warm support from well-wishers, as social activities thrive. Favorable Sun-Venus aspects are an important pairing in the Love Relationship Formula.

Venus Square/Oppose Sun—Distracted Feelings and Emotional Disadvantage
Minor Influence with Sun Square/Oppose Descendant

Your feelings are at a disadvantage when the Sun is in adverse transit to Venus. A certain moodiness prevails, leaving your social/romantic encounters ineffective. Still yearning for a sentimental exchange, your desires continue to be blocked. Too much emotionalism, however, warrants you avoiding entertaining on this day. Your charming self is seen as forced protocol. Meetings with your close social circle or lover should be postponed. The sensual pleasures in life are lacking, except for overindulging in food and drink, which is not recommended. Emotional displays should be kept in check as well.

Venus Conjunct Moon—Affectionate Feelings
Minor Influence with Moon Conjunct Descendant

Sensitivity in compatibility is strong when Venus and the Moon join together in aspect. You will want to express your feelings and be well received. Affectionate responses put you at ease as you know you are in the company of those who care. You can win the approval of others with a loving nature. Fond feelings are encouraged under positive Venus-Moon aspects, which are a valuable part of the Love Relationship Formula.

Venus Trine/Sextile Moon—Harmonious and Affectionate Feelings
Minor Influence with Moon Trine/Sextile Descendant

Feeling relaxed, you wish to share your feelings with those around you. The affectionate responses you seek will emanate from those who care.

Pleasant surroundings will induce a content spirit. The shared sensitivity that you experience persuades a more harmonious environment. Favorable Moon-Venus aspects are a highly supportive combination in the Love Relationship Formula.

Venus Square/Oppose Moon—Moody Feelings
Minor Influence with Moon Square/Oppose Descendant

A moody disposition will make relationships uneasy. Even if you are wavering with your own feelings, do be considerate toward others. Finding an emotional outlet will help channel this adversity. Moon-Venus angles at times require an emotional or sexual release. Otherwise, it would be best to work out unsettled emotions by yourself.

Venus Conjunct Mercury—Social and Affectionate Exchanges
Minor Influence with Mercury Conjunct Descendant

Congenial social interaction will be well received. Your charming self exudes a good-natured attitude that appeases the company you keep. Being yourself is quite attractive to those in your social circle.

Venus Trine/Sextile Mercury—Favorable Social and Affectionate Exchanges
Minor Influence with Mercury Trine/Sextile Descendant

Being content and socially appealing enhances your chances for a romantic advance. Encounters may easily lead to affectionate exchanges as you share your charming nature with others. You attract favors as you gain the approval of those around you. There will be an opportunity to relax and express yourself fully in agreeable surroundings.

Venus Square/Oppose Mercury—Social Disapproval, Feeling Disagreeable
Minor Influence with Mercury Square/Oppose Descendant

You are at a social disadvantage. Misunderstandings could be the result of vacillating feelings. A lack of information urges you to discuss ideas further. Disagreeable conditions will challenge you to try to bring some harmony into the environment. If you can not be tactful, keep your feelings to yourself. Displaying a polite manner will ease tensions and avoid criticism from others.

Venus Conjunct Venus—Congenial and Affectionate Exchanges
Minor Influence with Venus Conjunct Descendant

Your relaxed, easygoing nature will attract more considerate individuals. A gentle, friendly, and charming disposition is quite appealing as it creates romantic opportunity for your delight. Pleasantries are around you, so enjoy the good life.

Venus Trine/Sextile Venus—Harmonious, Congenial, and Affectionate Exchanges
Minor Influence with Venus Trine/Sextile Descendant

Social exchanges work to your advantage as your easygoing nature is well displayed. Others are agreeable and willing to compromise if need be. Although Venus attracts affectionate encounters your way, it doesn't offer romantic excitement. Enjoy the pleasant circumstances around you as they could always lead to something further. The sextile gains affection and approval as well.

Venus Square/Oppose Venus—Unaffectionate Exchanges, Moody Disposition
Minor Influence with Venus Square/Oppose Descendant

Social engagements may not turn out as planned. Your feelings are touchy, causing you to offend those around you. It would be wise not to overextend yourself or seek out affectionate exchanges. You are challenged to try to be agreeable and kind.

Mars Conjunct Venus—Social Exchanges, Romantic Desire
Minor Influence with Venus Conjunct Ascendant or Mars Conjunct Descendant

A Mars-Venus conjunction will always attract great attention. Active socializing may lead to an amorous exchange. Being emotionally receptive, the desires of Mars are enamored by the affections of Venus, lighting a romantic flame. The passion of Mars finds fulfillment through Venus (love). Mars is driven toward the attraction (Venus), both romantically and socially. As stressful situations ease, you may receive attention from romantic prospects. Positive Mars-Venus aspects are a strong pairing in the Love Relationship Formula. This loving dynamic creates an exciting moment that, if respected and nurtured, can last into the future.

Mars Trine/Sextile Venus—Favorable Social Exchanges and Romantic Desire
Minor Influence with Venus Trine/Sextile Ascendant or Mars Trine/Sextile Descendant

The smooth manner of relating to both sexes is very evident under favorable Mars trine Venus influences. You are motivated socially to connect with others, especially through parties or lively gatherings, and are well received with your charming persona. As you extend yourself, loving Venus is receptive to the desirous advances of Mars, creating quite a stir. One's flirtatious qualities are noticed, and a new romance is easily kindled. Amorous encounters entice a mutual exchange of excitement, as one's yearnings are met with great affection. Feeling romantically sexy, both parties are inspired to enjoy this meeting to its fullest, knowing that it may encourage a relationship to prosper into the future, especially if other supportive synastry connections are present.

Differences ease in ongoing relationships as loving feelings promote an affectionate exchange. Improving your personal appearance, perhaps with a new hairstyle, will enhance one's image. Remember that regardless of what transpires with onlookers, just having social/romantic appeal is a compliment. Romance is highlighted under Mars-Venus aspects, an essential combination in the Love Relationship Formula.

Mars Square/Oppose Venus—Unfavorable, Overly Aggressive Social and Romantic Exchanges
Minor Influence with Venus Square/Oppose Ascendant or Mars Square/Oppose Descendant

The lack of correspondence between couples is no more evident than when Mars squares Venus. Here, conflicting ideas of how to relate aggravate one another, causing separation as opposed to togetherness. What one needs (love) and what one desires (passion) do not blend easily. The loving feelings of Venus run into the blunt directness of Mars. A polite manner becomes easily irritated and quarrelsome. Romantic encounters made under this influence will eventually sour. Your date will not be what you expected, turning out to be something completely different than your imagined romance. An attraction may end up coming from the wrong person. The one you are interested in may be disagreeable or does not seem to notice you. A lack of passionate sex may only arouse arguments over the issues at hand. Releasing the emotional tensions through some type of lively activity, such as dancing, could be helpful. The idea in meeting someone is that the male and female energies need to get along socially, emotionally, and sexually. Otherwise, your work is cut out for you.

Jupiter Conjunct Venus—Encouraging Social Exchanges, Compliments, and Love
Minor Influence with Jupiter Conjunct Descendant

Since Jupiter wishes to expand upon the affections of Venus, the social/romantic ambiance is right for a positive connection to occur. Compliments and favors will come your way only to enhance your image. Feeling more attractive, you extend yourself to others with grace and confidence. Appreciation and love are expressed under favorable Jupiter-Venus aspects, which are a significant duo in the Love Relationship Formula. The strongest activation of this influence is seen in progressions and can lead to marriage.

Jupiter Trine/Sextile Venus—Encouraging Social Exchanges, Compliments, and Love
Minor Influence with Jupiter Trine/Sextile Descendant

It's a win/win situation as the two benefic planets unite in harmonious aspect. Jupiter will send compliments to your Venusian image, attracting great social/romantic appeal. A relaxed environment allows your feelings to flow, promoting a warm, inviting interaction with those around you. Social connections are optimistic, respectable, and full of goodwill. The rapport you establish with others may lead to a further engagement in the future. Your beauty and charm will inspire affectionate exchanges. Since Venus represents our persona, our self-esteem is highlighted by attracting only the best, socially and romantically. The positive image you have of yourself will only be more pronounced and attract what you deserve. The progressed aspects between Jupiter and Venus can instigate a marriage proposal, which is not surprising since auspicious Jupiter-Venus aspects are a vital part of the Love Relationship Formula.

Jupiter Square/Oppose Venus—Overwhelming Feelings and Social Life
Minor Influence with Jupiter Square/Oppose Descendant

Being overwhelmed with too much feeling is not helpful when you are hoping for a social/romantic exchange. Your image of how love is supposed to be is overrated, reeking havoc with your high expectations. Self-centered indulgences may prompt you to seek out more fun and romance, arousing your feelings toward sensual pleasures. You may long for more attention and approval, but not everything socially and romantically can turn out the way you envision. Emotions may need to be kept in check

Romanticism may entice you to engage in a love affair. But your efforts will soon be discarded as you realize this rendezvous is not what you thought. Emotional relationships may experience some upheaval as your partner is troubled, moody, hurt, or unsuitable for your needs. You may attract an inappropriate prospect, and have difficulty establishing a rapport with someone who interests you. Feeling personally frustrated, it would be in your best interest to relax and try to enjoy the niceties of life, as opposed to exploiting love.

Saturn Conjunct Venus—Serious or Unappreciated Love, Reserved Socializing
Minor Influence with Saturn Conjunct Descendant

Being at a social disadvantage is not a comfortable position from which to meet someone new. Your self-esteem may be low and a shy or awkward manner will be displayed. Personal insecurities may cause you to seem cold, thus causing others to be indifferent to your needs. The compliments or favors you are anticipating may not be forthcoming. It would be best to keep a low profile, especially since the odds are not in your favor. Spending time with familiar faces or having a quiet day by yourself is recommended. Be patient with a current relationship, for your partner is not able to appreciate you fully during this time. Couples usually don't meet under Venus-Saturn transits or progressions. However, they do stabilize relationships or get married under such influences, for this is where you need to acquire a serious attitude about love. I find more often than not that men in particular will settle down and/or get married when they are experiencing a Saturn-Venus crossing on either hard or soft angles. This combination in the Love Relationship Formula promotes a solid union, along with other favorable influences.

Saturn Trine/Sextile Venus—Serious, Stabilized Love, Reserved Socializing
Minor Influence with Saturn Trine/Sextile Descendant

Encounters under favorable Saturn-Venus transits may still experience some inhibitions. However, if you don't have a lot of expectations, and uphold a cordial appearance, the meeting should go relatively fine. A calm, responsible approach offers more security. You may find more support from ongoing relationships as there is a feeling of familiarity that allows you to relax and appreciate your loved one. Serious relationships are established under positive Saturn-Venus aspects, which are a solidifying influence in the Love Relationship Formula.

Saturn Square/Oppose Venus—Serious, Boring, or Rejected Love
Minor Influence with Saturn Square/Oppose Descendant

Although you may long for a secure love, this is not the time for a new romantic situation. Your advances will be rejected, which will leave you feeling even lonelier than you did before. Don't expect any romantic attention from others as you may not feel or look your best at this time. The discontent you feel socially and emotionally will require patience until this transit passes. It is best to keep your own company and, if you're already involved, be tolerant of a present relationship that is lacking any excitement. If you do attract someone, they may not be able to fully appreciate you or you them. Thus you will end up dissatisfied and continue to yearn for more. The solid relationship situation you long for will one day be there.

Uranus Conjunct Venus—Exciting, Unpredictable Attraction
Minor Influence with Uranus Conjunct Descendant

Surprise developments in one's social or love life may occur when Uranus conjoins Venus. Romantic sparks fly, creating an exciting attraction. Two people meeting under such influences will feel a magnetic enticement. A past love may want to reconcile with you. Unusual or rebellious encounters could be disruptive. Channel that restless energy by attending lively functions. Your monetary situation may experience sudden changes that allow you to enjoy life more. If nothing but an appealing social encounter happens, consider yourself fortunate. Romantic fascination transpires under Uranus-Venus aspects, which are an irresistible pairing in the Love Relationship Formula.

Uranus Trine/Sextile Venus—Positive, Exciting Attraction
Minor Influence with Uranus Trine/Sextile Descendant

Attraction is sparked by our sudden interest in another individual. We find ourselves in a moment of romantic intrigue that allows us to forget ourselves and feel a sense of rapturous wonder with another. Especially under Uranus trine Venus, a captivating attraction can occur that will sweep you off your feet. Out of the blue, an unexpected meeting will keep you gazing into the sparkling eyes of your romantic prospect. New feelings arise that will be explored through this exciting encounter. Old emotions will not be a deterrent, as a radiant, effervescent you is quite appealing. Being a part of the social scene will enable you to meet up with a significant someone who fascinates you. Since this vibrant attraction creates a lasting impression, there is more of an opportunity for a relationship to develop. A friendly new face, whose presence is short-lived, may inspire you to move in a promising direction. An ongoing relationship may experience new feelings that need to be explored. The sextile is subtler, yet still attracts favorable attention. The return of a past love during this influence indicates a positive reconnection. Yet both parties must be willing to resume the relationship in order for a successful tie to occur.

Better financial conditions will allow you to spend money on your appearance and enjoy lively social functions. The idea behind this transit is to bring out your best through compliments, love, and support. This highly significant Uranus-Venus combination in the Love Relationship Formula promotes a truly enchanting attraction.

Uranus Square/Oppose Venus—Unexpected, Unpredictable Attraction
Minor Influence with Uranus Square/Oppose Descendant

Love and affection find us in unexpected ways. At times there is an unstable variable that leaves us in more of a predicament as opposed to a promising romance. When transiting Uranus is in adverse influence to Venus, the outcome of love is unpredictable. The attraction will appear to be strong, but other factors may lead to uncertainty. Unless other influences warrant some type of stability, this romance may end almost as soon as it started. This proves that attraction is not enough to keep a relationship going. Attraction invites the meeting of two people, yet what follows could be anyone's guess under difficult Venus-Uranus aspects. In most cases, because of a dynamic magnetism, a fling or brief romance will develop that has no future, even though this meeting may affect you personally.

This erratic influence could also instigate the meeting of a past love. Chances are that your paths are not meant to merge together again as you both have grown in separate ways. Since Venus is a social planet, you may also find the Uranian force impeding your social life, making it either difficult to connect with anyone or only encountering people who do not interest you. Unusual contacts will come and go. Ongoing relationships could experience a temporary or permanent separation. A restless spirit could cause you or your partner to break off a trying relationship. Take the space and time to pursue individualized goals, then share these experiences with your partner if possible. This is one transit where love difficulties and financial difficulties may go hand in hand. Erratic spending may not help acquire the romantic goal. You could spend all the money in the world, yet love will still elude you.

Neptune Conjunct Venus—Idealistic, Platonic, or Deceptive Love
Minor Influence with Neptune Conjunct Descendant

The romantic encounter with Neptune and Venus depicts a scenario of heavenly love, as our dreams become our reality. Visions of the ideal soulmate come to mind, clouding our good judgment in an amorous encounter. The perfect relationship somehow seems attainable, and then drifts from our grasp. Rarely does the illusiveness of Neptune allow us to experience what we know to be true in love. Could it be that our expectations are unrealistic? In most cases a nebulous romance may never manifest into a substantial union, unless you accept a platonic alliance. When meeting under such influences, the spiritual connection presides over the relationship. If you can appreciate this bond for what it is, without expectations, you may enjoy the rapport of this union. Nevertheless, you could still be deceived if you fall into the throws of romance with abandon. Let a truthful ideal be your guide.

You may be attached to someone who is absorbed in their own pursuits and not there for you. Yet you are not inclined to be assertive, hoping that all will work out well. But the fact is that this vague connection could undermine your relationship if you do not attempt to interact with your partner. The dream phase will eventually dissolve, hopefully leaving you spiritually enhanced and not emotionally drained.

Neptune Trine/Sextile Venus—Favorable Idealistic, Spiritual, and Platonic Love
Minor Influence with Neptune Trine/Sextile Descendant

Although we are subjected to the illusive world of Neptune, favorable transits involving Neptune and Venus usually denote spiritual connections with others. Platonic love can always be a welcomed companion as long as expectations are kept in check and intimacy is not overdone. Still, a carefree attitude that somehow life will continue as planned is experienced. The ideal romance is sometimes described by Neptune trine Venus, yet only if this is not based on fantasy. Even then, the couple will most likely experience a platonic love. The term soulmate is sometimes attributed to the spiritual connection one feels with another. This bond has passed the portals of time and space, thus reuniting us with someone we have known from a past life. The mistake people make is that although you meet, you may not be destined to have a long-term relationship. Sometimes being good friends with someone is better than being their lover. We all must learn to appreciate relationship boundaries no matter what they are.

You can bet there will be times in your ongoing relationship when it temporarily becomes nonsexual. During these periods you want to develop the friendship of the relationship. What happens at times is that you feel you are drifting away from your partner, like two ships passing in the night. Some people begin to feel that they are falling out of love with their partner. Both need to develop the spiritual side of the relationship. If this cannot happen, the relationship may dissipate. One or both parties may decide the grass is greener on the other side. They will be equally deceived there, too! What you need to think about here is at what cost do you consider leaving your relationship. If implementing a spiritual approach does not work, then it may be time to let go. Due to the fact that this is a positive aspect, you have an opportunity to direct your relationship toward a more compassionate union that inspires a lifetime soulmate.

Neptune Square/Oppose Venus—Platonic, Deceptive Love/Fatal Attractions
Minor Influence with Neptune Square/Oppose Descendant

Men and women alike can be seduced by the sexual intrigue of fatal attractions. And there is none more deceptive than when tricky Neptune is in adverse aspect to the planet of love, Venus. It is not so much because we are encountering an illusion when Neptune influences Venus, but because we find ourselves in the midst of heavenly love and then we are totally deceived as the everlasting romantic fantasy turns out to be an emotionally devastating experience.

The problem with Neptune-Venus transits is that you start painting a romantic picture around someone that you feel attracted to and it's unrealistic. You are not seeing the person for who they really are, but for who you want them to be. Before this deception happens, you have convinced yourself that this is the one! Unaware of the romantic betrayal taking place, you proceed with becoming involved. When the veil of illusion has lifted, you finally see that you have been emotionally betrayed and are devastated.

Adverse Venus-Neptune transits herald imperfect results every time. What it teaches us is to be realistic in love, to attract stability into our lives instead of illusion. One can never be too careful in establishing a relationship with another.

Pluto Conjunct Venus—Intense Feelings and Deep Love
Minor Influence with Pluto Conjunct Descendant

When we experience a romantic encounter with the influence of a Pluto-Venus conjunction, our deepest feelings surface. The intensity that allows us to merge with another becomes an all-consuming love. If other favorable transits are present, this connection may last a lifetime.

You will find that personal feelings cause you to reflect on your love life, as you yearn for that deep, meaningful relationship. In alienating yourself from others, you are better able to understand such heartfelt emotions. An emotional, psychological transition will help you release old, buried issues. It may be such that repressed feelings from a past love will need to be resolved so that you can be open to the next relationship. This important Venus-Pluto aspect is a powerful combination in the Love Relationship Formula.

Pluto Trine/Sextile Venus—Deep, Meaningful Love and Relating
Minor Influence with Pluto Trine/Sextile Descendant

Pluto-Venus transits in favorable aspect encourage fated soulmate connections. Thus a longing for the perfect union will motivate you to seek out that special someone. Here, powerful influences will drive you toward a destined meeting. A like-minded spirit will bring the two of you in sync. You will be profoundly aware of the meaningful rapport. A deep friendship or a significant romance may develop that forces you to experience the gamut of emotions. You may find yourself overwhelmed with intense feelings of love. Because this is indicated to be a fated connection, if other planetary factors are supportive, this meeting has an opportunity to last a lifetime. A deep, evolved love will continue to inspire further growth. Harmonious Venus-Pluto aspects are a significant part of the Love Relationship Formula.

Pluto Square/Oppose Venus—Intense, Obsessive Love
Minor Influence with Pluto Square/Oppose Descendant

Meeting under a Pluto-Venus square will definitely intensify your feelings in a relationship. However, you may also become totally obsessed with the object of your affection. Because of the adversity of this aspect, you will be emotionally and sexually drawn toward this person, feeling a compelling drive to pursue until they are yours. You can become so fixated that your life starts revolving around the interest of your desire. Occasionally, the opposite occurs as someone you meet could become totally obsessed with you.

Either way, this forceful drive toward intimacy is not well received. What starts as an intense pursuit usually does not work out. Obsessive love that is unrewarded can lead to insane tendencies such as stalking and in extreme cases rape. The perpetrator is not willing to face up to their own issues and therefore projects them onto another, committing a horrific act. Beware of fatal attractions. This is obviously not what one cares to experience. It would be better to be alone.

The dichotomy with Pluto-Venus transits is that the influence will bring to the surface all of your buried feelings along with an overwhelming desire to involve yourself in a deep, meaningful relationship. Yet, this transit will not bring you the social/romantic satisfaction that you are looking for in another. So what is the purpose? These cosmic persuasions want to bring to the surface buried feelings from the past so that once and for all you can purge them from your life. Whatever old memory you have been holding on to, it's time to let go. These influences will also allow you to understand your deeper emotional and sexual longings. This will help establish a greater understanding of your intimate fears and desires. To do this, Pluto on some level will alienate you from others so you don't have a choice but to deal with past emotional issues and sexual yearnings. In the end you are transformed with a whole new peaceful outlook on love and values.

If you are in a relationship and experiencing a Pluto-Venus transit, allow for a lot of space and pursue soul-searching activities. You must get in touch with your deeper feelings under this transit. Otherwise you may lose your partner so that you finally do get in touch with those feelings one way or another.

Mars Transits/Progressions/Solar Arc Directions

Mars Conjunct Sun—Motivated, Passionate Goals
Minor Influence with Sun Conjunct Ascendant

The pride of Mars-Sun takes command in the pursuit of one's desires. You will be driven to assert yourself and initiate a response from the object of your affection. A challenge can be stimulating. Being an appealing leader and not a thug will win followers. Set an example for other romantic suitors. Positive Mars-Sun aspects are an active duo in the Love Relationship Formula.

Mars Trine/Sextile Sun—Successful, Passionate Goals
Minor Influence with Sun Trine/Sextile Ascendant

Your social circle will welcome your commanding appearance. You eagerly acknowledge friends and admirers. Your vitality and sex drive will encourage you to seek out the pleasures in life. A suave approach could bring a romantic exchange. If aroused passions are reciprocated, a genteel manner will be met with approval. Success is highlighted under favorable Mars-Sun aspects, which are an important combination in the Love Relationship Formula.

Mars Square/Oppose Sun—Frustrated, Passionate Goals
Minor Influence with Sun Square/Oppose Ascendant

Aggressive advances could trigger much dissent in partnership exchanges. Lusty behavior may need to be tempered to win any respect from others. Avoid taking risks as an impulsive, feisty nature will only aggravate those around you. A physical workout will channel this rowdy behavior.

Mars Conjunct Moon—Aggressive, Passionate Emotions
Minor Influence with Moon Conjunct Ascendant

Directing our emotions to get the most out of life can be quite challenging during this transit. Mood swings may override good judgment, causing a disruptive situation to occur. A restless nature may motivate you to accomplish set goals, yet not everything may turn out as planned. Lashing out in an argumentative manner will not benefit you. A passionate exchange may arise, but only with the right person.

Mars Trine/Sextile Moon—Passionate Emotions, Successful Actions
Minor Influence with Moon Trine/Sextile Ascendant

Your assertive nature will get results as Mars initiates a positive course of action. This can be a good time to start anything. Romantic advances in most cases will be well received. Passionate feelings are highlighted, especially in more amorous settings. A smooth approach brings about improved situations. Men may be successful in the company of women. The sextile will be productive as well.

Mars Square/Oppose Moon—Aggressive, Irritated, and Angry Emotions
Minor Influence with Moon Square/Oppose Ascendant

Impatience or a temperamental attitude will not fare well with others. You will need to direct this emotionally volatile influence, as mood swings may cause you to lash out when you least expect it. This is not a good time to start anything. You will find your plans going awry and causing much upset. Romantic advances will be rejected. Women may be overly emotional, demanding, or ill, and may require some assistance.

Mars Conjunct Mercury—Lively, Aggressive Communications
Minor Influence with Mercury Conjunct Ascendant

An active mind will promote intellectual exchanges. You will be ambitious about connecting with others and expressing your opinion. Enjoy others' company, but make sure your direct approach does not lead to rash behavior. Being overly aggressive is not attractive. You may need to take decisive action due to unexpected news.

Mars Trine/Sextile Mercury—Favorable, Lively, Aggressive Communications
Minor Influence with Mercury Trine/Sextile Ascendant

Mentally decisive, you will initiate a positive connection with those around you. Smooth verbal execution will stimulate more social interaction. You are apt to strike up a rapport with someone who is your intellectual equal. Motivating news will encourage you toward more productivity.

Mars Square/Oppose Mercury—Aggressive, Opinionated, and Angry Communication
Minor Influence with Mercury Square/Oppose Ascendant

You may not have success with new encounters. Others are not inclined to appreciate what you have to say as your aggressiveness arouses animosity. Impatience and misunderstandings create aggravation. Because you feel entitled to arrogantly voice your opinion, you may create a bad impression. Distressing news may be disruptive, but you will not fare well in lashing out at others. Try to keep a handle on your temper and wait for another time to approach disturbing situations if possible.

Mars Conjunct Mars—Aggressive Action/Passion
Minor Influence with Mars Conjunct Ascendant

Mars wishes to conquer, but its overly aggressive actions do not fare well with society at large. A disagreeable or hostile situation could erupt that leaves you feeling drained. Meet up with challenges directly so as to make them right. Your desire nature will create a strong restlessness that needs to be channeled. New acquaintances may feel threatened by your forceful approach. Your demands may be rejected. You will gain by being assertive yet compromising. Vigorous sex with a familiar partner can be satisfying.

Mars Trine/Sextile Mars—Positive Action/Desirous Passion
Minor Influence With Mars Trine/Sextile Ascendant

You may take aggressive action toward fulfilling your desires. Goals can be accomplished in a very expeditious manner. A sexual exchange may work to your advantage and be quite satisfying if you are longing for more passion in your life. A decisive, zestful approach addresses challenges directly. The more subtle sextile will still offer a lively exchange.

Mars Square/Oppose Mars—Excessive, Aggressive Action/Passion
Minor Influence with Mars Square/Oppose Ascendant

Overly aggressive actions may need to be tempered as emotions flare. Arguments and fights could easily erupt and leave you feeling drained. Although you are impatiently desiring a passionate exchange, sexual advances are abrupt and excessive. There is risk of infection even with protected sex. You may also experience hostility and possible rejection. If you're with the right partner, you may direct this energy toward lusty passion.

Jupiter Conjunct Mars—Zestful Drive, Passionate Desire
Minor Influence with Jupiter Conjunct Ascendant

Looking for adventure, your passionate drive may persuade you to extend yourself romantically. You will be well received. You may enjoy this arousal with a lusty spirit. But be clear about your motives, otherwise overindulgence may lead to a night of passion without substance. Encouraging Mars-Jupiter aspects are an influential coupling in the Love Relationship Formula.

Jupiter Trine/Sextile Mars—Positive, Zestful Drive, Passionate Desire
Minor Influence with Jupiter Trine/Sextile Ascendant

A highly recommendable time to meet is when Jupiter is in trine aspect to Mars. A zestful, sexy mood will attract prospects your way. The desirous Mars is greeted with romantic opportunity. As you are feeling good and looking good, chances are the encounter will work out to your advantage. Even the sextile is noted to stir up a passionate interest as favorable Mars-Jupiter aspects are a significant pairing in the Love Relationship Formula. A new relationship started at this time may reap many benefits in the future.

Jupiter Square/Oppose Mars—Unproductive, Impulsive Desires
Minor Influence with Jupiter Square/Oppose Ascendant

Although you may feel a restless urge to pursue romance, impulsive desires may be risky and not turn out as planned. Ideas about rough sex may not get you anywhere on a first meeting. Overextending yourself to others may be met with hostility. Unproductive results may leave you feeling even more frustrated. It would be better to channel your energy into another type of physical outlet. An ongoing relationship may enjoy magnified passions with discretion.

Saturn Conjunct Mars—Blocked Desires/Responsible Actions
Minor Influence with Saturn Conjunct Ascendant

People don't usually meet under Saturn-Mars influences due to the fact that Saturn lowers the vitality and passion. Hence, there isn't the drive to pursue romantic prospects.

Even if you were to extend yourself, you may not be well received, as Saturn will provoke a rejection of your affectionate advances.

What Saturn-Mars influences can do is give you a serious perspective on life. Since you are not being allowed to scatter your forces, you will find yourself concentrating on very specific goals that involve more responsibility. The focus is on work, not romance.

Many times when a person is under a Saturn-Mars transit, progression, or solar arc, and is involved in a relationship, they may feel that they are falling out of love with their partner. There is limited or no desire to have sex. Since the male libido is lowered, men in particular become worried and have difficulty understanding why they are not sexually attracted to their partner while they are under this influence. It's advisable to let the transit pass before making any impulsive decisions about ending your relationship.

Saturn Trine/Sextile Mars—Limited Desires/Responsible, Planned Actions
Minor Influence with Saturn Trine/Sextile Ascendant

Here again passions are limited, therefore you will not feel the impulse to pursue romance. Your work accomplishments, however, can be quite productive. You may find yourself acquiring a more realistic perspective on what you want in your love life. You will acquire results through patience and planning.

Saturn Square/Oppose Mars—Blocked Desires, Rejection, Abuse, Difficult Responsibilities
Minor Influence with Saturn Square/Oppose Ascendant

Due to a lack of motivation, a person usually does not feel the desire to be romantic. If they do, however, feel the need to extend themselves, they may experience a total rejection from the object of their affection. It is best to keep a reserved position, for overextending yourself can lead to trouble. Others will not take kindly to any aggressiveness. If you do experience a rejection, try not to take it personally so your situation doesn't end up in an argument or fight. If you are in an ongoing relationship, do not push your luck, otherwise a break-up may be in the offing. Channel this energy toward constructive goals.

Uranus Conjunct Mars—Overly Excited Passion and Hostility
Minor Influence with Uranus Conjunct Ascendant

Although you might exude an electric presence, the passionate encounter you attract is not likely to endure. Uranus conjunct Mars is just too volatile to support a long-term relationship. The erraticism of Uranus joins with the aggressiveness of Mars, creating a spontaneity that could turn hostile. You may encounter an unusual attraction, but this exhilarating meeting could end abruptly. A detached attitude will not fare well with any new meetings. If you are feeling the need to move in an independent direction, you may decide to terminate any relationship that you have either outgrown or that has become destructive. Unfortunately, meeting under a Mars-Uranus influence will unleash such volatile conditions. Taking the reins of your life is a constructive move against violent behavior. Be careful of attracting agitating circumstances with the casual passerby.

Uranus Trine/Sextile Mars—Exciting, Passionate Opportunity
Minor Influence with Uranus Trine/Sextile Ascendant

Where adverse transits involving Uranus and Mars usually lead to an affair or hostile situation, a new relationship venture started under a favorable Uranus-Mars transit has an opportunity to succeed, especially if other harmonious transits are present. Uranus will encourage you to be spontaneous in expressing your own unique self, which those around you will find quite appealing. You will be assertive in connecting with new people. Personal limitations will diminish, making it easier for you to meet that special someone. Many people will be charmed by your dynamic personality. As sparks fly, your excitement will be fueled by thoughts of a passionate rendezvous. Uranus emphasizes a new beginning toward an intimate exchange. Any stimulating encounters will be pursued. In most cases, the directness of Mars in trine aspect to Uranus will allow you to obtain what you want. Someone will most likely be there for the taking as your allure is captivating. The sextile is less enthralling, yet others will still notice your magnetic presence and wish to link up with you. Be ready for the attention you will receive.

Uranus Square/Oppose Mars—Love affairs/Spontaneous Sex/Hostility
Minor Influence with Uranus Square/Oppose Ascendant

Impulsive love usually leads to an affair. That is the impetus behind adverse Uranus-Mars transits. Under such influences, you feel the restless need to go out and perhaps show your wild side. The aggressive passion of Mars is spurred on by the excitement of Uranus. A tempestuous affair can easily be the result. If you are in a committed relationship, unexpected sex could be a welcomed break from your normal routine, with your partner that is.

Outside of a committed relationship, I do not encourage this sexual interlude. Uranus-Mars transits may provide a certain stimuli to have sex, but the planetary energies are so volatile that there is little chance, if any, of this intimate exchange having a future. This cosmic influence indicates complete reversals. Suddenly you meet and just as suddenly it could end. Even if a relationship were to ensue, eventually this influence would cause differences, arguments, and explosive situations that would be very difficult to resolve. Erratic behavior fuels a stormy relationship, which could become quite destructive. The spur-of-the-moment involvement turns into tremendous sexual tension that splits the affair apart. If you are in a current relationship that is becoming violently turbulent or that you have outgrown, you may want to break off the union completely. You may find your partner impersonal and uncooperative. Magnetic attractions may seem great in the moment, but if pursued as a relationship they may have a hidden agenda filled with sudden hostility and anger.

Neptune Conjunct Mars—
Illusive, Passionate Ideals and Desires, Possible Disappointment
Minor Influence with Neptune Conjunct Ascendant

The passions that are aroused under an illusive encounter may need to be closely followed. Your mysterious charm will attract popularity, but hidden feelings could lead you to be enticed by the unknown. What seems to be a romantic interlude could easily turn to disappointment, unless your passionate ideals match those of your partner. Here, both of you could enjoy an enchanting adventure. Exercising a level of integrity will keep you from drifting toward an unscrupulous rendezvous. Self-gratification may draw you to scandalous characters. Putting one's trust in another when the disguise is soon to be revealed is toying with temptation. The erotic lure of passion is intriguing yet dangerous. Unrealistic desires or seduction could lure you toward deception. The environment you succumb to will either take you into a magical world or lead you astray. Only you can make that choice.

It is best to participate in creative activities. Entertainment, especially involving music, the performing arts, or theatre, is encouraged. If the world of illusion interests you, maintaining high ideals will protect your reputation.

Neptune Trine/Sextile Mars—Inspiring, Illusive, and Passionate Ideals/Desires
Minor Influence with Neptune Trine/Sextile Ascendant

Being driven toward an illusive pursuit does not always reap the benefits for which we are hoping. Even under positive Neptune-Mars transits, we still encounter the cloud of illusion. However, more idyllic conditions can enhance a favorable meeting. The romanticism of Neptune is greeted with the passion of Mars. But you need to keep your wits about you, aiming toward pure motives that honor your integrity. To be carried away in an erotic escapade may not support an alliance into the future. Although the temptation may be there, know what you are getting into before accepting an invitation.

Harmonious Neptune-Mars transits are more easily handled in an ongoing relationship. You may commence with a romantic evening. Candle-lit dinners and a midnight swim are persuading antidotes to inspire a warm, intimate evening. Avoid evasive communication and create the satisfying ambiance that you both want to experience.

Neptune Square/Oppose Mars—Illusive, Disappointing Ideals and Desires
Minor Influence with Neptune Square/Oppose Ascendant

The lure of erotic love is laced with deception under adverse Neptune-Mars transits. Yielding to no one, the mysterious passions are unleashed. Seduction will be enticing, but will surely disappoint. Nefarious encounters could lead you close to danger. Sexual deception will erode your trust. In the worst-case scenario, sexual perversion, assault, or rape could occur. Do not acquiesce to the pressures of someone's compelling desires. Those with demanding passions may be reeking with dishonor. You might experience loneliness and disappointment, but hopefully you will have maintained your integrity.

Pluto Conjunct Mars—Intense, Passionate Drive
Minor Influence with Pluto Conjunct Ascendant

The pairing between Mars and Pluto may create an intense drive that will compel you to take action. From a positive perspective, this powerful force encourages you to seek out a desirous involvement with another. Although passion will need to be expressed, the Plutonian influences wish to transform any deep, hidden feelings. The moment of ardent intimacy awakens the soul to a more profound experience in being with another. This shared sexual experience instigates an emotional evolvement that will only strengthen the bond between you. Secret passions, however, could lead you down the wrong road. Manipulative power plays may erode good judgment as you are persuaded toward undesirable behavior. Deep-rooted issues could also sway emotions in an un-wanted direction, causing resistance. If this is the case, your partner may need some guidance to transcend destructive patterns.

Pluto Trine/Sextile Mars—Successful, Passionate Drive
Minor Influence with Pluto Trine/Sextile Ascendant

Favorable Pluto-Mars aspects will intensify your deep sexual desires. This over-whelming and determined feeling will zero in on the object of your affection and surely lead to a passionate exchange. Usually, both are willing. The ardent passion emanating from this planetary combination is experienced as the depth of souls merging in the night. Secret cravings become known as they arouse you to the height of passion. Al-though this driving force pushes you toward a driving intimate exchange, what you feel and experience actually become more important. Pluto-Mars transits will certainly ini-tiate arousal, but they will also encourage you to be transformed through the sexual ex-perience. Pluto is our planet of personal growth. It does not just seek out intense sex, but a shared sexual experience that will bring you to a greater awareness of evolving through intimacy.

Mars initiates love to secure an intense involvement with another (Pluto). Deep erotic feelings are acted upon. Passion (Mars) is transformed (Pluto) through a mean-ingful experience with another.

Pluto Square/Oppose Mars—Crazed, Passionate Drive or Sexual Denial
Minor Influence with Pluto Square/Oppose Ascendant

Assertive Mars coupled with the intensity of Pluto will compel you to be driven to-ward an end. This adverse influence will either force you into deep sexual denial or ag-gressive sexual desire. Being that this compelling force is not easily controlled, you could reek havoc on your life. Love games, power plays, jealousy, possessiveness, and manipulative tendencies may override good judgment. Sexual impulses may need to be kept in check. Putting pressure on someone to go along with your desires will only be met with resistance. Sexual power plays may seem to entice what you want, but later turn to sexual alienation. Erotic seduction could also lead to hostile, aggressive behav-ior. Trying to conquer your love interest to satisfy your sexual desires is not the idea be-hind sex. For in sex, there needs to be mutual consent for both individuals to be fulfilled. Here, selfish desire (Mars) wants a sexual exchange (Pluto). Since ultimatums in relationships do not fare well, I would not seek out this option. The resistance you will encounter will cause you to reevaluate your strategy toward intimacy. Sexual denial may allow you to transform your aggressive desires, thus leading to a more promising sexual exchange in the future. *If you have to manipulate love to get what you want, you have lost sight of the ultimate goal—a deep, meaningful, intimate exchange.*

Jupiter Transits, Progressions, and Solar Arc Directions

Jupiter Conjunct Sun—Supported Goals/Good Fortune

Better relations with the male sex are noted when Jupiter is in aspect to the Sun. A positive outlook supports your plans, especially in dealings with men. You will find them more cooperative and encouraging. An enthusiastic spirit is appealing to those around you. The confidence you project will attract appreciation your way from important individuals. Be open to exploring opportunities that will improve your status in life. Your ambitions are enhanced under Jupiter-Sun aspects, an important part of the Love Relationship Formula.

Jupiter Trine/Sextile Sun—Highly Supported Goals/Good Fortune

Great relations with men are inspired by a favorable transit from Jupiter to the Sun. The male sex in particular is happy to agree with your agenda, offering support along the way where needed. Feeling confident, you will attract the generosity of those around you. Important, successful individuals will recognize and appreciate your aims. Extending yourself will only further your standing in life. Enjoy the opportunity to gain the respect you desire. This uplifting Jupiter-Sun influence is a significant combination in the Love Relationship Formula.

Jupiter Square/Oppose Sun—Overrated Ideals

An overly confident nature is bound to lead to risky investments, especially with the male gender. What appears to be a good connection may be based on egotistical values of one kind or another. Inflated expectations are costly and will leave you feeling drained. Others are indifferent to your philosophy. They lack the awareness and support you feel you deserve. Try curbing self-centered desires. A more tolerant attitude is needed.

Jupiter Conjunct Moon—Optimistic Feelings/Good Results

The optimistic spirit of Jupiter encourages favorable relations. A happy mood will ease any stress and create a wonderful environment in which to connect with a special woman. There is an opportunity to reconcile any existing differences. A positive outlook puts luck on your side. As Jupiter-Moon aspects are part of the Love Relationship Formula, extend yourself, knowing that a confident you will be greeted warmly.

Jupiter Trine/Sextile Moon—Optimistic Feelings/Very Good Results

Harmonious relations with women are indicated when Jupiter is in favorable aspect to the Moon. This optimistic influence will improve your chances of enjoying the company of a special woman. A lively spirit will create an ambiance of happy times together. Jupiter has a way of affecting our mood to ease the pressure of a long day and allow us to look at the bright side. Positive, shared experiences could set a date off in the right direction. For ongoing relationships, this is an excellent transit for reconciling differences as well, which is why Jupiter-Moon aspects are part of the Love Relationship Formula.

Jupiter Square/Oppose Moon—Optimistic, Overextended Emotions

You may want to relax and enjoy yourself, but you will find yourself nurturing the emotional needs of another. Jupiter expands upon the emotions in a disagreeable way, making it quite taxing for those involved. Dealings with women may require more time and patience. Think of constructive ways to channel any emotional stress. Nevertheless, a sense of optimism will exist that will make the situation tolerable.

Jupiter Conjunct Mercury—Optimistic, Favorable Communications

Optimistic feelings will steer you in a positive direction. New contacts may assist you at the moment as well as in the future. Good communications will enliven your spirit, making you attractive to others. Prestigious connections are to be enjoyed and may enhance your position in life. Personal and economic expansion is greeted with success. Jupiter-Mercury aspects are an essential combination in the Love Relationship Formula.

Jupiter Trine/Sextile Mercury—Optimistic, Favorable, and Supportive Communications

Uplifting communications allow you to look at your future with a favorable outlook. New meetings will inspire you intellectually and personally. Ongoing relations will be more appealing as issues are reconciled. You will most likely prosper from decisions made at this time. You are optimistic about your progress and will also fare well with business dealings. Under Jupiter-Mercury aspects, a necessary coupling in the Love Relationship Formula, you will gain from extending yourself as you are well received by those around you.

Jupiter Square/Oppose Mercury—Overly Optimistic Communications

The intellectual rapport you are longing for is lacking. You may not share the same philosophy with others, making conversation somewhat strained, yet you may have to be entertaining for one reason or another. Unrealistic expectations may have you biting off more than you can chew. Although you are feeling confident that all will work out well, this may not be the case if you throw caution to the wind. I am all for a positive attitude, but to guard against mental highs that end up being disappointing lows, do attempt to keep everything in perspective. After you have overinvested yourself, you will realize you should have exercised good judgment.

Jupiter Conjunct Jupiter—Fortunate Advantage, Goodwill from Others

Since Jupiter tends to bring good fortune our way, when it is in positive aspect to itself, luck is on our side. New individuals met under this auspicious influence will greet you with respect. A more confident you will be on the receiving end of favors, good-will, and recognition. Your ideas will be accepted by those around you, as you attract opportunities your way. Although Jupiter-Jupiter transits are not known to be romantic, with such a lucky pair you may persuade your love interest to gladly accompany you. Any differences, especially in ongoing relationships, can be reconciled at this time.

Jupiter Trine/Sextile Jupiter—Fortunate Advantage, Goodwill from Others

You will attract auspicious opportunities that allow you to enjoy the good life. Support and backing will come from those around you. New individuals will honor you with favors, recognition, and goodwill. Your uplifting philosophy will be delightfully accepted, along with a newfound confidence. Since you will be well received by others, luck is on your side with romantic interests as well. You may benefit long-term from the good fortune that you reap as you have faith in your personal and business investments. You gain from reconciling any differences. The sextile also promises good fortune.

Jupiter Square/Oppose Jupiter—Overly Optimistic Goals

You may need to quell an overconfident nature as your tendency is to take on too much. Some goodwill is indicated, but your luck may be short-lived. Try not to overestimate your potential. You will have difficulty delivering on exaggerated promises. Great expectations may not come to pass, especially with new acquaintances. This is not the time to put your faith in anyone. New alliances may promise to be costly, personally and financially. Areas of personal growth may offer some benefit, but any undertakings are suspect. Delays may actually work out to your advantage, as you have more time to explore expansive options. If you can manage the expense of travel plans, then they can be pursued. Channel that optimism so you approach everything in moderation.

Saturn Conjunct Jupiter—Expansion of Long-Term Goals

A responsible attitude will allow you to advance toward a more secure future. This particular pairing of Saturn and Jupiter, an influential combination in the Love Relationship Formula, seeks out long-term goals that offer greater stability. If these influences are occurring in your fifth (romance), seventh (close relationships), or eighth (partnerships) house sector, there may be an opportunity to commit to a relationship situation. New individuals met at this time may be important, successful, and wealthy. Expanding your reputation through serious, ambitious goals will attract support your way. Older persons may be of great assistance to you.

Saturn Trine/Sextile Jupiter—Favorable Expansion of Long-Term Goals

Expanding your life experience to a more progressive and substantial outlook will attract a more stable foundation for your future. Solid relationship developments may occur with important, professional, and wealthy people. If one of these planetary influences is occurring in your fifth (romance), seventh (close relationships), or eighth (partnerships) house sector, there may be an opportunity to commit to a lasting relationship. An enduring bond will be established under favorable Saturn-Jupiter aspects, a combination in the Love Relationship Formula that enhances long-term security.

Saturn Square/Oppose Jupiter—Working Hard to Secure the Future

Work demands will require most of your time and energy, as you lay a solid foundation for your future. This is not the time to extend yourself socially. You may need to accept extra responsibilities that limit your freedom, but may lead to greater abundance. Applying yourself toward future aims may be the only avenue that makes you feel secure.

Uranus Conjunct Jupiter—Unexpected Good Fortune

An optimistic attitude attracts good fortune your way. The Uranus-Jupiter conjunction, especially in the fifth, seventh, or eighth house sector, may unexpectedly bring a romantic prospect into your life. A new, dynamic individual could cross your path. This person could be influential in encouraging you toward being individualistic, which will promote a new cycle of growth. You may also win the approval of others, generating an upscale crowd to satisfy your unique image. The odds of luck are in your favor. Be open to great expectations.

Uranus Trine/Sextile Jupiter—Wonderful, Unexpected Good Fortune

Luck strikes when Jupiter is in trine aspect to Uranus. Good fortune may offer new possibilities with romantic prospects, especially if one of the planets is activated in the fifth, seventh, or eighth house sector. A fortunate meeting is bound to occur that is quite stimulating and may offer a new direction in your life that is very appealing. As Jupiter wants you to expand your horizons, Uranus will suddenly open the door of opportunity. Be willing to extend yourself and make the most of your circumstances as change works to your advantage. You will most likely be well received as you gain the attention of those around you. In expressing your unique self, your buoyant nature will win the favor of important people. They may be willing to share their riches with you.

The sextile may be less exciting, but will nonetheless lift your spirits. A progressive attitude will land you in the company of sophisticated individuals.

Uranus Square/Oppose Jupiter—Overrated Good Fortune, Unfavorable Luck

When luck is not on our side, we need to be careful about taking chances. Our tendency with the presence of an adverse Uranus-Jupiter transit is to take the risk, yet the odds for a favorable outcome may not be in our favor. This enthusiastic transit indicates that promises will not be delivered. Therefore it would not be worth your while to proceed in this overrated direction. Someone's wild persuasions will cost you. A new individual may give the impression of success and trustworthiness, but turn out to be the wrong person for you to be involved with. You may only be able to rely on honorable connections. Guard against overoptimism. Erratic decisions may not bring you what you desire.

Neptune Conjunct Jupiter—Expansive Ideals, Exaggerated Hopes

You will find yourself in a more relaxed frame of mind as you consider original ideals. Trusted friends will offer their support. Creative opportunities encourage you to interact more with those around you. Outings or a journey will be pleasant, and new ideas may prosper. Enhanced fantasies are enjoyable but will not necessarily lead to a substantial relationship. Meditative practices may offer a clearer perspective.

Neptune Trine/Sextile Jupiter—Advantageous, Expansive Ideals
s that will attract goodwill.

Neptune Square/Oppose Jupiter—Overrated Ideals, Illusive Hopes
A vague sense of direction has you yearning for more. Yet overrated expectations may not manifest as expected, especially with romantic encounters. Since you are experiencing dissolving ideals, you must exercise caution in all of your personal dealings. Illusive, idealistic goals should be avoided, as others cannot be trusted at this time. Making humble sacrifices is regarded highly by those around you.

Pluto Conjunct Jupiter—Promoting Cooperation, Personal Growth, and Intimacy
Although Pluto-Jupiter aspects are known for their productivity in business, let's not forget that Pluto also rules over partnerships and sex. When both or one of these planets are in the fifth, seventh, or eighth house sectors of romance, relationships, and partnerships, respectively, your chances for intimacy increase. A confident attitude will easily persuade others to your point of view. Your eagerness to enjoy life to the fullest needs to be in cooperation with others for the greatest benefit.

Pluto Trine/Sextile Jupiter—Favorably Promoting Cooperation, Personal Growth, and Intimacy
Jupiter wishes to expand your personal growth by generating an enthusiasm for partnerships in business or pleasure. If intimacy is what you are looking for, this influence will enhance your chances for an intimate exchange either now or in the near future. The sextile may only offer subtle support from others.

Pluto Square/Oppose Jupiter—Challenging, Unproductive Personal Enterprises
Our experiences with adverse Pluto-Jupiter combinations have taught us that overextending ourselves may get us into trouble. Whether it be in business or pleasure, this is not the best time to invest your time and energy. Your eager approach may only work if you cooperate with others. Even if you gain, you may feel manipulated as your trust is wavering. Evaluate areas of expansion and personal growth carefully and have faith in your own beliefs.

Unromantic Outer Planets in Transit

The outer planets do not usually attract romantic opportunity or benefits unless in aspect to Venus, Mars, or Jupiter. Since Saturn, Uranus, Neptune, and Pluto are known as planets of guidance, we have much to learn from their impact on our lives.

Saturn-Sun—Serious, Difficult Goals

You will be concerned with building a stronger foundation in your life by accepting more responsibilities to further your aims. Although new encounters, especially with older persons, offer some sense of stability, romance is clearly lacking. For women, men may be distant, selfish, or unsupportive, personally and financially. You are better off focusing on constructive goals. Relationship developments may be at a standstill until this transit passes. Stabilizing your life will help build a reliable, solid foundation under favorable transits. Familiar and older individuals can be of some assistance. Although romance is not forthcoming, you may acquire a more realistic idea of what you want. Careful planning will bring success.

Adverse aspects may indicate a difficult time for your career and reputation. Since everyone is scrutinizing your efforts, this is not the time to be overextending yourself. Your work load is extremely demanding, exhausting you so that you have no incentive to seek romance. You may be feeling underpaid, overworked, abandoned, and lonely. Men in general will be disappointing, in trouble, or will not be supportive to your needs. Have faith that this will pass and your life will be better for the experience.

Saturn-Moon—Serious, Blocked Emotions and Outlook

The conjunction of this pair does not bode well for romantic developments, as the emotions are suppressed. You will feel restricted in connecting with those around you. When you finally do, an uneasy warmth may not bring the desired result. A matter-of-fact approach may be the only way to get through the day. Exercising caution, you will be emotionally protective of yourself. Save emotional and financial investments for another time. Women may be worrisome, lack sensitivity, or brush you off.

Harmonious transits will encourage you to be productive. You gain by making improvements to your familial relations. You are emotionally centered and will have a more realistic approach to new encounters. A conservative, dignified image will be respected, especially by older individuals. You appear responsible to those around you.

When you are under difficult transits, worry and exhaustion will block you from pursuing a social life. Feeling limited, it would be in your best interests to stay home and attend to chores. Anyone met at this time would only be draining and anxiety-ridden and not offer you the emotional understanding you may desire. You may be seen as distant, reserved, or cold. Try to avoid depression by doing something constructive. If anything, you could be a source of support to someone in need.

Saturn-Mercury—Serious, Practical, and Restricted Communication

Feeling industrious, you can make solid plans for the future. Applying self-discipline, you will put paperwork in order and better organize your life. Your conversations with others will be of a more serious nature, even with new individuals you meet. But you are not interested in socializing or concerning yourself with amorous thoughts. Make that date for another time. Pursuing intellectual aims will be far more productive.

Even positive aspects may bring social blocks and challenges to your status. If you have to mingle, keep the conversation matter-of-fact and limit your interaction. You would be wise to consider intellectual ambitions that enhance your long-term interests. Carry out your work in a methodical manner that is fulfilling.

Under adverse influences, this is a terrible time to socialize, as personal limitations may sour your reputation. Feeling unpopular could cause a serious depression. Social exchanges will mentally exhaust you at this time. You need to be with yourself, organize your life, and address tedious chores. Double-check for mistakes as your thinking is not up to par. Aiming toward building a solid foundation will sustain you.

Saturn-Saturn—Securing Stability/Pressured, Difficult Times

Building a foundation is usually accomplished by a lot of hard work. Relationships take work too. The reality of your situation in life will be further recognized. You may find that either you appreciate who you are with, or you don't. I have seen couples get married with a Saturn Return occurring in their seventh house sector of relationships. This aspect was not what they met under, as most Saturn-Saturn transits will limit one's interaction romantically with another.

Favorable influences are supportive, offering more stability. Your efforts will be rewarded. In personal relationships, you may have to care for another in worrisome need. If you feel blocked extending yourself to others, try a more conservative approach. Still, others may seem detached and uninterested.

Inharmonious transits will restrict you from social interaction. People met at this time may be impersonal, burdened with problems, or disappointing. It would be best to keep a low profile and stick to tedious chores. Your work load may be demanding, yet through accepting responsibilities, a more solid foundation can be built. If you are feeling lonely and insecure, deal with the obstacles that are preventing you from achieving success.

Saturn-Uranus—Realistic Future Goals, Restricted Freedom

Bringing a more structured format into your future ambitions will only add to long-term investments. Responsible planning will give you the freedom you desire. A new meeting could encourage you to pursue your individualistic incentives. A steady partner may be of concern to you. All work duties are in a shifting pattern at this time.

New people encountered under harmonious angles could be very intriguing. You may meet an exciting individual who offers a long-term rapport that is uneasy yet thrilling. Changes within your work schedule might be challenging, but help further your goals. You may be relieved of your responsibilities toward another person.

Adverse aspects indicate that you may experience some upsetting changes that leave you feeling insecure and ill at ease. A familiar face could leave your life, while a new individual may stimulate you toward the pursuit of unique ambitions, but lacks the romantic incentive. Someone may require your support during this time. Extra duties or adjusting to another's schedule may limit your call for freedom. If you are caught in the middle of tradition and unconventionality, work out your obligations before moving forward.

Saturn-Neptune—Reality Undermines Romanticism/Love Turns Sour

Even at their best, Saturn-Neptune transits still cast a shadow over romantic meetings. Too much realism blocks the idealistic feelings of Neptune. Once reality undermines romance, life becomes dull. This lack of luster restricts us from realizing our dreams. Illusions of love are always reflected in Neptune's presence, but Saturn has a way of steering us in a more functional direction that eludes romance completely.

Whatever the angle between these two planets, you will find yourself feeling bored by the end of the evening, if not before. Even if there are moments of excitement, they will surely be impeded by the confines of Saturn. When we are prevented from pursuing an objective, Saturn is clearly telling us that it is just not meant to be. If you force the issue, you will only be disappointed. Realistic circumstances (Saturn) hinder romance (Neptune) from occurring. Nebulous Neptune finds no-nonsense stability through Saturn, which causes an overcast outlook.

Life at times will travel a dreary road. Yet amidst it all, we still need to be grateful for what we have. You could say that this is a time of taking stock of what you possess, realizing that the best has yet to come.

Saturn-Pluto—Securing or Restricting Personal Growth and Intimacy

You will find yourself concerned with security issues, where accepting more responsibility will build a stronger foundation. Intimacy will lag behind, for you are not ready to extend yourself until this work cycle is completed. Even favorable aspects between Saturn and Pluto will persuade you to develop your work potential. Securing your position on the job will require a focused and compromising attitude, so you gradually acquire status. You can gain from long-term goals that deal with the reality of relationships as well. Lock in that dependable partnership. Hidden or manipulative issues will surface so you can exercise greater control.

Conflicting influences, especially the square aspect, will bring a tremendous challenge, as your work duties are overwhelmingly demanding at this time. Accept the responsibilities that are required of you. You will be extremely limited creatively and personally. Fears of being alone may be all-consuming, as intimacy is lacking. Manipulative tendencies may keep you restrained. You are at a standstill with close relationships, so do not overextend yourself. Forced demands will lead to an ultimatum or ending. If you have an opportunity to secure a commitment, consider it carefully.

Uranus-Sun—Exciting, Unpredictable, and Detached Relations

Discovering new insights will open up your perspective on life as interesting individuals show you the way. A sudden, unpredictable infatuation may be encountered that causes great excitement. Your feelings may prompt you to escape from a boring, dissatisfying situation. But your romantic intrigue is short-lived when the other party unexpectedly pulls away to pursue other interests. Although this is not an enduring combination, it nonetheless inspires you to break out into new directions. Sometimes other people act as a catalyst for growth and are only meant to be a brief part of our life experience. Ongoing commitments will experience estranged relations.

There is a certain thrill experienced when you meet under a Uranus trine Sun transit. The enthusiasm generated will cause you to wonder whether this is the romantic prospect for you. Infatuations will be fleeting, so keep your emotions in check. The dynamic individuals met during this period will stimulate you to further personal growth. Relationship developments may occur if other transits and progressions are supportive. Even though Uranus transits to the Sun are not known to be enduring, in most cases you will still come out ahead regardless of the outcome. The more subtle sextile from Uranus to the Sun inspires some excitement, but does not have the same impact as Uranus trine Sun.

Unusual and dynamic individuals may cause quite a disruption in your normal routine. Most encounters will be too volatile, erratic, or impersonal to pursue. Yet a surprising, unexpected encounter may sweep you off your feet as you desire to move into the future with your new attraction. Throwing caution to the wind, you are so stimulated that you have no qualms about getting romantically involved. Then as suddenly as you meet, the initial excitement fades into disappointment as you realize that it's suddenly over. Uranus comes into our life to stir up old, worn-out conditions, yet it's objective is unpredictable, especially when in adverse aspect. Usually you experience a complete reversal that you had not anticipated. Of course you were feeling so good with all of the excitement, how could this happen? Breaking out into a new direction with a new love always has its risks. But with an adverse Uranus-Sun transit, it is a risk not worth taking. Continue to be independent. More growth is needed to attract your significant other.

Uranus-Moon—Exciting, Unpredictable, and Detached Emotions

Feeling restless, you are inclined to be out mingling with others. A changeable disposition could have you on a social merry-go-round one minute or wanting to check out a new environment the next. A lively, effervescent personality will attract attention. New meetings may seem exciting, yet may not be enduring. A detached and independent manner will have you headed in a different direction without delay.

Positive angles will bring excitement and inspiration into your daily routine. New and unexpected encounters will lift your spirits, and may even invoke some romantic thrills. Yet longevity is lacking. Your sparkling persona will be noticed, so enjoy the moment but keep expectations in check.

Challenging aspects will create unexpected, erratic situations that have you in a whirlwind. Mood swings may cause you to feel unsettled and indecisive. Persons met under this volatile happening may seem vibrant and intriguing at first. Then, a change of heart occurs that causes one of you to break out of this alliance. Strained relations and sudden endings may transpire.

Uranus-Mercury—Mental Intrigue/Exciting, Unpredictable Communications

The conjunction will stimulate conversation in social situations that includes progressive ideas. Even though you will be feeling restless, you can still extend yourself as well as improve your work position. Scheduling changes may cause some tension, but you will quickly come up with an original plan of action. You may find encounters with others to be intriguing, but do not expect an affectionate advance. Nevertheless, intellectual exchanges can open you up to new insights.

Exciting ideas will motivate you to further your work ambitions under harmonious angles. Good publicity will enhance your standing and attract new connections. Accept all invitations, as favorable news may come your way through social as well as work situations.

With adverse contacts, you will experience a high level of stress. Unexpected scheduling changes may throw you into a tizzy. You will be plagued with indecision, changing your mind from one minute to the next. Sudden social developments will push you to act promptly, as you come up with a spur-of-the-moment agenda. You will not benefit from radical or impulsive decisions. Others, including new meetings, are unreliable, so keep your expectations in check. Unexpected publicity is unstable and may create unsettling conditions in your life. Alter only what is needed, for new situations are subject to reversals.

Uranus-Uranus—Sudden Change, Exciting Future

You will be persuaded to break up old patterns and move into the future. A new relationship, full of intrigue, may inspire but may not endure. Current relationships may be permanently broken. The excitement felt will convince you to act impulsively. Do hold onto that which you value. Uranus perpetuates a cycle of change when we have become too settled in our life experience. For your own individualized growth, you need to purge yourself of any impediments.

Change will work to your advantage under harmonious transits. Be open to exciting, progressive opportunities. Unique individuals will come your way to enhance your future ambitions. Someone impressive may be a strong influence in your development, offering uplifting insights. Ongoing relationships improve as tensions are eased.

Unexpected changes will create much disruption with adverse transits. Your need for freedom is strong and may push you into a rebellious mode. You will capitalize upon individual aspirations and release that which is holding you back. Relationships will be too unconventional or unpredictable to be pursued. Someone may briefly be a part of your life and suddenly leave you. Stress may break a once compatible bond. You will need to come up with an original plan to handle the reversals of activity that could turn your life upside down.

Neptune-Uranus—Original, Unusual, and Illusive Ideals

Sudden ideals may come alive and progress through creative inspiration. Yet romantic encounters may be colored with nebulousness, causing you not to know where you stand. You may strive for idyllic conditions, but may experience unexpected disappointments. New persons are fascinating yet unstable, causing much uncertainty about the future.

You are inclined to feel that dreams will come true under favorable transits, besides being able to enjoy life more as pressures ease and your outlook is inspired. New persons could encourage you toward your future vision and may steer you toward friendship. Be open to a propitious outcome, realizing that strange feelings of dissatisfaction will have you yearning for more in life.

Under difficult aspects, you will want to detach and escape from your routine to pursue a vague ideal that somehow offers you something better than what you think you have. But this ideal is not founded on realistic concepts. Nevertheless, anxiety will continue to urge you toward impulsiveness. New individuals met at this time will seem intriguing, but these encounters could suddenly dissolve, leaving you with unsettling discontent. Just when you think everything is fine, unanticipated cheating or deception may appear. Expect the unexpected, because it is going to happen.

Uranus-Pluto—Close, Unusual Bond/Compromising Your Independence

Compromising your freedom, you are better able to integrate a sense of unity so that everyone benefits. There will still be a desire to be intensely independent. An unusual attraction may pass your way, yet cultural and conditioned influences may deter you from becoming romantic allies.

The harmonious trine and sextile aspects allow a collective force to come together in the sharing of unique, progressive ideas and incentives. An unexpected and unusual bonding with another, with whom you feel an unspoken affinity, may appear and draw you close together regardless of personal hindrances, traditional customs, or geographical barriers. A lifetime connection can be established.

These two planets of transformation in challenging aspect will prompt you to change your lifestyle and direction with any relationship. You will want your freedom and not feel inclined toward making a commitment of any kind. The need for personal growth is strong and encourages you to make a break from any limiting conditions. Unconventional connections may occur that are intriguing, yet not progress in the direction that you would like. If you want to keep your significant other, be sure to meet your partner halfway for the best results. Be willing to compromise, even as you maintain a margin of distance. You may feel the pressure to conform to a relationship situation, and although freedom calls, you will need to cooperate to keep unity, even if it means you acquiesce.

Neptune-Sun—Ideal, Illusive Goals

You will want to escape into secluded surroundings, as you dream of getting away from it all. Life will seem unfair, as what you reach for eludes your grasp. Unless they share your vision, those around you are not reliable and seem to be disappearing right when you need them. Men who are not spiritually grounded and respectful of your needs may be selfish, impractical, evasive, or involved with drugs and alcohol. They may need to prove themselves before you agree to a relationship. You may desire to retreat into seclusion. You will benefit from pursuing spiritual progress and maintaining your integrity.

Positive transits assist you in bringing your ideals into reality. You will meet persons who encourage your vision. Look for advantageous opportunities that improve your circumstances. Romantic relationships that are founded on mutual love and respect may prosper. Keep starry-eyed meetings in perspective. Creative and spiritual activities will increase your awareness of worldly compassion.

Under adverse transits, you will be highly disappointed in the pursuit of your goals. The ideals you expect to achieve may fade away. Although you desire the perfect romance, you are likely to be deceived by your lover. Beware of scandal, impotency, unconventional sexual acts, or adulterous situations. Clandestine affairs will promise more than they deliver. No one gains from deceiving themselves or others. Men, especially, are evasive and lack the supportive sensitivity you need. If you are attracted to meditative environments, before becoming too involved, feel in your heart what you know to be true. You tend to be more passive than usual. You should keep a low profile and avoid potentially deceptive circumstances. Never sacrifice your reputation or pride.

Neptune-Moon—Compassionate, Spiritual, and Confused Emotions

You are apt to be more sympathetic and understanding with people when influenced by the conjunction. Your compassionate nature will succeed with others in easing their ills. If a moody persona overcomes you, retreat into meditative silence to recapture your essence. Women may be emotionally sensitive or not there for you at this time.

When in favorable aspect, compassionate feelings embrace those around you. A grateful attitude helps you relax and rely on spiritual persuasions. Due to a broader outlook, you will utilize your creativity and prosper. Women will be sensitive, compliant, and understanding with you.

Challenging influences, such as the square and opposition, create overemotionalism that causes confusion with your incentives. Avoid extending yourself to others, as you will experience disappointment or rejection. You may want to escape your present environment yet lack the clarity to make improvements. Women are not dependable under this influence, so consider relying on yourself, tempering your own emotions where needed.

Neptune-Mercury—Creative, Vague, and Deceptive Communications

There is always a level of deception when Neptune is involved with our interactions with others. The conjunction will try to manifest a more creative rapport if your connections are trustworthy. Yet a nebulous state of mind may weaken direct communications, causing misunderstandings to manifest. Under this influence you risk being misrepresented, so new meetings may not pan out. Better to enjoy a secluded environment that allows your imagination and spirituality to grow regardless of vague interruptions. Monetary upsets may also require your attention.

Creative connections and environments are appreciated with positive transits. Even as you relax, you may be inspirational to those around you. Your imaginative and spiritual insights prosper and will be encouraged by new individuals. Social acquaintances can be charming, but you may prefer more reclusive surroundings.

Difficult transits are completely adverse. You will be misrepresented and deceived. Postpone important decisions. Someone close to you may have intentions to undermine you. You are not privy to this scheme and much could be at stake. Business dealings are surrounded by uncertainty. You may be distraught by a financial setback that may take time to unravel. New meetings are clouded in deception and will not prosper. Disappointments are likely. Although you are dissatisfied with your present circumstances, stay in meditative seclusion until this influence passes.

Neptune-Neptune—Idyllic, Deceptive Goals and Dreams

Your imagination will capture you, and you are hopeful that your wishes will be granted. But vague assumptions will prevent your dreams from becoming a reality. Harnessing this creativity might be challenging yet rewarding, as old conditions dissolve to be replaced by new conditions.

Favorable transits allow your dreams to manifest. Your resourceful thinking will spell out how you can improve your life. Whatever idyllic quest you pursue can be attained. People in your close surroundings will share in your vision. They will put you at ease as you enjoy their company. Romantic developments are infused by your imagination. You will be inspired by creative or spiritual pursuits.

Adverse influences will cause great uncertainty, as you are dissatisfied with present conditions. You may yearn for more, but have a vague sense of direction. You will encounter deceptive circumstances and people that will undermine your efforts, causing distress and disappointment. What you thought was a stable situation may dissolve. New individuals with misleading intentions are not to be trusted. Romantic fantasy may be deceiving, especially clandestine love affairs that end up being a disenchanting letdown. You will have to rely on intuitive and spiritual insights to be your guide. If a motive is not pure, don't go there.

Pluto-Sun—Intense Goals, Total Transformation, Endings and Beginning Life Anew

Major changes take place when we need to eliminate that which we have outgrown to further our potential in life. Climactic endings that seem to be out to destroy us rush through our soul. All along we are being reshaped to assist us in evolving to the next stage of our existence, which we would rather avoid. Plutonian transformations can be quite traumatic. In the end, a complete metamorphosis occurs.

When you are experiencing positive influences, change, although dramatic, may work to your advantage. If anything, you are being given an opportunity to empower yourself by moving into a stronger position with work and relationships. Others may see you as a leader or one who is able to handle a principal role with your constructive use of power. Accept their admiration with gratitude. Your self-expression is easily projected, bringing you to a more purposeful place with your goals. You can be persuasive and determined to achieve what you desire. An important man may assist you in your future direction. Romantic developments are also likely with the right person.

During challenging transits, you may go through the depths of hell to gradually find more purpose in your life. You must be willing to rid yourself of persons and situations that have run their course and could be undermining you. You are completing an old cycle and will approach life differently from this point on. Weed out what you need to, but hold on to that which has value. You may confront conflicts, uncooperative circumstances, and power plays. However, you must compromise if you are going to maintain unity. You may be swayed by others' decisions that defy your own findings. People who criticize you, undermine your efforts, debase you, or abuse you should be cast aside forever. Possessive and jealous lovers may be lurking. There will always be temptation with power and desire. Let your integrity lead the way. Men may be forceful and manipulative. Stressful relationship issues may leave you feeling drained. Your creativity and self-expression are blocked, causing a strained discontent that forces you to take a stand and address needed changes. Yet you will not gain from ultimatums. In order for us to be purified we need to finalize karmic experiences and be reborn. This transformation may make or break you, but will definitely take you to a new dimension of your existence.

Pluto-Moon—Deep, Intense, and Manipulative Emotions

Inner feelings will allow you to understand situations on a deeper level. You are more aware of your responses to and from those around you. Familial situations may arouse tension. This may be a time to consider resolving conditions from the past. Do not let intense issues get the best of you. Stay focused and allow these innate emotions to be your guide. A powerful woman may be very influential, persuading you to her point of view.

Beneficial transits offer deep insight into your experiences. You will be keen on finding answers to questions. New individuals met will be understanding and offer helpful information. Spiritual connections may occur that are rewarding. You will have the upper hand in relating to others. It is to your benefit to be cooperative and seek unity. You also gain by releasing old issues and correcting the past. Any unsettled family issue will be appeased through your willingness to compromise. An advantageous change of environment or residence is possible.

Arduous transits will be emotionally disturbing. Manipulative relationship situations may arise that are difficult to resolve. You will find yourself searching high and low for answers. You must try to trust your intuitive insight to help you. People will have expectations that leave you feeling emotionally drained. Unresolved issues could surface and cause friction. If someone leaves your life, it may be for the better.

Pluto-Mercury—Deep, Intense, Manipulative Thought and Communications

You may find yourself engrossed in deep thought, looking for answers and pondering your future direction. If involved in a social situation, you may have to cooperate with others even though you are feeling manipulated. Conversation on a more evolved level will be revealing. There may be someone you can connect with who understands your perspective. Psychological groups may offer good interaction and personal transformation.

Supportive aspects still promote compulsive, repetitive thought, yet you are also able to come to some good conclusions. Communicative exchanges will be on a deeper level that offers insight into your life experience. New individuals met will be impressed with your compromising approach and powerful mental aptitude.

When in adverse aspect, you will find yourself in constant, repetitive thought as you look relentlessly for answers. Somehow you must guard against a lack of good judgment. Decisions made at this time may not benefit you in the future. New meetings are not apt to go as planned. Communication difficulties will leave you feeling frustrated and drained. Stress felt in a relationship situation will reach its breaking point, especially if hidden motives are suspect. Ties are broken. An ultimatum will also lead to an ending. Before you act, be aware of the outcome.

Pluto-Neptune—Powerful, Transformed Ideals/Deceptive Involvements

Positive aspects encourage you to bring your ideals into a powerful reality. You may meet people of different cultural backgrounds who further your vision. A close, spiritual bond may materialize with someone special. You may be compelled to involve yourself with unexplained phenomena or wish to withdraw into meditative silence.

Unfavorable influences will persuade you to retreat into seclusion to recharge your personal resources. This rejuvenation may be necessary to help you take charge of your destiny. People met during this time may be from different cultures and not share in your philosophy or way of living. Be aware of manipulative or deceptive tendencies from others. Finding those you can relate to on a deeper level will be challenging. You may pursue deeper insights into life's mysteries, but avoid underground fantasies.

Pluto-Pluto—Intense Transformations, Finalities and New Cycles

Positive transits encourage a personal transformation where a new cycle in one's life is begun. Releasing old issues will bring better order into your daily existence. You, along with others, will be cooperative in business as well as more intimate relationship situations. You will benefit from agreeable partnerships that are supportive of your growth. Relationship concerns are easily resolved, whether someone is coming into your life or departing. A powerful individual may sway your opinion.

Discordant angles generate difficult partnerships where your partner is keen to manipulate you to satisfy their needs. You may feel compelled to cooperate with a convincing, iron-willed person. Intimate relationships will need to evolve to a new level of understanding, or face a parting of the ways. New persons met at this time will always retain an uncompromising stance, thus making getting along quite taxing. It is advisable not to become involved with new partnerships of any kind, as you will only be dealing with power struggles down the road. You will consider reevaluating your life goals, ridding yourself of anything or anyone hampering your progress. Dormant ambitions can now be pursued to your benefit, as you let go of that which has run its course. Your attitude about life, death, and where you fit into the universal plan is transcended into a whole new perspective. You will find yourself living with greater purpose in the pursuit of your aims.

27 ♥ Meeting and Marrying under Mercury Retrograde

Meeting during a Mercury retrograde period can be very precarious as this influence does not always support plans following through to the anticipated result. Thus, the desired long-term relationship may not manifest. Most couples end up struggling to keep some stability in the union that seems destined to be short-lived even when the Love Relationship Formula is present.

Marrying under Mercury retrograde can also be risky. A famous example of this was the marriage of John F. Kennedy, Jr., and Carolyn Bessette, which took place in secret at a quaint church on Cumberland Island off the coast of Georgia. The date was September 26, 1996, and Mercury was retrograde. Although Neptune was in favorable trine aspect to Mercury, Mars was in adverse semisquare aspect and Uranus was in sesquiquadrate aspect to Mercury, creating even more volatility toward what may transpire.

This event involving Mercury retrograde would play itself out in the most unfortunate of tragedies. On July 16, 1999, at around 9:30 PM, their small plane crashed near Martha's Vineyard, ending the lives of John, Carolyn, and Carolyn's sister Lauren. Never should we tempt the fate of Mercury retrograde.

You will find Mercury retrograde appearing in solar and lunar returns. When it falls in the seventh-house sector of close relationships or the fifth-house sector of romance, you will be inclined to reevaluate your current position on relationships and romance. You may not be able to move forward with any decisions until the solar or lunar return with Mercury retrograde has ended. The planetary influence will be present, but not able to proceed in carrying out the activity involved in this sector. You will consider changing how you are applying yourself as you reassess where you stand. Even though you might be at somewhat of a standstill, the underlying motive will persuade you to move ahead. Personal frustrations will slow down the process. You will experience insecurities until you look at the problems in this romantic area that are holding you back from experiencing more fulfillment. In life, we often encounter difficulty acquiring what we want. If the goal is not within our grasp, then we need to go back and change our pattern or approach to this relationship goal so that it can be attained.

♥ meeting under a
void-of-course moon

The Moon is the fastest-moving planetary influence in our universe as we know it. Every twenty-eight days it journeys around the earth, traveling through each of the twelve constellations that we refer to as zodiac signs. In the course of a day, the Moon makes many aspects to the other planets and specific points of interest. Its influence will only last a couple of hours and sometimes less with each contact it makes, as the Moon moves 1 degree every one-and-three-quarters to two hours. Since there are 30 degrees with each horoscope sign, it will take the Moon approximately two-and-a-half days to travel through each sign. During this brief journey through each sign, the Moon will make various angles until it reaches the last major angle it will make before it moves into the next consecutive horoscope sign. After the Moon makes this final angle or aspect to a planet or significant astrological point, it is said to be wobbling in its orbit, or *void of course (v/c)*, until it reaches the next sign.

Since the Moon reflects our feelings, our emotional instincts are said to be out of sync whenever it goes void of course. If we are not in tune with ourselves, we feel uncentered, scattered, and confused. Lacking good judgment, we are prone to making mistakes. More often than not, plans go awry. It seems that our approach has missing links that keep us from achieving our goal.

What is started under a void-of-course Moon usually does not pan out even when the Love Relationship Formula is present. Therefore, if you meet someone under a void-of-course influence, this encounter is not destined to have a future. It would be best to plan any get-together when the Moon is not void-of-course for a better outcome. Otherwise, you will be disappointed when the connection dissolves and and you have wasted a lot of time and energy.

When the Moon is void of course, it's okay to pursue routine tasks. But more importantly, it is a good time to mull over your plans and take inventory of what is happening in your life at this time. Then, when the Moon moves into the next sign, take action toward what you would like to accomplish, such as setting up that romantic date.

29

♥ The Love
Relationship Formula
in a First Meeting Chart

The first meeting chart will give us a very good description of a couple's future. Every planetary influence will affect the outcome of the relationship. When the Love Relationship Formula is present, the relationship prospers.

First Meeting Chart of Jared and Lynn

"Jared" and "Lynn" met on January 25, 1987, at 4:00 PM in Garfield, New Jersey. The placement of the Sun in the seventh house of marriage sets the stage for future events. Jupiter is in semisquare contact with the Sun, creating opportunity for a relationship to prosper, as long as they don't overextend themselves. Jupiter is also in favorable trine aspect to the Ascendant, a Mars Point, and sextile the Descendant, a Venus Point. Jupiter's good fortune supports this auspicious meeting when in aspect to the angular cusps on the horizon. The semisquare aspect between the Sun and Venus emphasizes an affectionate exchange, as long as one's feelings are not filled with expectations. The romantic passion is highlighted as well, with Venus in wonderful trine aspect to Mars, and the Moon in trine contact to Mars. The Moon conjunct Venus denotes caring and sensitivity between them. When the Moon, Venus, and Mars influence each other positively, a couple encounters one of their greatest loves. Saturn conjunct Venus promises a long-term commitment, yet Saturn trine Mars emphasizes a more dutiful alliance. Saturn is also in semisquare contact with the Sun, conjunct the Moon, and in square aspect to Jupiter, creating a serious, obligated perspective on building a life together and developing a solid friendship. Jupiter in square aspect to Venus denotes a happy couple who enjoy an active social life. A strong, exciting, lasting attraction is indicated with Venus conjunct Uranus. Even more enthusiasm is generated from the Jupiter square Uranus aspect, which encourages the couple toward self-discovery.

Communication is enhanced with Mercury in wide conjunction to the Sun, in sextile to the Moon, Venus, Mars, and Saturn, and in semisquare to Jupiter. Mentally they would get along brilliantly, agreeing to a diplomatic and practical approach to their goals. Only Mercury in square aspect to Pluto would be somewhat challenging, as they would be persuaded toward deep, repetitious thought and possibly coercive behavior. Chances are their intuitive insights would not allow for bad judgment as Mercury is exalted in Aquarius and in fine contact with several other planets.

Mars in square aspect to Neptune, and also in T-square aspect to the MC and IC, indicates nebulous developments in home, career, and love. Luckily their career goals have a creative, healing essence and their conservative home is a Neptunian, spiritual haven as well. The romantic connection of Mars trine Venus helps channel any vague moments. Mars inconjunct Pluto might indicate some resistance between them that is easily resolved with a cooperative attitude and good interaction. Venus in semisquare contact to Pluto intensifies the love bond. Uranus is in contact with all of the angular points, stirring up the unexpected along with something new to be experienced. Pluto square the Sun and in sesquiquadrate aspect to Jupiter presents situations that force them to evolve to a new level, unless they are already doing this for themselves.

The monetary picture is at times stressful due to Pluto in square aspect to Mercury in the eighth house of joint financial handlings. Yet the Moon in Sagittarius trine the second-house cusp of earned income, along with Venus, Mars, and Saturn, has helped substantiate their finances. The three children they have is a reflection of Jupiter in square aspect to Venus in the fifth house, and of the Moon and Venus in Sagittarius, which promotes abundance. Both agree that they have been happily married for twelve years.

Aspects in the First Meeting Chart of Jared and Lynn
(Love Relationship Formula aspects underlined)

Sun 5°21' Aquarius conjunct Mercury 14°16' Aquarius (wide)

Sun 5°21' in the seventh house semisquare Venus 18°47' Sagittarius

Sun 5°21' Aquarius semisquare Jupiter 22°02' Pisces

Sun 5°21' Aquarius square Pluto 9°53' Scorpio

Mercury 14°16' Aquarius sextile Moon 13°30' Sagittarius

Moon 13°30' Sagittarius conjunct Venus 18°47' Sagittarius

Moon 13°30' Sagittarius trine Mars 12°08' Aries

Moon 13°30' Sagittarius conjunct Saturn 17°57' Sagittarius

Mercury 14°16' Aquarius sextile Venus 18°47' Sagittarius

Mercury 14°16' Aquarius sextile Mars 12°08' Aries

Mercury 14°16' Aquarius semisquare Jupiter 22°02' Pisces (wide)

Mercury 14°16' Aquarius sextile Saturn 17°57' Sagittarius

Mercury 14°16' Aquarius square Pluto 9°53' Scorpio

Venus 18°47' Sagittarius trine Mars 12°08' Aries

Venus 18°47' Sagittarius square Jupiter 22°02' Pisces

Jupiter 22°02' Pisces sextile Descendant, a Venus Point 23°30' Capricorn

Venus 18°47' Sagittarius conjunct Saturn 17°57' Sagittarius

Uranus 24°58' Sagittarius semisextile Descendant, a Venus Point 23°30' Capricorn

Venus 18°47' Sagittarius semisquare Pluto 9°53' Scorpio

Mars 12°08' Aries square Neptune 6°36' Capricorn

Mars 12°08' Aries inconjunct Pluto 9°53' Scorpio

Jupiter 22°02' Pisces trine Ascendant, a Mars Point 23°30' Cancer

Jupiter 22°02' Pisces square Saturn 17°57' Sagittarius

Jupiter 22°02' Pisces square Uranus 24°58' Sagittarius

Jupiter 22°02' Pisces sesquiquadrate Pluto 9°53' Scorpio

Uranus 24°58' Sagittarius semisquare Pluto 9°53' Scorpio

Uranus 24°58' Sagittarius inconjunct Ascendant, a Mars Point 23°30' Cancer

Neptune 6°36' Capricorn square MC 6°01' Aries

Neptune 6°36' Capricorn square IC 6°01' Libra

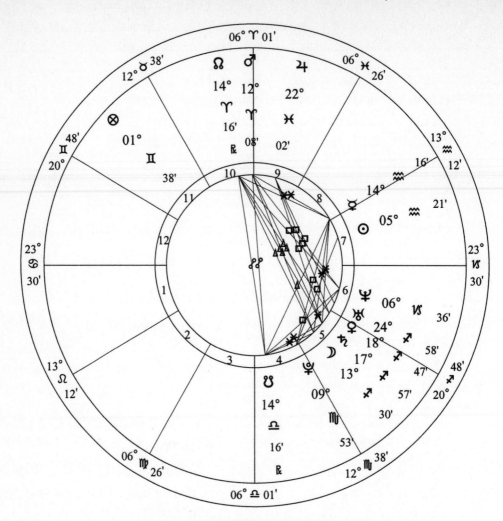

First Meeting Chart of Jared and Lynn
January 25, 1987 / Garfield, NJ / 4:00 PM EST
Placidus Houses

30

♥

the love
Relationship formula
in a marriage chart

Marriage Chart of Paul Newman and Joanne Woodward

Choosing an auspicious day to get married can influence the longevity of your relationship. Paul Newman and Joanne Woodward were married on January 29, 1958, at 6:00 PM in Las Vegas, Nevada. The Love Relationship Formula exists in the chart on this particular day, regardless of the angle between the planets. The Sun and Moon are in trine aspect, harmonizing the relationship right from the start. There is a strong, fortunate Sun-Venus conjunction that attracts love, affection, and respect for them as a couple. This loving influence offsets adversity and encourages a lasting, affectionate bond. Although the Sun is in wide conjunction to the Descendant, a Venus Point, it still offers some support. A Sun-Mars aspect creates a passionate drive that sparks some competition. A favorable Moon trine Venus sensitizes the relationship, where there is considerable care and understanding. The connection of Mars and Venus, even on a semisquare, enhances the romantic dynamics. A Mars-Jupiter sextile augments the passion and overall motivation of the relationship. The Moon inconjunct Jupiter promotes their enthusiasm, which may come and go but is still present. Jupiter in wide square to the Sun emphasizes the success of their goals along with their high expectations. A Venus-Jupiter aspect invites an uplifting social circle and adds a complimentary appeal between them. Feeling comfortable in each other's company and establishing a long-term union is indicated with Venus in strong aspect to Saturn. A supportive friendship is attributed to a Jupiter-Saturn aspect. The pairing of Venus and Uranus instigates a powerful attraction on an opposition, yet some space is needed for their own individual development. Venus inconjunct Pluto coaxes an intense involvement as long as they are both willing to cooperate. There are some influences that present a challenge, such as Sun square Neptune, Sun opposite Uranus, Mercury sesquiquadrate Pluto, and Mars conjunct Saturn, among others. But the Love Relationship Formula gives the marriage what it needs to confront any issue and come out winning. This couple certainly did.

Aspects in the Marriage Chart of Paul Newman and Joanne Woodward (Love Relationship Formula aspects underlined)

Sun 9°41' Aquarius trine Moon 2°13' Gemini (wide)

Sun 9°41' Aquarius conjunct Venus 7°37' Aquarius

Sun 9°41' Aquarius semisquare Mars 26°39' Sagittarius

Sun 9°41' Aquarius square Jupiter 1°14' Scorpio (wide)

Sun 9°41' Aquarius semisquare Saturn 22°28' Sagittarius

Sun 9°41' Aquarius oppose Uranus 9°37' Leo

Sun 9°41' Aquarius square Neptune 4°46' Scorpio

Sun 9°41' Aquarius conjunct Descendant 21°57' Aquarius (wide)

Moon 2°13' Gemini sesquiquadrate Mercury 18°59' Capricorn

Moon 2°13' Gemini trine Venus 7°37' Aquarius

Moon 2°13' Gemini oppose Mars 26°39' Sagittarius

Moon 2°13' Gemini inconjunct Jupiter 1°14' Scorpio

Moon 2°13' Gemini inconjunct Neptune 4°46' Scorpio

Moon 2°13' Gemini square Pluto 1°36' Virgo

Mercury 18°59' Capricorn sesquiquadrate Pluto 1°36' Virgo

Venus 7°37' Aquarius semisquare Mars 26°39' Sagittarius

Venus 7°37' Aquarius square Jupiter 1°14' Scorpio

Venus 7°37' Aquarius semisquare Saturn 22°28' Sagittarius

Venus 7°37' Aquarius oppose Uranus 9°37' Leo

Venus 7°37' Aquarius square Neptune 4°46' Scorpio

Venus 7°37' Aquarius inconjunct Pluto 1°36' Virgo

Mars 26°39' Sagittarius sextile Jupiter 1°14' Scorpio

Mars 26°39' Sagittarius conjunct Saturn 22°28' Sagittarius

Mars 26°39' Sagittarius sesquiquadrate Uranus 9°37' Leo

Mars 26°39' Sagittarius semisquare Neptune 4°46' Scorpio (wide)

Mars 26°39' Sagittarius trine Pluto 1°36' Virgo

Jupiter 1°14' Scorpio semisquare Saturn 22°28' Sagittarius

Jupiter 1°14' Scorpio conjunct Neptune 4°46' Scorpio

Jupiter 1°14' Scorpio sextile Pluto 1°36' Virgo

Saturn 22°28' Sagittarius sesquiquadrate Uranus 9°37' Leo

Saturn 22°28' Sagittarius semisquare Neptune 4°46' Scorpio

Uranus 9°37' Leo square Neptune 4°46' Scorpio

Neptune 4°46' Scorpio sextile Pluto 1°36' Virgo

North Node 5°41' Scorpio conjunct Jupiter 1°14' Scorpio

North Node 5°41' Scorpio conjunct Neptune 4°46' Scorpio

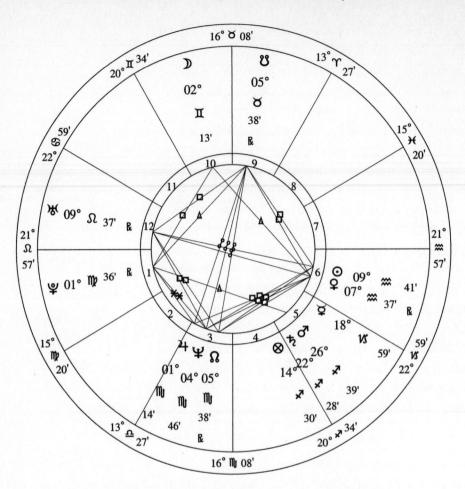

Marriage Chart of Paul Newman and Joanne Woodward
January 29, 1958 / Las Vegas, NV / 6:00 PM PST
Placidus Houses

♥ the love
relationship formula
in the composite chart
and solar return

Since romantic relationships are the most common reason why we use the composite chart, when it encompasses the Relationship Formula the results may seal together a lifelong union. We may also benefit in other ways. In synastry, weaker influences from the natal charts can be strengthened in the composite chart. If a person has Saturn square Mars in their birth chart, and in the composite chart of the couple there is a Jupiter trine Mars aspect, it will ease the personal restriction of the natal Saturn square Mars aspect. If the Love Relationship Formula is present, this may be an excellent relationship for the Saturn-square-Mars person to be in to alleviate the drawback of the planetary adversity. In most instances, a relationship exists so two people can fulfill a need in each other. This is part of the attraction. When Saturn square Mars is viewed as a lack and therefore a need, this need is fulfilled by the Jupiter trine Mars in the composite chart.

In a relationship analysis, it's always important to analyze the natal charts of the two people involved. This will give you valid clues as to what kind of a relationship the two people are looking for. Then see if the composite chart is a reflection of this vision and includes the Love Relationship Formula.

When the Love Relationship Formula exists in the solar return chart, there is opportunity for love. The formula can be present in various sectors of the chart, with a seventh-house emphasis involving the Sun, Venus, and/or Jupiter. The first (self), fifth (romance), seventh (relationships), and eighth (partnership) house sectors are the more significant areas that support relationship advancement if encouraging planets and aspects are involved. The Love Relationship Formula needs to be present in some capacity to help solidify a wonderful, long-term union. If love continues to elude you, astrocartography and relocation charts can assist you in finding a desirable place for positive relationship developments to occur. In exploring the possibilities, check your compatibility, transits, progressions, solar arc directions, and solar return to be sure that all astrological influences are working in your favor, especially The Love Relationship Formula. For love may be closer than you think.

Appendix

Create a Love Relationship Formula Report
Using Your CD-ROM Program

First you need to install the program. Just remove the CD-ROM from its folder and place it in your computer's CD-ROM drive. The program will begin to install itself.

If it does not install automatically, click on the Start menu and then select "Run." In the Run menu dialog box, type in your corresponding CD-ROM drive followed by the filename SETUP.exe. Typically, the CD-ROM is set up as D:\

D:\SETUP.exe

The install wizard will run and guide you through the rest of the process.

For an alternate method, you can access your CD-ROM drive by clicking on "My Computer" and then the CD-ROM drive (typically D:\). Double-click the SETUP.exe icon.

You will see an introductory splash screen with the name of the program (it flashes on and off very quickly), and then you will see a screen called "The Love Relationship Formula."

The Love Relationship Formula is a basic astrology program, designed around the most so-phisticated astrology programming available. Cosmic Patterns, in collaboration with Llewellyn Worldwide, has developed this program to provide you with birth charts (the circle with all the astrological symbols), and also to provide basic romantic interpretations for two people (seven-to ten-page printouts of information about a couple's charts).

Let's discuss the choices you have:

- The Start button is used to create your charts.
- The About button provides information about the CD-ROM program; about Llewellyn Worldwide, the publisher of *The Love Relationship Formula;* and about Cosmic Patterns Software, the designer of the program.
- The Quit button allows you to exit from the program.

To use your program, select "Start" from the menu, then select "New List of Charts (New Session)." If you are returning to the program and want to see the last chart you made, select "Continue with Charts of Previous Session."

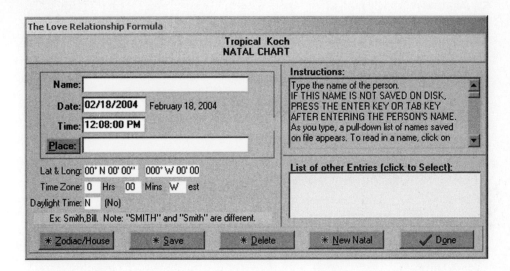

This is where you enter your birth information. There are some simple instructions on the right side of the screen, similar to what follows here. Let's make charts for Bill and Hillary Clinton as an example.

- In the Name box, type "Bill Clinton," and then Enter.
- In the Date box, type "08191946" (for August 19, 1946), and then Enter. You will notice that as you enter the date (in mm dd yyyy format), the cursor will skip to the next part of the date field for you.
- In the Time field, type "085100 AM" (his 8:51 AM birth time in hh mm ss format), and then Enter.
- In the Place box, type "Hope, Arkansas" (the birth place). As soon as you type the word "Hope," a list drops down. You will notice that "Hope, Arkansas" isn't in the list, but Hope is close to Texarkana, Arkansas. Begin typing "Texarkana." When you have typed "Tex," "Texarkana" appears at the top of the list. Select it. The drop-down list disappears, and you see "Texarkana, Arkansas" in the Place box. You will also see information filled in the boxes below it: the latitude is 33N26 00, the longitude is 094W03 00, the time zone is 6 hours 0 minutes West, and the Daylight Saving Time box is marked "N."

A number of cities are included in the program's atlas. If your city does not automatically come up, you can use a nearby city from the list. You may also look up your birth place in an atlas to find the latitude and longitude, time zone, and daylight saving time information, and fill in this information. Generally, a city close to the birth place will have a longitude and latitude close enough for your purposes, and will also be in the same time zone. If the time zone information is different, your chart could be off by an hour, one way or the other. Depending on the distance your choice is from your actual birth place, your chart will be slightly different. You can obtain the correct longitude, latitude, and time zone information from a time table book for astrology.*

- The Zodiac/House button allows you to select a different house system. The program automatically selects the tropical zodiac and the Placidus house system. Experiment with the other choices to see what changes on the chart wheel. In this program the interpretation will only change if you select the sidereal zodiac.

- Select the "Save" button at the bottom of the screen to save the chart (you can delete it later if you need to).

- Then select the "Done" button. If you forget to save and go directly to the Done button, you will get a prompt asking if you want to save the data. In fact, all the way along, prompts appear to help you enter the data.

- You now see an Information box that says "You will now be prompted to enter the data for the second person." Click "OK." Follow the same procedure again by typing "Hillary Rodham Clinton," "10261947," and "080000 PM" (Hillary was born on October 26, 1947, at 8:00 PM in Chicago, Illinois). In the Place field, type "Chicago." You will see Chicago Heights and Chicago in the drop-down list. Select "Chicago," "Save," "OK," and "Done."

The screen on the next page is what you see when you have chosen the "Done" button:

---

* Two possibilities include *The American Atlas,* compiled and programmed by Neil F. Michelson (San Diego, CA: ACS Publications, 1978 and newer editions); and *The International Atlas,* compiled and programmed by Thomas G. Shanks (San Diego, CA: ACS Publications, 1985 and newer editions).

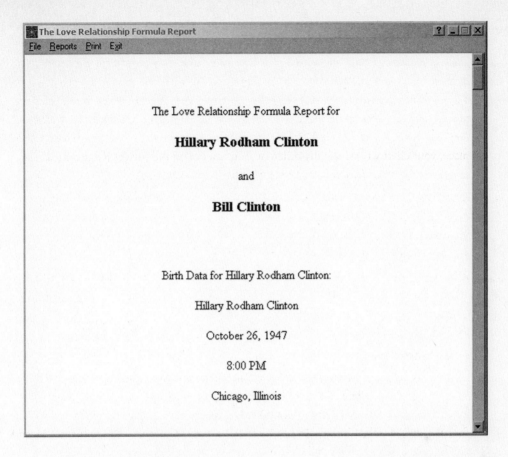

- If you scroll down, the names of the charts you just entered appear. You can see Bill and Hillary's names and birth data. If you scroll down, you can see more information lists, and then the interpretation.
- If you select "Wheel" from the Reports menu, a form appears. It contains a chart for Bill at the top and one for Hillary at the bottom.

- At the upper left it is labeled "Chart Wheels." This form should look just like the one printed here.

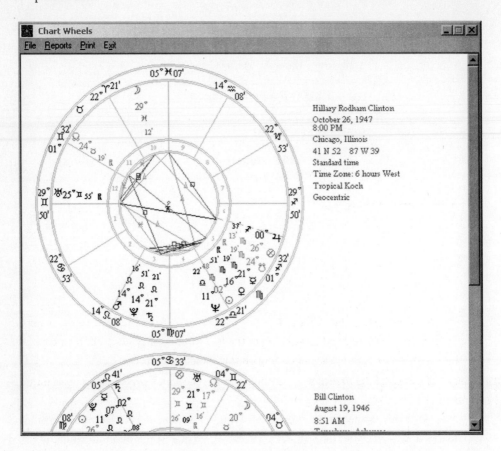

- Select "Print" and Print Current Report" to print either the wheel or the interpretation report. Only the item on the screen prints. Select the other option on the Reports menu to change the screen.
- Select "Exit" and then "Yes" to go to the opening screen. From here you can either exit the program, or select "Start" to make another chart and interpretation.

That's it! You can now create charts and interpretations for any birth information you want. This program is so easy to use, you won't need much help. Still, we have included step by step instructions for those of you who haven't used an astrology program before.

 glossary

Angular Houses—The angular houses are the first, fourth, seventh, and tenth houses. Planets in these house sectors are referred to as being in the foreground. They hold a lot of weight and therefore can help or hinder one depending on the planet and aspects to the planet.

Ascendant—The cusp of the first house, pertaining to the self, one's personality, physicality, approach to life goals, and first impression made on others, located on the horizon line. Angular power point abbreviated ASC.

Aspect—When a planet by degree interacts with another planet or significant astrological point thus forming a geometry angle such as 0 degrees, 60 degrees, 90 degrees, 135 degrees, or 180 degrees, with outer space as the backdrop.

Astrocartography—Plotting geographic locations on a global astrological map, which emphasizes the use of power points, the Ascendant, Descendant, Midheaven, and *Imum Coeli,* that indicate where you will be able to maximize your potential. A planetary mapping method used to relocate to ideal astrology zones.

Astrological Karma—Karma that is designated by the astrological influences.

Astrology—The study of the stars, including planets, zodiac signs, and house sectors, to help us understand the past, deal with the present, and guide us into the future.

Belief System—What you think, and therefore attract and become. The ideas that you store mentally that reflect your view of people and life.

Benefic—A planetary influence that attracts opportunity, favors, and benefits. Jupiter and Venus are known as the two benefic planets.

Cadent Houses—The cadent houses are the third, sixth, ninth, and twelfth houses, and are known as the background houses. Here the planetary influences are considerably weak, and therefore may not be able to support or undermine you, depending on planet, sign, and house placement.

Conditioned—Programmed in one's environment to act in a specified way, which creates learned emotional and behavior patterns. Trained to believe that one must behave in a certain restrained manner.

Dysfunctional—Not able to function normally due to disorder, in some context, in one's environment.

Co-dependent—A mutual compulsive need to lean on each other for support in some manner, which restricts the individuals in becoming independent.

Descendant—the cusp of the seventh house, pertaining to close relationships and marriage, which is located on the horizon line of the astrology chart. Angular power point abbreviated DSC.

Dyad—A relationship of two, and only two, such as male and female. Usually this duality is based on the polar opposite of the other.

Element—Fire, earth, air, and water are the four elements used in astrology to describe each planet or significant astrological point.

Exalted—Each planet has an exalted sign. A planet in its exalted sign experiences an elevated rank or dignity. Here the planet and sign are positively expressed, thus creating a magnified experience. Example: Jupiter in Cancer.

Fall—When a planet is in the opposite sign of its exaltation, it is said to be "in fall." Example: Jupiter in Capricorn.

Golden Ratio—The formula of transcendence that concurs with "Phi"—1:16:18—and appears in all life forms.

Holy Grail—The magnificent formula of all formulas that transcends life itself.

Houses—Divided sectors of an astrology chart that describe an area of one's life. There are twelve house sectors in a chart. This is where the experience happens.

Karma—A universal law that suggests that you are held accountable for all of your actions, even in previous lifetimes. Karma determines one's destiny.

Imum Coeli—The cusp of the fourth house, pertaining to home, property, and one's roots, which is on the meridian line that divides the astrology chart. Angular power point abbreviated IC.

Malefic—A planetary influence that is nefarious in context. Inferring evil intent. Saturn is known as a malefic planet, especially in adverse aspect to Mars and the outer planets.

Midheaven—The cusp of the tenth house, pertaining to career and social status, which is on the meridian line that divides the astrology chart. Angular power point abbreviated MC.

Midpoint—The middle point degree between a pair of planets or other significant astrological points of interest.

Nodes—Commonly known as the dragon's head (North Node) and the dragon's tail (South Node). The Moon's North Node indicates the future direction in which you should be headed, for that is in line with your destiny. The Moon's South Node indicates what you have experienced in a past life, and are consciously moving away from to experience something new. We need to release the symbolism of the South Node and reach for the symbolism of the North Node to attain our highest potential.

Orb—The allowed degrees within an aspect. The distance between an astrological angle that emphasizes an influence.

Phi—Represents an etheric, mathematical formula for transcendence, 1:16:18.

Pythagorus—Greek philosopher and mathematician. Created the Pythagorean Theory.

Quadruplicities—Groupings of four signs that emanate a similar approach to goals pursued in life, and based on the beginning, middle, and end cycle of the seasons. The quadruplicities are cardinal signs—Aries, Cancer, Libra, and Capricorn; mutable signs—Gemini, Virgo, Sagittarius, and Pisces; and fixed signs—Taurus, Leo, Scorpio, and Aquarius.

Part of Marriage—An astrological point that refers to marriage. The Part of Marriage is the same distance from the Descendant as Venus is from the Ascendant, yet located on the same side of the horizon line as Venus. It is calculated by adding the longitude degree(s) of the Descendant to the longitude degree(s) of the Ascendant, and then subtracting the longitude degree(s) of Venus. For example, if Venus is 20° above the Ascendant, the Part of Marriage will be located 20° above the Descendant. If you find Venus 11° below the Descendant, the Part of Marriage will be 11° below the Ascendant.

Planets—Cosmic bodies in our solar system. In astrology, planets are the experience.

Sun—Represents the self, vitality, and one's goal or purpose in life.

Moon (for convenience, referred to as a planet)—Represents emotions, sensitivity, habits, mother, female associations, and the past.

Mercury—Represents intellect, communication, understanding, learning, and analysis.

Venus—Represents values, attraction, love, romance and affection, self-esteem, beauty, financial prosperity, artistic values, and femininity.

Mars—Represents desire, energy, identity, passion, aggression, and masculinity.

Jupiter—Represents expansion, opportunity, abundance, good fortune, optimism, travel, and religion.

Saturn—Represents limitation, reality, discipline, maturity, responsibility, and authority.

Uranus—Represents sudden change, progress, the future, excitement, the unpredictable, unconventionality, and individuality.

Neptune—Represents illusion, idealism, creativity, spirituality, deception, and dissolution.

Pluto—Represents intense involvement, power, transformation, endings yet new beginnings, obsession, manipulation, elimination, and regeneration.

Progressions—Transits used to predict future developments that are calculated by using an ephemeris and counting a day for a year of your life, after the Greenwich Meridian Time has been refigured and an Adjusted Calculation Date derived.

Relocation—Moving to a particular latitude and longitude, different from your birthplace, that is astrologically indicated as an improved place to live. Relocating your birth chart to another geographical area.

Signs—Referring to the zodiac, of which there are twelve signs: Aries, Taurus, Gemini, Cancer, Leo, Virgo, Libra, Scorpio, Sagittarius, Capricorn, Aquarius, and Pisces. Horoscope signs always describe the experience.

Solar Return—A significant astrology chart that is based on when your Sun returns to the exact degree, minute, and second of your birth, which indicates the trends that will play out in your life for that particular year.

Soulmate—A person whose soul you have been close to in a previous lifetime. Someone with whom you feel a spiritual and/or romantic bond that is upheld through time.

Succedent Houses—The succedent houses are the second, fifth, eighth, and eleventh houses. They constitute the middle ground and hold less weight.

Sun/Moon Midpoint—A significant astrological point that represents the male and female energies that is calculated by changing the zodiacal degrees of the Sun and Moon to the 360 degrees of a circle of notation, then adding them together and dividing by two.

Synastry—The study of relationships based on astrological compatibility.

Transits—Planets in motion in our solar system that, in traveling through the constellations, form aspects (mathematical angles) to other planets, be they stationary or in motion themselves.

Triads—A relationship of three, such as mind, body, and spirit, that exemplifies the idea of bringing a dyad relationship together with a spiritual conception, be it God or a higher divine power. A grouping of three elements.

Trinity—From a religious perspective, this triad is the union of God the Father, Son, and Holy Spirit. The union of three people, things, or ideas moving toward a common goal, which is usually one of spirituality and truth.

Triplicities—Groupings of the elements of fire, earth, air, and water that form a geometric triangle by degree that relates to three compatible horoscope signs. The fire triplicity includes Aries, Leo, and Sagittarius; the earth triplicity includes Taurus, Virgo, and Capricorn; the air triplicity includes Gemini, Libra, and Aquarius; and the water triplicity includes Cancer, Scorpio, and Pisces.